JUMPING THE ODDS

JUMPING THE ODDS

Memoirs of a Rastafarian Showjumper

Oliver Skeete

with the assistance of Peter Holt

HEADLINE

First published in 1995
by HEADLINE BOOK PUBLISHING

10 9 8 7 6 5 4 3 2 1

British Library Cataloguing in Publication Data
Skeete, Oliver
Jumping the Odds
I. Title II. Holt, Peter
798.25092

ISBN 0–7472–1277–5

Phototypeset by Intype, London

Printed and bound in Great Britain by
Mackays of Chatham PLC, Chatham, Kent

HEADLINE BOOK PUBLISHING
A division of Hodder Headline PLC
338 Euston Road
London NW1 3BH

To Susan, Chanelle, Zarra, Oliver, Aloma and Keilly,
and Mum and Dad

CONTENTS

Acknowledgements   ix

Preface   1

1 Bajan Child   3

2 Rude Boys and Blues   19

3 The First Time . . .   49

4 Bunny-hops Down the M1   67

5 False Dread   87

6 Working the Door   113

7 The Lone Rasta   129

8 Banged Up in Chelmsford   159

9 Famous, but Skint   175

10 'The Showjumper From Hell'   197

Postscript   211

ACKNOWLEDGEMENTS

First, I'd like to thank all those companies who have shown faith in me and come forward with sponsorship of all types in my hour of need. It's thanks to their support that I've been able to continue riding – even when I've been down to my last fiver! So a big thank you to: Cliff Barnsby Saddles; R. H. Mears (jackets); Allen and Casewell (boots); Balanced Horse Feeds; Thermatex (rugs); Gorringe (jodhpurs); Misbourne (horsebox); Tack Track (tack marking system); M. M. Farmkey (freeze marks).

I'd also like to thank Margaret Cooper, British West Indian Airways, The Barbados Tourism Authority and the British Show Jumping Association. I wouldn't have got anywhere in this immensely competitive sport had it not been for the hours of help that were freely given to me by professional riders. Here my deepest gratitude goes to Barry Fox, Nigel Goddard, Nick Smith, Nat and Liz Heal and Tracey Hedges.

Many friends have helped me to keep going with words of encouragement during some difficult times, notably Errol and Faith John, Brian and Sally Knight, Dick and Sasha Strutton, Mike and Angie Hedges, Pat Newton and Norman and Theresa Jackson. And, of course, I'd like to thank my mother and father for their support and endless patience.

Finally, thank you to Peter Holt, who listened to my rather chaotic story from beginning to end and then put it into some sort of order!

PREFACE

I'm told that the Queen was astonished when she first saw me on the showjumping circuit.

'Who is that black man with the hair?' she is said to have asked one of her courtiers as she watched the jumping from a box at the Royal Windsor Horse Show.

'Actually, they're known as dreadlocks, ma'am.'

'How on earth does he fit them under his hard hat?'

'Presumably it's a very big hat, ma'am.'

Well, I don't know if the story's true or not, but it's what one of my horsey friends told me and it made me laugh. And the courtier was right. I *do* have to wear a very big riding hat – indeed, I own the biggest hat you can buy.

Her Majesty first saw me at the Royal Windsor Horse Show in 1994. We didn't meet but I was sitting just three boxes away from her. That might not sound like much of a claim to fame, but it meant everything to me. I was brought up in a West Indian family of ten; I've slept rough on the streets of London's West End, and I've got a criminal record stretching back to when I was thirteen. So I'm the last person you'd expect to find in the rich, upper-class world of showjumping. The sport lies at the heart of the establishment and black people are not supposed to be involved in this sort of thing.

I have absolutely no idea why I developed a love of horses. They are not in my blood and I certainly didn't like them as a child. The only member of my family who had anything to do with horses was my Uncle Sylvan, my father's brother, who was the mounted

1

policeman responsible for law and order in my family's village in Barbados.

Uncle Sylvan was not a big man, but when I was growing up he looked to me like a giant in his uniform astride his horse. He was the dominant figure in the village, patrolling his patch on a massive charger that glistened with foam from the heat.

Everyone was frightened of Uncle Sylvan, particularly the children. Whenever we heard his horse's hooves we would take off and hide. Sylvan, you see, had a formidable reputation. Like most policemen in Barbados in the 1950s and 1960s he had a solidly old-school approach to crime. Rather than deliver offenders to the courts, a process he considered an unnecessary waste of time, he would administer punishment himself – he simply gave them a good beating. Having set about you with his truncheon, he would give you a vicious ticking-off before sending you and your bruises home. And it took little to anger him. Everyone was a potential criminal in his eyes and it made no difference if you were family.

For years I associated horses with Uncle Sylvan and the fear that he instilled in the village. His mount was the biggest creature I had ever seen. Once, when he was in one of his gentler moods, he lifted me up and placed me in the saddle in front of him to see what it felt like. I seemed to be miles from the ground and I couldn't wait to get down.

But now, more than three decades later, horses have become my life. And when the Queen found out more about me I'll bet her reaction was the same as everyone else's: 'A Rastafarian showjumper who didn't start riding until he was thirty-five? And in eighteen months he's on the professional circuit? Oh c'mon, man, don't be ridiculous.'

But that's the truth. And it amazes me, too. Sometimes I have to pinch myself when I remember how far this extraordinarily elitist sport has taken me from my roots.

1

BAJAN CHILD

I was eight years old when I left Barbados. My parents had emi-
grated to England a few years earlier and now I was being sent for.
'Sent for' was an expression that we children knew well. It was as if
the West Indian piccaninnies were little parcels to be popped in the
post at the adults' convenience. My friends were always being 'sent
for'. I didn't really understand what it meant, other than that I would
never see them again.

My schoolteachers had shown me England on a map but it didn't
mean a thing to me. I'd been told that England would be cold but I
had no concept of what cold was. To be cold in Barbados was to
wake in the middle of the night to find the sheet had slipped off the
bed, the temperature outside had dropped to 75 Fahrenheit and a
breeze was blowing through the window.

A few weeks after my eighth birthday, Grandma dressed me in my
short-trousered Sunday suit and a white nylon shirt. Accompanied
by a couple of my aunts, she took me to Seawell Airport. This was
several years before the island's tourist boom and the airport building was little more than a hut. I hugged Grandma and my aunts
goodbye. They sniffled into their handkerchiefs and told me to be
good. I kicked my feet, bewildered by their distress and impatient to
board the plane.

A stewardess held my hand during the long walk across the tarmac
to the aircraft. The plane was sleek and shiny. It was the most
exciting thing I had ever seen.

I was wide-eyed throughout the entire flight. For ten hours I fidgeted in my seat and didn't drop off to sleep once. The air steward-esses fussed about me, fetching glasses of orange juice. I remember that one of them had a Scottish accent. She sounded so foreign. I'd never heard anything so funny.

In the seat next to me was a thirteen-year-old white Bajan girl. I can't remember her name, but her face has stuck in my mind. Even at the age of eight, I noticed that she was pretty. She was the first attractive white girl I'd seen. She looked after me all the way to England, doing drawings and sums to keep me amused. She lived with her parents in Barbados and was returning to boarding school in England. What confused me was that although she was so dark she was a white girl. She had a deep suntan, and I couldn't under-stand the concept of a tan. Surely your skin was either black or white and that was that. Or was it?

I found her fascinating. I'd met very few white people before and I began to think that if they were all like my new friend life in Britain was not going to be too bad. It felt strange being so close to a girl. I'd had no contact with girls except for my big sisters, and like big sisters everywhere they had gone out of their way to avoid me.

When the cabin staff wheeled out the food trolleys I began to have second thoughts about leaving Barbados. They served up little bits of tasteless fish. Fish in Barbados was seasoned to the limit, but this was white and colourless. If this food was anything to go by, I reckoned that I must be heading for a place very different from the one I had left. I had the disturbing feeling that a big change was on the way.

After we had landed at Heathrow Airport the aircraft door swung open. I cautiously walked out on to the landing steps and was hit by the cold of a late February afternoon. The white girl said goodbye and skipped down the steps. I was left alone staring at Heathrow's bleak buildings. I began to cry.

One of those airport nannies, a bossy lady of fortyish known as an 'international aunt', hurried me through Immigration and Customs. Then I was in the Arrivals Hall and falling towards the arms of my mother. She ran up to me brandishing a cardigan. She wrapped it around my shoulders, gathered me into her arms and burst into tears.

I had not seen her for two years. My mother recalls that my first words to her were: 'It's cold, but I'm glad to be with you, Mum.'

Then came the journey from the airport into London, in a car owned by a friend of my parents. Like all the other vehicles on the road it was black. I sat in the back next to my mother and gazed out of the window in amazement at the number of cars. Back in my village in Barbados, only two or three people had their own cars, and they were considered very grand.

As we approached west London it got colder and colder. Mum fretted over me, making sure my cardigan was buttoned tight. I pushed her away. I wanted to concentrate on what was going on outside the car. The buildings were so dark and the people so dismal. Everybody was in grey and black. What was my family doing here? Why had they left the Caribbean? What was the attraction of this place? I couldn't work it out. Because yesterday in Barbados everything had been so colourful . . .

I was born on 26 March 1956 at my parents' shack in a hamlet called The Whim. I was the seventh in a family of ten and the heaviest baby of them all.

The Whim – population 150 in the 1950s and now around 300 – lies in the parish of St Peter at the north-west corner of Barbados, near the port of Speightstown. No one knows for certain how the village got its name, although one suggestion is that both pedestrians and vehicles have always been at the whim of the steep hill that leads up to the village. In the 1950s the road was little more than a track. It was just about passable up to the brow of the hill, where it became a treacherous muddle of boulders, ruts and pot-holes. It was even worse after the deluges of the rainy season.

My family had lived in this square mile for years. I don't know where our name came from. There was a British judge named Skeete in Barbados during the seventeenth century and perhaps my ancestors were his slaves and took his name. Or maybe there was a Skeete among the indentured servants from England, Scotland and Wales who settled in Barbados as plantation overseers from the time of Charles I. These settlers often inter-bred with the African slaves so it is possible that my family is descended from one of them.

The Whim is one of the tiniest villages in Barbados and it has a special character of its own. Because it is so inaccessible, many Bajans have never even heard of it. The community is tightly knit and fiercely independent. Few outsiders ever settle there and you hardly ever see a tourist.

When I was growing up, everyone in the The Whim was related in one way or another. Almost everybody was called Skeete – villagers would jokingly greet each other with the question: 'Are you my mum or my sister?' This was mainly thanks to my paternal great-grandfather, known as Count Philip, a man with an exceptional libido.

Count Philip, who lived at the turn of the century, was the night-watchman at the local Stanhope Plantation. In those days there were serious punishments for theft. Anyone caught stealing from the plantation was arrested and locked up. But there was much poverty in The Whim and the peasants supplemented their diet by scrumping mangoes from the plantation's orchards. They were often caught. Count Philip reasoned that it was foolish to lock up the culprits: so many people were raiding the plantation that if he stuck to the rules the entire village would end up in jail.

My great-grandfather devised a simple alternative that was acceptable to everyone. He gave any women he caught stealing the option of either being taken to the police or sleeping with him. They all settled for the latter. The Whim's menfolk caught on and thereafter always sent out their women to steal mangoes rather than going themselves. The men reasoned it was better for the girls to end up in Philip's bed than in the hands of the police. As a result, Philip sired numerous illegitimate children. To this day, any man in the village with a large family is nicknamed Count Philip.

One road bisected The Whim. The houses were reached by dirt paths, their verges a colourful swirl of bougainvillaea, hibiscus and oleander bushes. The village was dotted with banana palms and surrounded by sugar cane fields. Each house had its own mango and sugar apple trees. Chickens scratched in the dust and pigs snuffled over discarded mango skins. There were monkeys everywhere.

At the time of 'cropover', when the cane was cut, most of the villagers worked on the plantation. For the rest of the year work was limited. The men sat in the rum shops spending their meagre sugar earnings and wondering whether to start new lives abroad.

There was neither electricity nor running water in The Whim. We lit our homes with oil lamps and candles and one water tap served the whole village. You filled your bucket from a pipe cut into the rock at the side of the road. If you wanted a shower, you lay down under the pipe and let the water gush over you.

Our house nestled in the shade of an almond tree on the grassy plateau above Whim Hill, overlooking the Caribbean. It was a typical Bajan 'board 'n' shingles' shack with sun-bleached clapboard walls and a rusty corrugated-iron roof. Chipped stone steps led to a tiny verandah. The building was balanced on breeze blocks to stop the floor from rotting and to keep out the night-time army of frogs. There was a yard at the back and behind that the bath house, made of hastily assembled bricks. The toilet was simply a hole in the ground.

That toilet was the scene of a big drama when I was about six. My sister Glenda, who was eighteen at the time, had recently married a man called Noel. One day Noel came home with a piglet which he planned to fatten up and sell. But he was a lazy man and couldn't be bothered to tie up the animal. 'Piggy' wandered around the yard for a few hours and eventually plunged into the hole, squealing terribly. He landed twenty-five feet down in the shit.

A friend lowered down Noel on a rope and pulled him back up clutching the piglet. Both man and animal smelled vile and my sister wouldn't let either of them in the house for a week.

The house had two cramped bedrooms. I shared one with my brothers. My sisters Judy, Sandra and Jennifer had the other. I had two older brothers, Kennedy, born in 1949, and Bentley, born a year later. Ricky was born in 1957 and Elvis in 1959. Glenda, the eldest, born in 1945, had left home following her marriage. My little sister Claudia was born much later, in London in 1969.

My brothers and I slept on mattresses on a bare wooden floor that bore the traces of peeling lime-green paint. I had no privacy. I used to lie awake at night longing to escape my brothers' grunts and groans. We were all scared of the dark and we would huddle up to each other if we heard anyone walking past the shack at night. One night a man reached in through the window and tried to grab my little brother Ricky. We knew who he was. He was a guy called

Butter and he was drunk. We screamed and he ran off. I grew up to hate drunks. People who drank that much rum got stupid.

My mother, Iris, was a woman of incredible mental strength. She was having children from the age of seventeen until she was forty-two yet she always worked to feed her family. She was very pretty. I remember her in a flowery dress and a pinafore and no shoes. She had a part-time job in a local shop called Elmer's. She dressed up to go work and looked smarter in the shop than she did at home.

Mum was also the village seamstress. When one of the village girls got married she was always commissioned to make the wedding dress. I have an indelible image of her hunched over an ancient Singer sewing machine with her glasses on the end of her nose and a thimble on her finger. I was always getting in her way. I would try to climb on to her knees while she pounded the foot treadle. She would say things like, 'Boy, get off me lap. Don' you see me tryin' to work?'

According to my mum, of all her children I was the one closest to her. I wouldn't let her out of my sight. I was always getting in her way, hanging on to her apron, sucking my fingers and staring up at her face. She expected me to turn out the best, yet when I grew up I was to become the worst behaved of us all. During my teenage years I was the one who was to drift furthest away from her.

There was a dance at the time called The Dog. It was the latest thing in Barbados and at the age of four I was really good at it. Mum would put the record on and her friends would give me a few cents for dancing to it. Even then I liked showing off – and I can't say that things have changed much. I made a real name for myself with The Dog. It was a sort of calypso and you wiggled your hips. Mum couldn't stop giggling at me. I was overjoyed that I made her so happy.

My father, Rupert, was not a big man, about five foot nine. But when I was a child he seemed enormous to me, and I grew up in terror of him.

Dad worked for a plantation in St Andrews. He drove a sugar cane lorry, a battered Bedford RL army truck. He was one of the few people in the village with a car, a long, black Vauxhall with front doors that opened backwards. He did not own the vehicle himself. It belonged to a friend who could not drive and Dad had it on permanent loan.

Dad was a heavy drinker when he was young. In the evenings he would hang out with his friends in the rum shops in Speightstown. At around 9 a.m. he would come home and we'd hear his curses as he staggered through the village, tripping over the pot-holes.

He carried a huge cutlass that he used for trimming the bundles of sugar cane on his truck. Laughing crazily, he would lurch around the outside of the shack, pushing the blade through the wooden shutters and rattling the slats. We were terrified and sometimes I ran out of the house and hid in the cane field. My sister Judy, her eyes wide with fright, would cower in a corner holding a coathanger in front of her for protection. I never understood what good a coathanger would do.

At weekends Dad held court on a flat rock under a tree in front of our house. He doubled as the village barber and was famous for his hair-cutting skills. He was very rough, especially with us children. He would slash away at my hair with scissors and then shape it with a cut-throat razor. I would end up with little bloody nicks around the sides of my head.

Black people's hair easily becomes knotted and we tend to be careful with the comb. Dad had no such graces. He would grab hold of my forehead and take the comb from back to front in one swipe. If I cried, he called me a cissy and told me to shut my mouth. My brothers suffered the same fate. We may have only been children but he was determined to treat us like men.

I didn't like my father and I had confused ideas as to what a dad was supposed to be for. I grew up thinking that dads were supposed to beat you and that small boys were supposed to hate them.

West Indian parents of the 1950s and 1960s were very tough on their children. You had to grow up fast in Barbados and child psychology was unheard of. Children had been brought up the same hard way for years. Their ancestors had been beaten by the slave-owners and a couple of centuries later grown-ups were passing on the same treatment to their children. It was the only way they knew.

My father was brought up in a strict, disciplinarian household and he would not tolerate rebellious behaviour. Old-fashioned Christian values included beatings, usually with his belt or a piece of rope. It was painful at the time but I didn't resent it because to me it was normal – most of my friends in Barbados were brought up in the same way.

Later, when I first moved to England, I used to go to my white friends' houses after school. I couldn't believe it when they shouted at their parents and told them to shut up and leave them alone. I couldn't talk to my mum and dad like that – no way. It was 'Yes, Mum, yes, Dad.' I'm not like that today with my own children. My kids walk all over me. I shout at them sometimes like my parents did, but they take absolutely no notice of me.

I would never hit my children. If my dad told me to do something and I turned away and ran upstairs in a temper, he would come after me and beat me. If I tell off my daughters, they run upstairs and shout, 'I hate you.' I sigh and think, 'Oh God, here we go.' I can't take their tantrums too seriously and I never run after them. I know how frightening it is to grow up with a parent who wants to beat you the whole time.

Dad was not a warm man. I don't remember him showing much affection to anyone, although he once kept a dog as a pet. It was a massive thing. It used to sleep on the warm tarmac in the middle of the road until it was run over by a lorry one day.

When I felt brave enough to leave my mother's skirts I was off as fast as I could go. I was always running across the cane fields and climbing trees. After the initial shock of my new-found independence, I began to enjoy myself. I loved the freedom of running around in no shoes and a torn T-shirt. I threw stones at monkeys and played football with breadfruit. When I was hungry I trotted home and Mum would be there to give me food. They were happy days and I never thought they would end.

My easy life began to change in 1961 when I was five. I can't remember Dad actually leaving but suddenly he was no longer in the house. After a couple of weeks without him I began to grasp what had happened. He had gone across the sea to this place called England to start a new life with a job in a sausage factory.

My father had been planning to leave Barbados ever since he had had an accident with his sugar cane lorry. One day, as he drove down from the hills of St Andrews, the brakes failed. The truck turned turtle with ten tons of cane on board. Thankfully, the steel driver's cab held the vehicle's weight or my father would have been crushed. Dad vowed that he had had enough of this dangerous work. The sugar cane lorries were badly maintained and were often involved in accidents. By the end of that sugar season he had quit his job.

I did not miss him, especially since my brothers, sisters and I now had our mother to ourselves. As far as I was concerned, life was getting better and better.

A year later, however, I suffered a devastating blow. My mother couldn't stop crying. She talked about how my father needed her. I couldn't work out what the fuss was about. Surely Dad would come home?

But then she was gone too.

Her departure to Britain must have had an effect on me but I can't recall much about it. She flew to London by plane but I can't remember seeing her off, or whether I cried. I know that for a few days I could think of nothing but her. I kept hearing her voice calling me from the yard and feeling her arms around me as she put me to bed. They are sad memories and I often think about that time today.

My parents' shack was barred and shuttered and we children went to live with my maternal grandmother up the hill. The hurt of Mum's departure began to lessen as I got used to her not being there. Since we had not been able to afford to have our photographs taken I had no picture to remind me of her. Mum never wrote to me from England, although she usually put little messages to all of us children at the end of her letters to my grandmother.

I spent the next three years with Grandma. And life with her was very different. From being a quiet, carefree child I turned into a little monster.

If you were generous, you might describe Grandma as a character. But to us children she was a tough woman who wanted her grandchildren to grow up fast. In her favour, she was hard-working and went out of her way to ensure that we were properly fed and clothed. Grandma came from a farming family. Her dress was tied up with a piece of string and she wore a scarf around her head, the knot tied on top. She smartened up on Sundays when she put on a billowing cotton frock and straw hat for church.

She had a heavy snuff habit and her fingers were mottled and yellowy. Little lumps of snuff stuck to her nose and her hankies were always stained brown. There was always a brown patch on her dress by her hip where she wiped her hands. Sometimes I sneaked a pinch of her funny powder, but it only made me ill.

The transformation between life with Mum and life with Grandma was horrendous. Like my father, Grandma saw corporal punishment as the answer to everything. If you didn't toe the line, you were beaten. Any lip, any answering back, and you received a thrashing. Simple as that. Beating came naturally to Grandma. She had already tried out her methods on my mother and her sister and she reasoned that because they had turned out OK there was no reason why her grandchildren shouldn't be the same.

Grandma called me Junior. She used to say, 'Yer tryin' to kill me, in't ya, Joon-yaar?' That's a favourite expression of elderly people in Barbados. When I had done something wrong, such as being late for a meal, she shouted, 'When you come here, boy, I'm goin' to lambase' yer backside.' Then she would grab me and cry, 'If you can't hear, boy, you will feel,' and the blows would rain down on my bottom. Her house was a hard place to be growing up, especially as the memory of my father's punishments had dimmed and since his departure my mother had only occasionally smacked me. Nobody in the village disapproved of Grandma's behaviour because it happened in every other family.

I can remember people in Barbados being either fat or skinny. There was no in-between. Grandma was decidedly fat. She was a strong, big woman with the largest, strongest pair of legs I'd ever seen. She carried buckets of water on her head with no hands, and furthermore she walked down Whim Hill without spilling a drop. Very occasionally I got words of praise from her. If I helped fetch and carry her shopping she gave me a few cents to buy a bottle of soft drink from the kiosk that one of my aunties owned. Or I'd get a stick of sugar cane or a mango.

Some of Grandma's frustration was justified. She turned on me only when I wouldn't do as I was told, which was frequently. As I said, I had become a difficult child after my mother left. I took virtually no notice of what Grandma said and I always answered her back. I couldn't stand being dominated by this powerful woman.

We fought about everything. When I heard her call me back into the shack I ignored her and stayed outside playing. I was usually late for meals. During cropover I'd go and roll in the mountain of sugar cane thrash that had been left in the fields. I would come home a filthy, sticky mess. Grandma would drag me in for a bath and scrub me hard with carbolic soap. My skin would be scratched from the cane and the soap stung. I would scream my head off and try to escape the old woman's grasp. Grandma would lose her temper and beat me round the head. It was like that every evening during cropover.

My reluctance to attend Sunday School created more friction between us. On Sunday mornings I would hide in the cane fields and Grandma would be forced to go to church alone. When she returned and I had reappeared she would beat me. Sometimes I would be caught before I escaped from the house and she would drag me to church. That was like losing the battle. It always gave me a great sense of failure.

My grandmother tried to force me to eat food I didn't like. If I refused to eat I was beaten. Her speciality was the Barbados national dish, 'cuckoo' and flying fish. Cuckoo was cornmeal, like couscous, and I loathed it. She mixed it with okra, which made it feel slimy as it slipped down my throat. To this day I hate cuckoo. My mother says she ate cuckoo every day while she was pregnant with me. Perhaps that is why I detest the stuff.

We seldom had meat. My great-aunt Emelyn kept pigs and occasionally she killed one of them. I remember her sticking a skewer in a pig's neck and draining the blood out of it. The animal screamed and kicked up the dust for several minutes before it died. The incident put me off pork for a long time.

Life in The Whim wasn't all bad, though, and the beatings didn't affect the good times. And for someone who turned out later to be an academic disaster zone, I have fond memories of my Barbados schooldays.

I was five when I went to Speightstown Boys' School. Until then, the village was all I knew of the world. It was as if nothing happened outside The Whim. Bridgetown, the capital of Barbados, was as far removed as New York and Speightstown, barely a mile away,

13

scarcely seemed closer. School, then, was a big adventure.

My route to school took me down the hill and through the gully below The Whim. I regarded the gully as my own little jungle. It was a deep ravine thick with mahogany and silk cotton trees. Long creepers hung down to the forest floor. Even in the daytime the gully was dark and forbidding and I wondered what lurked beneath the undergrowth. Children never went down there at night. It was pitch black and the grown-ups warned us off with tales of 'duppies' (ghosts) and 'heart men', who pounced on you and cut out your heart.

In one part of the gully there was a deep drop below the path. My aunts tell a story about my great-grandmother, Janie, who was walking back through the forest from Speightstown one rainy night during the wet season. The path was so narrow that you had to put one foot in front of the other. My great-grandmother slipped in the mud and lost her footing. She plunged off the path into the abyss. Luckily, she was unhurt and managed to pull herself back up, but ever since the spot has been known as Miss Janie Hole.

The teachers at Speightstown Boys' were terribly strict. They shouted at us and smacked our hands with rulers. First your knuckles, then you turned your hands upwards and they flayed your palms. It was all 'Yes, sir' and no talking out of turn.

The school was an old wooden colonial building. The classrooms had long wooden benches with no back rests so you had to sit up straight. I wore the uniform of blue shirt, khaki shorts and grey socks, all made for me by my mother before she left. They had been sitting in the cupboard until the day I started school. While the uniform was compulsory, shoes were not. I went barefoot everywhere.

The lessons were boring but playtime was fun. A drainage ditch ran along the back of the school. We put stones on the end of a piece of string and caught crabs hiding in holes in the ditch. Grandma sometimes gave me a few cents and at lunchtime I went to a shop owned by an Indian called Bata, who sold Coca-Cola and cheese rotis.

After school I played with my cousin Eddie, who was the same age as me. We had no toys and had to make do with whatever flotsam was lying around the village. When we weren't fighting, we played with sticks and old bicycle wheels. We would put a stick in a wheel and run it up and down the road. Sometimes we played football with a tin can. This was a dangerous sport since we were barefoot and the cans often cut our feet. One of the village boys, I remember, lost his toe: it was sliced off by a can that he kicked too hard.

This was the early 1960s and the great emigration to Britain was in full flow. At that time it was typical for big families to leave the West Indies in dribs and drabs. There wasn't the money to pay for flights for everybody, let alone to support the family immediately they all arrived in England. So the fathers or parents would go first to get a job and home set up. Then they would save up to bring over the rest of the family when they could.

We were no different. Judy went first, then Sandra and Jennifer. I remember my sisters disappearing from Grandma's house; suddenly they were no longer there. The house seemed so quiet without the girls. I knew they had gone to live with Mum and Dad but I couldn't quite work out where. I don't remember missing them much – I don't think I was a particularly caring child and, like most members of my family, I certainly wasn't prone to displays of sentimental emotion.

I still had my brothers, but I wasn't especially close to them either. Kennedy and Bentley were much older than I was, and they wanted little to do with me. Ricky and Elvis were too young to join in my games, and at times it felt like I was an only child. It might sound callous but it was as if my brothers were little more than friends who happened to share the same house as I did.

My parents had intended to send for Kennedy and Bentley next, but because I was getting on so badly with my grandmother they decided that I should go before my brothers. Grandma could not cope with me and she told my mother in an urgent letter that she had put up with this disobedient child for long enough.

I was ambivalent about leaving Barbados. The main thing was that I wouldn't see Grandma any more and that was good. The teachers at Speightstown Boys' tried to tell me about Britain but I don't think they knew much about the place themselves. They gave the impression that London was smoggy and dirty, but I think they had picked this up from Sherlock Holmes books. I learned about things like Buckingham Palace and the Changing of the Guard. I also knew that the buses in London were red and double-decker. I certainly didn't know anything about the royal family. I was more interested in Martin Luther King because my mother had been a great fan of his and had his picture hanging in the house. Perhaps Martin Luther King lived in England. Now that was an exciting thought.

And the English? My view of white people was that they owned everything. My dad worked for a white man and his dad had worked for a white man. The white people owned all the big houses up in the hills so presumably everybody in England was just as rich. I had no bad feelings towards white people; it was just the way things were. I don't remember people in the village being anti-white. On the contrary, the locals would rather protect the plantation-owner's land from their own people rather than protect you from the plantation-owners. That was the attitude then, and it's not much different today, except that now the whites own the hotels, not the plantations.

Before I left for England, the village held a special church service for me. They did this for everyone who was going to a new life overseas. The whole of The Whim turned out to say goodbye to me. The Pilgrim Holiness Church was another wooden shack with a gnarled corrugated roof topped off by a white wooden cross. It wasn't much of a church. There was a piano, but it was warped by the humidity and permanently out of tune.

All the old women were singing and crying at the same time. Spirituals like 'God Take Care' filled the church. Everyone from the vicar to my aunts was praising the Lord and blessing me. They filed up, shook my hand and kissed me on the head. They prayed that I would get to England safely. I think they had great doubts about the reliability of air transport.

During the hymns I stood next to my Grandma. She seemed proud to be my grandmother and for a moment I remember thinking that she liked me really. I was the only member of her family who stuck up to her. I had character and perhaps she secretly respected me for it.

I looked up at Grandma and saw that she was crying. My sister Glenda, on my other side, was sobbing, too. Behind me, Great-Aunt Pearl was heaving and sighing and choking back the tears. I couldn't understand what the fuss was about. Why were they so upset? Adults could be so strange. I couldn't wait to leave the church – it seemed such a waste of good playing time.

2

RUDE BOYS AND BLUES

The Skeetes were no different from most West Indian families who immigrated to Britain in the 1960s. Like everyone else who flocked from the Caribbean looking to improve their lives, we suffered from near-poverty and overcrowding.

My parents began their new life in a bedsit in Shepherd's Bush. But when the children began arriving from Barbados they moved further west across London to a two-bedroomed first-floor flat in a terraced house in Graham Road, Acton. It was a short, tree-lined road and all the cars parked in it were black, like the one which had brought me there from the airport. The front doors were in alleyways to the side of the houses. It was not a glamorous address.

My parents had great difficulty finding somewhere to live. Landlords did not like West Indians and properties for rent often had signs stating 'No blacks, no dogs'. Mum and Dad had come to London expecting great things, but the streets had been paved not with gold but with rubbish. My mother was incensed by the racism. 'At school we were led to believe that England was our mother country and that English people would love us,' she says. 'But when we got there we found they didn't want us.' Yet despite the harassment, I can see why my parents' generation wanted to leave Barbados. There were no jobs there except for work in the fields. Even a racist Britain was better than that.

By the time I arrived, the flat was home to my parents and my sisters Judy, Sandra and Jennifer. Since both bedrooms were full, I was given a folding bed in the sitting room.

After the drive from the airport Mum sat me down and poured me a glass of Mauby, the Barbadian national drink made from the bark of the mauby tree. The bitter-sweet taste made me feel at home. I held on tight to the glass as if it were all I had left of my old world. Mauby still conjures up my happiest memories of Barbados. I still love the stuff, although my children won't touch it.

My sisters were delighted to see me. They danced around, hugging and kissing me. Their welcome puzzled me. I'd almost forgotten about them in the time we had been separated. They enveloped me in their arms and pressed their lips to my cheeks, crooning about how much I had grown. As an eight-year-old boy I was not keen on kisses. I felt childish and embarrassed. I struggled to escape their grasp.

The celebrations lasted a couple of days. Then it was back into the old routine. I was little brother again, issued with strict orders to mind my manners and keep out of the girls' room. The flat was so small that everybody was very protective about their space. I was restricted to the settee and a few square feet around it.

The day after my arrival I developed chickenpox and didn't leave the flat for two weeks. So my first days in Britain were spent lying on the settee with my face plastered in calamine lotion. It was a good excuse not to go out into the horrible, cold weather.

My sister Jennifer also caught the disease. Chickenpox created a bond between us and we quickly became good friends. She was beanpole thin and I called her names like 'Boneyard' and 'Skinny Winny'. When we got better we played football together in the flat, kicking the ball around the furniture until my father yelled at us to stop.

I wasn't happy about being in England. I think I must have felt as depressed as an eight-year-old boy can feel. Everything was so dismal after Barbados. I didn't want to go outside. I suppose I was too frightened. The streets looked forbidding and uninviting, and nothing like the emerald-green cane fields of The Whim.

I remember looking out of the window and seeing our neighbours playing in their front garden across the road. They were Anglo-Indian and I found them fascinating. They had what seemed like an endless supply of toys, something I had never had. There was even a swing in their garden. I watched them enviously from behind the safety of the curtains. They shrieked and whooped and looked as though they were enjoying themselves hugely.

It took me several weeks to summon up the courage to say hello to them. I shyly called out of the window one day and they invited me to come down and play. I remember kicking a football around with them for a few evenings, but I never got to know them properly and now I can't even remember their names. It wasn't long before they moved.

The hardest part of my new life was getting on with my father. My status as prodigal son returning to the bosom of the family lasted all of about two days. It was not long before Dad was back on his old form, shouting at me and putting me in line.

Back in Barbados, whenever my grandmother had hollered at me I had run out of the house and hidden. But hiding places were limited in a two-bedroomed flat in Acton, and furthermore it soon became clear that whereas I could run circles around Grandma, my father was not going to let me get away with anything.

The last time I'd seen Dad was in 1961, when I was five. I had lost three years of him and I had developed a personality of my own, which he didn't seem too happy with. It was hard to behave myself in such a small place where there were no gullies to run to, no trees to climb.

Dad had definite views about how to bring up his son. He was a forceful man and he was determined to be the dominant figure in the family. He shouted at me all the time: 'Come here, boy . . . do this, do that . . . time to get your hair cut . . . go and have a bath.'

I was sure that my parents had changed. They seemed to be less carefree, less happy. City life did not suit them after the Barbados countryside. There everybody had known everybody; in England, nobody knew anybody. We were restricted to a cramped flat with a handful of friends my parents had known back home. That was our world.

My father had become dour and reserved. Life was difficult in Britain. Like so many West Indians of his generation he had a far harder life in Britain than he would have had back home – or at least that's how I saw it. His life was all work. He never went out with his friends and he didn't have the heart for recreation. He might have been poorer in Barbados but I think he would have been happier.

He'd spent a year in London by himself preparing the way for the family. He had found a job on the production line at the Wall's sausage factory in Acton, but he complained that he was always being given all the menial tasks. At the time he was convinced that this was because he was black. He cheered up later when he realised that there were also white people in the same lowly jobs.

After briefly working in a laundry, Mum had found a job with London Transport as a ticket-collector on the underground. She was a born survivor. In Barbados she had made dresses and cakes to earn some extra cash, and she would support her family if it was the last thing she did on earth. It was no different when she arrived in Britain. She worked long shifts, often at night, but she never complained and there was always food available for us whenever we wanted it.

There was a temporary feel to our household. My parents had originally intended to stay in Britain for only five years. The plan was to make enough money to return to a comfortable life in Barbados, but the cost of supporting such a large family never made that possible. In the end, they stayed for twenty-five years.

When my last chickenpox spot disappeared I started school at Rothschild's Primary in Acton.

My first day at school was terrifying. I didn't know anybody and I was convinced that because the teachers were white I was going to be beaten. The teachers in Barbados had been white and they had regularly beaten me, so I couldn't see why it should be any different in England.

Of the 300 pupils, only about twenty were black, and I felt like an outsider. There were three black children in my class. One of them, an African girl called Meannie, was the first person outside my family with whom I became friendly in England. Meannie was tall and strong and spoke with an African accent. I was fascinated by her. I'd never met an African before. I'd heard about them and vaguely knew that hundreds of years ago my family would have come from Africa, so to get so close to an African was a small thrill.

Our form teacher, Mr Pearson, was a tall, thin man whose head seemed to touch the ceiling. I was surprised when he shook my hand and said he hoped I would be happy at the school. Teachers weren't supposed to be like that. I began to wonder whether perhaps I might not be beaten so often after all.

Mr Pearson gently introduced me to my class. 'This is Oliver. He is from Barbados.' A titter went round the room. 'Be nice to him,' Mr Pearson said firmly. 'He is a long way from home.'

I can't remember much about my first lesson except that towards the end Mr Pearson asked me to demonstrate my reading skills. I had learned to read back at Speightstown Boys', but I did not enjoy it.

Mr Pearson strode up to my desk and gave me a book. It was a collection of Bible stories written for children. He flicked through the pages until he reached the story about Samson and how he slew 1,000 men with the jawbone of an ass.

I looked up at him beseechingly. Did he really want me to go through with this?

'Stand up, Oliver.' I slowly got to my feet. The pages in front of me seemed to go fuzzy. I could feel the eyes of the whole classroom upon me. Mr Pearson returned to the front of the class. 'Now you may read,' he said.

I stuttered: 'An' Sarm-sun came outta de cave and saw de Philistines . . .'

As soon as I opened my mouth the kids started laughing. They found my Bajan accent hilarious. I felt stupid and undignified. Tears appeared in my eyes. I wanted to dig a hole and climb into it.

Mr Pearson told everybody to shut up but the giggles continued. There was nothing I could do. I carried on.

'An' Sarm-sun took de jawer-bowan of an arse an' he kilt one t'ousand sold'ers widdit.'

My pronunciation of the word 'ass' was too much for my classmates, who shrieked louder than ever. It was one of the most humiliating experiences of my life.

After school finished each day I would go home alone. I had no one to play with except for Jennifer. We developed a routine of playing football every evening out in the street. She was a formidable opponent. We were always fighting and making up. She was a tough girl and she knew how to throw a punch. If I hit her, she hit me back twice as hard. Yet of all my family Jennifer was the one I got on best with. My sister Sandra was three years older than me, which was a big gap. She was always giving me orders and I treated her more as a grown-up than as a friend. My second-oldest sister, Judy, was seventeen and had an office job. Although she lived in the flat I had very little to do with her. She was a 1960s girl with false eyelashes and a beehive hairdo. I found her baffling and we hardly ever spoke. My four brothers were still in Barbados.

I forgot about Barbados pretty quickly. I soon realised that although I didn't have as much freedom in London, at least I had a chance to learn new things. The black boys were different here. They were a lot more clued-up and streetwise. And so I began making friends and getting up to tricks.

The children who had laughed loudest during that first lesson soon learned that I was not to be messed with. I may have been a disaster in the classroom, but in the playground I was a terror. I simply beat up anyone who took the mickey out of my accent. And I quickly earned respect as one of the best footballers in the school.

I hated lessons. I just wanted to play football. I was always running with a ball and competing with the other boys to see who was the fastest, the strongest. Almost immediately, I was picked to play for the school soccer team.

One of my earliest football-playing friends was another West Indian called Frederick Barry. Frederick was an excellent footballer, but his parents were strict Pentecostalists and they dragged him off to church every Saturday and Sunday. This meant he was unable to take part in Saturday matches. I couldn't understand how somebody could miss football for church when we needed him on the team. I called him a cissy for obeying his parents and I wanted to beat him up.

I remember another boy called David Cheeseman. He was white and spoke broad Cockney. He nicknamed me 'Ollyocks. David's parents lived in a little terraced house in Acton with a toilet in the backyard. David kept pet mice in his bedroom. I was appalled. The mice smelled terrible and I thought they were filthy and unhygienic.

He also used to swear at his mum and dad. I couldn't work that out. If I had sworn at my mum and dad I'd have been limping for a month.

I had another white friend called Ian Duer. His family were typically working-class English. They went on camping holidays and wore army-surplus clothes. Ian's house was very old-fashioned: bathtime was once a week in a tub in the kitchen.

I idolised Ian because he had a bicycle. Mum and Dad couldn't afford to buy me one and so I used to ride on his crossbar. I longed for a bike. Mum finally bought me a second-hand Raleigh for my ninth birthday. I had it for twenty-four hours before I left it in the alleyway next to the house and somebody stole it.

My greatest friend was Clyde Macallam, a slim, powerfully built Jamaican with closely cropped hair. He was not a good-looking boy. He had a long, protruding lower jaw that gave him a determined appearance. He spoke quickly without drawing breath. He was demanding and argumentative and his favourite expression was 'Gimme dat!'

Clydie was the fastest runner and best footballer in the school. We teamed up and were always chasing each other round the playground. If other boys were playing football we would break up their game and take the ball off them. They had no hope of getting it back because we were so good. And when we tired of that we teased the girls mercilessly.

Clyde had arrived in England a couple of years before me. He was a year older and I was deeply impressed by how much he knew about Britain. This boy knew the ropes, no question. He became my first teacher in street life.

At weekends we went scrumping apples on the allotments in Acton. Sometimes we even found strawberries and blackberries. There were a surprising number of open spaces in Acton and Ealing in the early 1960s, mostly old bombsites which had not been redeveloped. But it's all changed now – blocks of flats everywhere.

With our bellies full of fruit, we played chicken on the railway line, running back and forth across the rails waiting for trains to come. Or we'd climb into people's gardens and steal their gnomes.

Our favourite spot was a ramshackle adventure playground on the

South Acton Estate. We called it The Wreck because it was so broken down. Going to The Wreck was exciting. Most of the inhabitants of the South Acton Estate were white. The fathers were teddy boys and their sons were skinheads. They didn't like black people on their territory.

This was my first experience of racism. The white boys called us 'nigger' and 'gollywog', and we were always getting into fights, which we usually won. When they learned that black boys defended themselves, they went off and picked on Indians and Pakistanis instead. Terrible place, the South Acton Estate. In ten years I watched it go from being totally white to a totally black area where white people couldn't walk.

We stood up for ourselves more than the white boys did. You'd often find one of us fighting gangs of three or four whites. If one of them had done something to us, we would walk alone straight into the middle of the group and beat the hell out of him. White boys didn't do that. It was usually a case of six of them against one of us.

Clydie taught me how to look after myself. We ruled the playground at Rothschild's and anybody who dared say anything nasty to us was in trouble. He taught me every survival skill a black boy needed in London. The only thing he couldn't teach me was how to do my school work, because he was no good at lessons either. I visited Clyde's home and learned the differences between the Jamaican and Bajan cultures. The food was different, the language was different and the Jamaicans tended to be more aggressive and go-getting. I secretly wished that I had been born a Jamaican.

Not surprisingly, my parents were appalled by this new influence in my life. They didn't like Clyde in the house and were always beating me for not doing my homework. They tried to introduce me to 'nice' Bajan boys like my cousin, also called Clyde, who was strait-laced and priggish and accompanied his parents to church without argument. I wasn't interested. My cousin was as boring as church.

They thought I might get on with a chap called Briggsy, also from Barbados. He was good at school and a proficient musician. Mum invited him around with his trombone in the hope that some of his talents might rub off on me. I hated the sound of his trombone. I couldn't wait for him to go home.

My mother and father had a desperate time trying to send me to Sunday School. They were not great churchgoers themselves, but they thought it would do me some good. On Sunday mornings I dressed in my suit and then pretended to go to Sunday School. I never went near the place. Instead I would kick a tennis ball around the local park until it was time to come home. Sometimes I'd put my suit on over my pyjamas, so that when I returned home I could go straight back to bed and watch the television.

There had been no TV in Barbados and I found it fascinating. I spent hours glued to the screen, soaking up the adventures of *Dr Who* and *Thunderbirds* and sniggering at *Sooty and Sweep*. My first memory of British television was that Rediffusion star and someone singing 'Re-di-fu-sion Lon-don.' When you switched off the set the star disappeared slowly into a white dot. I couldn't work out how they'd done that.

My biggest problem in England was coming to terms with the weather. After I had acclimatised to the British winter I thought I could still run around outside in shirtsleeves as I had done back in Barbados. My mother would dress me up in warm clothes before packing me off to school, but as soon as I was out of her sight, I tore off my cardigan and tied it around my middle. I never wore my duffle coat. I put the hood over my head and let the coat flap behind my back like Batman.

One day in December 1965 when I was walking home from school I felt so hot that I thought I was about to catch fire. I got home and told my mother I didn't feel well. She called the doctor and I was rushed to hospital with pneumonia. I spent my first Christmas in England in hospital with the family crowded around my bed, convinced that I was about to die. Mum spent her last pennies on a tin robot to cheer me up. She forced me to wear my duffle coat after that.

Now that I had made a few friends I was enjoying myself more. In the evenings, Clyde or other boys would call at my house and we'd go to the park.

Like many West Indian parents, my mother and father were very strict about the times I kept, but as both of them worked nights so often I was able to do what I wanted. My sister Sandra was supposed to look after me. And what a grass she was, too.

'TV off at nine o'clock,' she'd say before going to do her home-
work in the girls' room. At 10 p.m. I'd still be in the sitting room
glued to the telly. Sandra would storm in, unplug the TV, take away
the indoor aerial and order me to bed. I discovered that sticking a
knife in the aerial socket worked just as well as the aerial itself.
Sandra would go mad when she discovered I had fooled her. Next
morning she'd tell Dad, who would beat me yet again.

Cash was tight and my parents never gave us pocket money. I was
particularly envious of friends who had no brothers or sisters: it
seemed to me that if you were an only child you always received a
few shillings a week. When I first started playing football, Mum
couldn't even afford my boots. I think a neighbour gave me a pair.
She couldn't afford to give us a normal Christmas, either. My Christmas presents came from London Transport. The company held
Christmas parties for their employees' children and at the end we'd
be given a toy. The LT handout was the only Christmas present I had
for several years.

I wasn't bothered that my parents had so little money because that
was normal in working-class London in the early 1960s. None of my
friends, black or white, ever had any money. The only way to get
sweets was to steal them. Clyde and I made a good team and I was
breaking the law by the age of nine. One lunchtime I tried to pinch a
bar of chocolate from a sweetshop on the way home from school.
The shopkeeper was nowhere to be seen and I presumed he was in
the back storeroom.

Wrong. I seized the chocolate bar – and suddenly a hand shot up
from behind the counter. The shopkeeper had been hiding there all
the time, lying in wait because he had been robbed so often.

He grabbed my hand and tried to haul me over the counter. I was
very frightened and struggled and screamed. But I was quite strong
for a nine-year-old and I managed to pull away. Clyde and I legged it
out of the shop and down the street.

The shopkeeper knew which school I went to. He reported me to
the headmaster, who told my parents. My father gave me a vicious
beating, but I didn't care. He said he was ashamed of me but his
words went over my head. The experience had taught me only one
thing: don't get caught.

When my parents had saved up enough money they sent for the rest of the children. My brothers Kennedy, Ricky and Elvis arrived from Barbados in 1965, when I was nine. Bentley came over a few months later. I was not happy to see them and I resented losing my status as the only boy in the house. Worse, my two older brothers, Bentley and Kennedy, were almost grown up and much better behaved than I. They got on well at school and did their home-work.

Kennedy was hard-working and good at sport. He also sang and played the guitar. Bentley was argumentative and angry with every-body. He was nicknamed 'The Bishop', partly after a Bajan cleric called Bishop Bentley and partly because of his self-righteous manner. Ricky was a sensitive boy. He hated people touching him or looking at him when he was eating. He had a mania for cleanliness and he couldn't drink from a glass until he was sure it had been washed thoroughly. Elvis was a skinny five-year-old, a cry-baby and Mummy's boy.

Much to the relief of my parents, none of them had my rebellious streak. But I was able to teach them a few tricks. They all had Bajan accents and looked and behaved like 'ignorant foreigners'. They regarded me with awe. They saw a very different Oliver from the unsophisticated country boy who had left them a year earlier. My Bajan lilt had almost gone and I had an impressive command of English slang.

I viewed my brothers as pathetically backward. I teased them with an inexhaustible supply of pranks that I'd learned from my English friends. One afternoon I tried out a trick on Ricky and Elvis while we played out in the street. I put a football on the pavement. I told Ricky to go ten yards one side of it and Elvis to go ten yards the other side. Then I told them to run for the ball. The first one to kick it would be the winner. They rushed for the ball but as they reached it I kicked it away. They ended up kicking each other and you could have heard the screams two roads away. I got another hiding from Dad for that.

A few weeks after my brothers' arrival my parents bought their first house. We left the flat in Graham Road in a dreadful state. My younger brothers and I had discovered what fun it was to use our beds as trampolines, and the day before we departed the ceiling collapsed in the flat below. The landlord couldn't wait to see the back of us.

Home was now a late-Victorian terraced house in Adelaide Road, Ealing. When we first moved there, there were no more than ten cars in the whole street. These days you can't find a parking space.

The council had just planted trees along the pavement. My mother hated the trees because dogs pissed on them. They tried planting one outside our house, but Mum ripped it out. They planted another. She ripped that one out as well. And so it went on until the council gave up. There is still no tree outside that house to this day.

The place hadn't been touched since the turn of the century. The walls were lined with dado rails and heavily embossed wallpaper which had been overpainted a million times. Cracked black and white tiles covered the hallway floor. The staircase banisters threatened to collapse at any moment.

Dad slowly renovated the house. Every bit of his spare time was spent in redecorating and knocking down walls. There was still barely enough space for all of us. Dad moved the kitchen into the dining room in order to make another bedroom. There were beds everywhere and it seemed to me that the house was one big bedroom. Looking back on those days, I think I resented the fact that I had nowhere quiet to retreat to. I had no privacy growing up and it's something that I value very highly today.

I shared a double bed with my younger brothers, Ricky and Elvis, until Dad could afford to buy me my own bed. Elvis and Ricky were always fighting in their sleep. Bentley and Kennedy had their own room and the girls another. My parents had the top front room overlooking the street.

Dad struggled to pay the mortgage as well as supporting seven children. At one point he was working sixteen hours a day. At night he was at the sausage factory. He'd come home for breakfast, sleep for an hour or two and then trudge off to a job in a bakery. The strain showed in his face and he became sad and permanently exhausted.

Mum filled the house with items discarded by London Transport. The initials LT were engraved on every knife, fork and spoon we ate with. The cups, saucers and plates were made of thick, white china and bore the same legend. And I'm sure that some of the grey trousers I wore to school were cut-down underground guards' trousers. Mum was not proud. She regarded hand-me-downs as a necessity if she was going to bring up such a large family on so little money.

When my parents began earning more Mum had a fitted kitchen built. The cupboard doors were dark blue. My friends would come to the house and say we must be rich. Mum was also proud of her windows. In 1972 she became the first person in the street to install aluminium double-glazing. She thought she was very smart.

By now, my mother had become a loud, dominating woman. She always wore her grey London Transport uniform and shouted at us as if we were passengers who hadn't paid their tube fare. She ruled the house. My friends were scared of her because she wouldn't tolerate any nonsense. On shopping days she picked on whoever was nearest to her to pull her basket. Whenever I knew shopping time was coming up I would go and hide, but she'd drag me out and I'd have to pull her groceries home. I dreaded my friends seeing me because it was such an uncool thing to do. My brothers used to laugh at me because they knew it hurt my pride so much.

Mum was not a particularly emotional woman, although I remember her sadness on the day that Martin Luther King was assassinated in 1968. We were in the sitting room when the news came over the radio. Mum burst into tears. It was like the end of the world for her. Martin Luther King was her hero. Like many of her generation, she saw him as a speck of hope in a racist world. She was always reading books about the rights of black people and considered herself a supporter of black rights.

Mum loved European pop music and I grew up listening to Lulu, Tom Jones and Cliff Richard. Her favourite was Jim Reeves. She forced us to listen to Jim Reeves' Christmas album every Christmas morning. But in the kitchen she stuck to her native cuisine. She always cooked Bajan food and I couldn't eat anything else. Sometimes I went to my English friends' homes where I was given sausage and chips. Food like that tasted horrible and I couldn't eat it.

Meals were a battle, though. We had to fight for our food. If there were two chickens and you got to them last the best bits were gone. Luxury to me today is having whichever part of the chicken I want.

By now I resented the poverty. Because of my brothers and sisters I felt I was missing out on the good things in life. I used to say to Mum: 'Why did you have so many children? Because I can't have what I want.'

'Hush, Oliver,' she'd reply sadly. 'Ain't you a selfish boy, wantin' everythin' for yourself?'

My father was quieter than my mother now – hardly surprising since he must have been permanently tired. He spent much of the time sleeping in his armchair, feet up, trying to escape from his family. Or he'd come home from work and go straight to bed. Because he worked nights we had to be quiet when we came home from school. That was hard. He never went to the pub. All I can remember him doing is getting up to go to work and coming home and sleeping. He couldn't have afforded to have done anything else, even if he'd had the energy.

Dad became uncompromising about money. We couldn't waste anything. There was trouble if we threw food away. He didn't have a car and even if we could have afforded one, he wouldn't have had time to drive it. We never had pets, although for a brief period he kept an Alsatian chained up in the back garden. It was only there as a deterrent to burglars and I'm not sure if it even had a name.

My most distinct memory of my father is at the breakfast table. He would hide behind his newspaper – always the *Daily Mirror* – pretending not to notice us. Sometimes he would peer over the top and stare at me. Perhaps he was wondering whether or not I would play truant from school that day. He seemed to be always observing us. I can imagine his thoughts as his children made a mess of the table, spilling their cornflakes everywhere. He must have thought, 'Christ, look at this lot. Did I really bring them into the world?' And then he'd give a sorry smile and return to his paper.

If I wanted anything as a child I had to beg for it and if Mum agreed to my demand she had to save and save. We never went on holiday, except for an annual day trip to Blackpool with London Transport's West Indian Social Club. The coach left from Shepherd's Bush Green and everyone brought huge picnic baskets stuffed with fried chicken and plantain.

I hated those trips. Mum would make me wear my suit and a

plastic clip-on tie. I couldn't wait until we got home when I could tear the thing off. Throughout the journey everyone sang and danced to calypso music played on tinny tape-recorders. The other kids had stupid Bajan accents and I spent most of the time avoiding them.

We'd have our picnic in the coach park at Blackpool before going down to the beach. All the English people would be in their swimsuits, but not us. The men were stuffed into their Sunday suits and the women wore their church hats, flowery dresses and cardigans. We must have looked so out of place. It was totally inappropriate dress for a day by the seaside.

In spite of the deprivations, I look back on the age of eight to eleven as a generally happy time without too much tension. But as I grew older I was changing – and it was not for the better.

On my first day at Twyford Secondary School, Acton, I somehow managed to be two hours late. My lack of punctuality has plagued my life ever since. You could say I'm a stickler for being late – it's what I call Mexican Time.

Everybody was in class when I eventually walked through the gates. I hung around until break at 11 a.m., when the pupils spilled out into the playground. Some boys were playing football. I stood there watching. A mixed-race guy came up and asked me if I wanted to join them. He was called Tony Shankster and he became my first friend at Twyford. He was three years older than I.

I started kicking the ball. I ran up and down the playground with it. The other boys tried to tackle me but nobody could get the ball away from me.

Tony congratulated me. 'Man, you're good,' he said. He took me over to the games teacher, Mr Parker, and before I'd even started my first lesson I was being picked for the school football team. I was getting my priorities right, you could say.

I spent the next fifteen minutes in the playground running rings round the rest of the boys. It was the same later in the gym. I was able to do back-flips and somersaults and climb ropes quicker than anyone. I was just a natural athlete and that was all I enjoyed for the rest of my schooldays.

The worst thing about my first day at Twyford was that I was still wearing short trousers. Some of the children laughed at me. 'Nobody wears short trousers here,' they jeered.

That evening I told Mum. 'No, boy, you are not big enough for long trousers,' she said. 'You wait till I tell you when you can have 'em.'

I hated my mother for being an ignorant Bajan. All my white friends had long trousers but the Bajan parents couldn't understand this. This attitude was shared by the parents of all my Bajan friends: boys wear shorts until they are twelve. I felt I was dressed like an idiot because my parents came from the West Indies. They were still living in the 1950s. They didn't have a clue about how to live their lives in Britain.

I worked out how to avoid my shame. The next day I left the house with a pair of Bentley's cast-off long trousers rolled up in a newspaper. I changed out of my shorts in an alley at the bottom of the road and arrived at school looking like everyone else. I did this every day until I was in my teens, when Mum finally decided I was grown up enough to wear long trousers.

My parents found it hard to come to terms with bringing up children in England. Everything was moving too fast for them. When I look back on it, Mum and Dad had trouble keeping up with me from the moment I arrived. In Barbados a boy of eleven does as he's told – but I wasn't in Barbados, and the shouting matches which had started between Dad and me got worse.

My form teacher at Twyford was a woman called Miss Sadler. She had black hair and was a timid, softly spoken woman. You could take diabolical liberties in her class. She was incredibly patient and would continue to teach even when the classroom was in uproar. She hardly ever lost her temper and on the rare occasions she did she would only send you to the headmaster.

I spent the next four years in Miss Sadler's class, coming last in every subject. I couldn't be bothered to learn and I always sat at the back. I just wanted to play football and fool around with my friends.

My only white friend at Twyford was a guy called Gordon Bartlett. I was generally wary of white boys since I had little in common with them. The only reason Gordon and I got on was because we were both good footballers. He was a more powerful player than I and could kick the ball much harder. His family lived near us in Ealing and we'd take the bus to school together. My parents approved of him and I was allowed to go to his house after school.

The Bartletts lived in an ordinary house like ours but I was convinced they had money. Gordon had a bike and even his own bedroom. He had everything I wanted.

Sitting at a table having beans on toast for tea felt very strange. I was amazed when Mrs Bartlett served us. We didn't have meals like that at home. We ate when we wanted to eat. We just took our own food from the oven or the fridge and sat down with our bowl and spoon. People hadn't had dining tables in Barbados and we didn't have one in England. You just sat in an armchair and had your dinner on your lap.

I still feel uneasy around a dining table – it's simply not the Bajan tradition. My children eat on their own at the breakfast bar in the kitchen and we only use the table if we have friends round. These days I get invited out to dinner with friends in the horse world. The tables are often set with a ridiculous number of spoons, knives and forks. I've learned to start from the outside and work my way in, but to start with I used to think: how the hell do they know which fork to use?

Twyford was a tough school. I soon made friends with the black boys. Our enemies were the white boys, whom we dubbed the South Acton Mafia. We were always fighting them.

My behaviour became worse and I was forming some questionable friendships. Clydie had gone to another secondary school and I lost contact with him. I fell in with a group of West Indians who lived in Acton. My new friends made Clyde look like a choirboy. I used to hang around with them after school and I was frequently late getting home to Ealing.

I earned a reputation for organising playground fights. One afternoon a battle nearly broke out with the skinheads over a couple of white twins. I liked the girls but they refused to mix with black boys because they lived on an all-white estate and had been brought up to hate West Indians.

A friend of mine touched up one of the twins and she told the skinheads. Word went round that there was going to be a big fight when school was over. It got back to the teachers and that evening every member of staff was on the front gate. The fight never happened, but the teachers accused me of being the ringleader. I was suspended from school for a week.

After a couple of terms I started bunking off school. I either went to the cinema or mooched around in a park smoking cigarettes. But the pictures and cigarettes cost money and I had none. I started making a few bob by selling my dinner ticket. Or I'd buy ten No. 6 and sell them singly for a profit. Otherwise I'd simply steal Dad's packets of Piccadilly from under his pillow when he was sleeping. But it still wasn't enough.

To finance this new lifestyle I started a protection racket. The Indian boys at Twyford couldn't defend themselves. Worse than that, they didn't *want* to defend themselves. They were victimised terribly. The white skinheads constantly picked on them and every day another Sikh or Bengali was beaten up in the playground. This was 1967, and the era of 'paki-bashing' was in full swing.

I had a reputation as a good fighter and I wasn't frightened of the white boys. One day I talked to one of the Indians, a boy called Nirinda Kurana, and suggested that I could make sure he wasn't beaten up in return for a small amount of sweets.

Nirinda was a short, skinny Sikh. At eleven, he was too young to wear a turban, so he wore a hankie on his head instead. We thought it looked ridiculous and the other children were always trying to pull it off. All the Sikh boys wore hankies on their heads, and they were teased mercilessly.

Nirinda cheerfully agreed to my offer. His father was a rich importer-exporter and he sent his son to school with plenty of pocket money. Nirinda was an excellent badminton player and footballer and we became good friends. We used to go to the sweetshop together and he'd buy me a chocolate bar or a bottle of Corona.

We spent four years together in Miss Sadler's class. Nirinda was a brilliant student and let me copy his work. The only thing against him was his smell. To me, Nirinda smelled terrible. He used to put a viciously pungent concoction of oils on his skin and hair. It took great resolution to occupy the desk next to him.

One morning a skinhead tried to steal Nirinda's dinner ticket.

I spotted the fracas from the other side of the playground. The skinhead had pushed Nirinda against a wall and was spitting in his face. I ran over and challenged the white boy.

'Fuck off, nigger,' the skinhead growled.

I grabbed him in an arm-lock and threw him to the ground.

'Who're you calling nigger now?' I said. I punched him hard in the stomach.

The skinhead pissed himself. I let him go and he staggered off, a wet stain spreading down his trousers.

Nirinda was grinning like a madman. 'Very good, Oliver. Oh yes, very good indeed.' He was so pleased he gave me £1.

That became the norm. Once a week Nirinda gave me a quid and I stopped him from getting beaten up. Then his friends all wanted the same service. It wasn't long before most of the Indian boys in the school had West Indian minders.

Nirinda began to grow and by the age of twelve he was able to defend himself. He gained a lot of respect because of his academic and sporting achievements and the boys who had once picked on him became his friends.

A mixed-race boy called Orlando arrived at Twyford. One day I caught him stealing money out of my white friend Gordon's coat. I beat him up and the fight was eventually stopped by a teacher. Gordon got his money back and after that Orlando and I became good friends and I used to go to his house. He was the first black boy with a white mother I had known. It was weird seeing a white woman who knew so much about black people. She even cooked West Indian food.

But Orlando and I were not friends for long. He started growing dreadlocks at the age of thirteen and became one of the first Rastafarians in London. Overnight he went from speaking proper English to proper Jamaican. Yet he'd never been to Jamaica in his life. I stopped hanging around with him because this was not my scene. It was to be a few more years before I turned to Ras Tafari.

My elder brothers, Kennedy and Bentley, were also at Twyford. Kennedy used to sing along to Elvis Presley records in his bedroom and do his homework. He would lock himself in the bedroom so he could study in peace. We younger brothers used to play cowboys and

Indians on the banisters and he was always storming out of the room and telling us to be quiet.

Kennedy was the most boring man I'd ever met and he later became a Jehovah's Witness, which proves my point. We get on OK now, but it took a long time. He didn't like me and I didn't like him. He was on a lifelong crusade to reform me but he never got anywhere. He married and went to live in Abingdon. I never went to see him. It was as if we weren't from the same parents. He hated me for upsetting Mum and Dad and was always trying to turn my other brothers and sisters against me.

I resented Kennedy a lot. As it became obvious that I was not destined to become a scholar by any stretch of the imagination, my teachers would constantly nag me, 'Why can't you be like Kennedy? Such a polite boy and so hard-working.'

Kennedy was deputy head boy when I arrived at Twyford. Almost every day the headmistress, Miss Cook, would call me into her office and give me a ticking off. 'You've had two brothers at this school and why can't you be like them?' she'd say. 'They're both doing so well but you don't seem to want to learn anything.'

During Miss Cook's lectures I'd stand there, saying nothing and staring out of the window. I longed to escape from her office. To me, my brothers were the most boring people I'd ever met. I certainly did not want to be like them. Oh yes, I knew exactly where Miss Cook could put my brothers.

Miss Cook tried to tame me by giving me a part as a Roman soldier in the school nativity play. I was dressed in a pair of tights and a thigh-length tunic that looked like a skirt. Mum came to watch me. She thought I looked lovely. I nearly died of embarrassment. Here was the hard man of the school dressed up in tights. My mates took the piss out of me for weeks after that.

Kennedy was the brainiest boy in the school. And Kennedy was such a goody-goody that Miss Cook trusted him enough to allow him occasionally to teach classes himself. He took me once for maths. Can you believe that? Being taught by your own brother? How humiliating!

I gave him hell. I skulked behind the raised lid of my desk and lit up a cigarette when he wasn't looking. When he saw the clouds of smoke billowing from the back of the classroom he exploded in fury. No brotherly love here. He kicked me out of the class and ordered me to write out 500 lines – 'I will not smoke in school.'

I refused to do them. That evening he came home and told Mum that I had been smoking in class and that I wouldn't do my lines. My mother gave me a smack round the head. She sent me to my room and ordered me to take the punishment like a man. Borrowing from a trick I had learned from the Bash Street Kids in the *Beano*, I taped three pens together and hastily scribbled out the lines. This trick might have worked for Plug and his chums, but it did not work for me. Mum made me rewrite them properly because they were such a mess.

Bentley was not much better than Kennedy. He had gone straight to Twyford the moment he arrived from Barbados. He was tall, skinny and quiet. He used to get picked on constantly and was always coming home with a bloody nose. When I got to Twyford boys used to come up to me and jeer, 'My brother used to beat up your brother.'

Bentley might have been a weed, but the family honour was at stake. 'Well, you can take this, then,' I'd snarl. And I'd beat up boys for having a brother who'd beaten my brother.

Of all my brothers Bentley was the most like me. But he kept his rebellion to himself. When he was seventeen he could stand my father's domination no longer. He announced that he was leaving home to join the RAF. I asked him, 'What do you want to join the RAF for? Now everyone with a stripe is going to be your father. You'll have hundreds of Dads.'

The year 1969 was a bad one. In July my sisters Sandra and Jennifer were walking across the Great West Road on their way to a youth centre in Brentford. A car doing around 70 mph hurtled down the road towards them. The driver jumped the red traffic lights and smashed into them. They were sent flying seventy feet.

Sandra took the full impact. She broke her pelvis, legs and arms. She suffered brain damage and was in a coma for nine months. Jennifer broke her arm and shoulder. Both were in hospital for a long time.

The driver was caught and it turned out he was drunk. Sandra received compensation from his insurance company but it didn't help her much. She was crippled for life and still has to wear a leg brace.

At the time of the accident my mother was pregnant with my youngest sister, Claudia. Judy was also in hospital, having an operation. My father was cracking up. I remember he and Mum having such violent rows that Mum threatened to leave home. It was the worst year in the life of the Skeete family.

Until that time I'd just been naughty and a bit of a rebel. Now I went totally off the rails. I wanted to kill the man who'd hurt my sisters. I was thirteen years old and I wanted to kill everybody.

In the summer of that year I went on a school day trip to France. We took the ferry from Dover to Calais and I was seasick for the whole journey.

We spent the day in Calais. The first thing I noticed about France was the smell. I remember eating French food and thinking that it was disgusting. Some of the kids wanted to try frogs' legs, but I wasn't having any of that. I was used to flying fish and rice and anything different was the food of barbarians.

But the shops were great. You could buy things that you couldn't buy in England. Like flick knives.

I was becoming increasingly aware that white people were being nasty to me because of my colour. A flick knife was the perfect deterrent.

I bought one knife for myself and another to sell at a profit when I got home. My knife was the best thing I'd ever seen. It had a blade that popped straight out from the handle and was lethally sharp. But even better, it was strictly illegal back home. And anything illegal made me feel like a man.

I returned to England 'tooled up' for the first time. Nobody stopped us at Customs – they didn't expect a school party to be returning with knives. We had to do a project about the trip but I wrote nothing in my exercise book. My French teacher said it had been a waste of time me going to France. Little did she know . . .

Back in London I put a handkerchief in one back pocket, my shiny new knife in the other – and became a rude boy.

All my black friends were rude boys. It was the only way to be.

A rude boy didn't stand for any nonsense. He didn't run and he didn't take racist shit from anyone. If people called him a black bastard, he stabbed them. Simple as that. If you ask a white boy from the 1960s why he picked on Pakistanis rather than West Indians, he'll say that it was because the West Indians carried knives.

The irony was that we dressed in the same way as the skinheads. We even listened to the same records, like 'Moon Stomp' by Judge Dread. We all wore Levi sta-press trousers, Ben Sherman shirts and Crombie coats. On our feet were ivy brogues and on our heads trilbys. Rude boys had crewcuts like the skinheads, yet we were avowed enemies. It was really bizarre.

I joined my rude boy friends on trips to a club in Richmond called the Boat House. The skinheads also went there. There were often fights and people were always getting stabbed and sliced up.

Some of my West Indian friends were influenced by America and got into flares and Afro hairstyles. But I hated flares – the rude boy look was the only look for me.

The best thing about rude boys was that they were Jamaicans. It was far cooler to be Jamaican than it was to be Bajan. Jamaicans called Bajans 'small-island boys' because they were sleepy and boring; Jamaicans were aggressive, hyped-up and streetwise.

I took to the Jamaican culture easily. I dressed like a Jamaican and I began to talk like a Jamaican. If you spoke like a Bajan you were a nerd. But speak like a Jamaican and you had instant street credibility.

I took to greeting my father with: 'Iree, Dayaid. Yarra arrite, marn?' I learned to gently 'kiss' my lips before speaking in a lazy drawl. My family were baffled. They couldn't understand a word I said.

Dad detested everything about my new look and voice. 'Gore 'bline ya, boy. Don't talk to me like dat. If you can' talk English, don' talk at all.'

And I'd say, 'But me issa speakin' English.'

'Where was you born, boy?'

'Barbados, Dad.'

'Den why de hell you talkin' like a Jamaican for?'

And so our squabbles went on. My Jamaican accent stuck until my

late teens, when my Bajan pride, and consonants, returned. A few of
the sounds have stuck, though, and even now many black people are
genuinely surprised when I say I'm from Barbados. I have to put on
a Bajan accent to convince them. Bajan is the most difficult of all the
West Indian accents to do and you won't find many Jamaicans who
can mimic it.

My parents' loathing of my Jamaican accent had much to do with
the fact that they knew no Jamaicans in their first years in Britain.
Bajans stuck with Bajans.

Until secondary school my misdemeanours had been restricted to
nicking a few sweets. Dad was never called in to the headmaster's
office when I was at primary school. Now that I was at Twyford he
was hardly out of it.

By the age of thirteen I was sneaking out of the house at night to
go to 'shebeens' and 'blues' in north London. Shebeens and blues
are an essential part of West Indian culture in Britain's cities. A
shebeen is an illegal drinking club held on the same premises each
night. Blues are itinerant paying parties that can be held anywhere –
in houses, council flats, garages.

You heard about blues by word of mouth. Boys used to stand by
the school gates during the lunch break and whisper, there's a blues
tonight at such-and-such. Blues were illegal because the organisers
were charging money for drink without a licence. If the police turned
up the organisers hid the money and all of a sudden it became a
'private party'. The police were powerless to do anything except
order the DJ to turn down the music.

I used to wait in my bedroom until midnight, when I went out.
Once my sisters were asleep I climbed down the drainpipe and met
my friends in the park. One of them would have a stolen car and
we'd drive to north London. Since my parents usually worked nights
I had to be back by 6 a.m. One morning I'd only just got in from a
blues when Dad surprised me and came into my room. I was standing on my bed taking my trousers off before going to sleep.

'You're up early, Oliver,' he said.

'Yeah, aren't I, Dad.' And I pretended that I had just got up and
was getting dressed. I pulled my trousers back on.

'Happy that you ain't playin' truant today,' Dad added.

'Yeah, time I learned somein'.' I conned him beautifully. He was delighted that I had reformed and was making an effort to get to school on time. A few years later I told him how he'd been tricked. He laughs about it now.

The first time I pulled my flick knife was in a blues at a council flat on the sixteenth floor of a block in Brentford.

It was like many blues I had been to. You could hear the music a mile away and the landing outside the flat was packed with people drinking Special Brew and smoking spliffs. I paid my £2 entrance to the two heavies on the door and pushed my way inside. There must have been 300 guests and it took twenty minutes to get down the corridor to the sitting room where the sound system was set up. The crush was so bad that the place would have been a death trap if a fire had broken out.

There were loudspeakers in every room and I could hear nothing but the thump of reggae. There were virtually no lights and I couldn't see where I was going. I was fighting my way to the bathroom when a large man stepped on my toe. 'Oi, mind your fuckin' feet,' I said.

He looked round to see this snotty thirteen-year-old. 'Who the fuck you talkin' to, yo blud clot,' he spat.

Blood clot, ras clot, bumba clot and pussy clot are all Jamaican insults of the worst kind. I drew myself up to my full height, which wasn't much more than five foot. 'Me a talk to you, ras'hole.'

'Fuck off, kid.'

I drew my knife. 'Jeez man, you's a cunt or wa'. You say sorry.' I pressed the button on the side and the blade sprang out.

His eyes bulged with fright. 'Hey man, sorry. Put dat knife away.'

He took off through the crowd. I chased him but I couldn't catch him. It all sounds so stupid now but I was astonished by the effect that a knife could have. I learned something else that night: when somebody's chasing you with a knife you find that extra speed to get away from them. I've never hurt anybody with a knife, but a weapon certainly deterred people from getting in my way.

The first time a knife was drawn on me was at Ealing Common funfair when I was fourteen. There was a boxing sideshow. You paid 50p and went into the ring, where you fought your opponent in three one-minute rounds. The winner got £2.

My friends and I scraped together the money and I went into the ring with another guy called Norman. We planned to mess about and then one of us would pretend to lose. Then we would share the winnings. But Norman forgot we were supposed to be faking. He hit me hard. So I belted him back. We continued to hurt each other and I won the fight. Outside the ring, Norman was livid. He pulled his knife out and waved it at me.

'Oh, put it away,' I said. I wasn't frightened. I didn't think for one minute he would cut me. We became friends after that.

It's funny, but I met most of my friends through fighting them. Errol was another one. We ended up brawling in the park after boasting about who was the best footballer. I suppose my aggression says something about my psychological state as I entered my teens. The natural thing was to fight and make up, just like dogs. I wasn't a great fighter, but I was thick-skinned and scared of no one.

I was now drinking Special Brew and smoking weed regularly. I can't deny it, can I? Well, didn't most people smoke dope when they were young? I bet that there were some cabinet ministers, maybe even members of the royal family, who had a few spliffs in their teens. Everybody I knew smoked dope when they were growing up. Cannabis was OK, but I never did other drugs.

As I approached the age of fourteen I began to stop fighting my friends. Instead, I began to fight the system. The first time I got into serious trouble was over a bicycle. I stole a bike from a back garden behind our house. I'd been looking out of the window at this gleaming machine for weeks. Eventually, I couldn't resist taking it.

I put it in our back garden. When the owner looked out of his window he could see it. Pretty stupid, huh?

The police arrived at our house. They told my father that I was suspected of theft.

'Is it true, Oliver?' Dad asked me.

I adopted my cool, Jamaican attitude. 'Narra, marn. 'Snart me bike, marn. Issa me maeet's bike.'

'English, Oliver.'

'Er, OK. It's my mate's bike.' I blamed somebody else. Anything to wriggle out of trouble.

No one believed me. The owner got his bike back and my unglamorous dive into the world of crime landed me in a magistrates' court for the first time. I was found guilty of theft and let off with a caution.

Mum reluctantly attended my hearing. But she told me not to expect any more support from her. 'Let me tell you something,' she said. 'This is my first time in a court and I'm goin' to make it my last. If you go stealing ag'in, count me out.'

Dad gave me a few smacks round the head. 'You got me vexed, boy, and you gonna get yourself in big trouble,' he said. 'You be goin' to prison along with all your Jamaican friends.' He and Mum were deeply upset. When we got back home Mum sat in the kitchen and cried. She kept asking herself where she had gone wrong.

I hated the police from the first time I got into trouble. They were the enemy of all black people and they deserved to be treated like the pigs they were. I know I was in the wrong, but by the end of the 1960s the London police were overstretching the mark where West Indians were concerned. If there was any trouble, black boys were automatically to blame. If anything was stolen we were the culprits; if a house was burgled it was us; if anybody was beaten up, it was us.

I was on the police files after the bike incident. I was in the system and there was nothing I could do about it. If anything in my area was nicked, the police came knocking on our door. They also warned the school about me. If a pupil's fountain pen went missing, I was the first one that the teachers questioned. I could have been on the other side of London at the time, but they still thought it was me.

If you can't beat 'em ... fuck them over, I thought. Good 'n' proper. And so I began to steal cars.

I had learned to drive in Acton when I was eleven. A postman called Jack lived in the flat beneath us. He had a Mini. I was mad about cars and Jack used to let me sit in the passenger's seat while he showed me how the pedals worked. Sometimes he paid me a shilling for cleaning his car, inside and out. He would give me the key and then walk to work. When no one was looking I would get in the driver's seat, start the car and take it around the block. It was the biggest thrill of my life.

By my teens I was hooked on driving. My first attempt at joyriding came when I was thirteen. Some friends and I took a Mark I Cortina

GT. I'd been eyeing this car for several days and it was so easy to break into and hot-wire. None of my friends could drive so I was put in charge. About seven of us piled in and I drove it through Ealing. Two policemen in a patrol car spotted us. They gave chase, blue light flashing, siren screeching.

I drove even faster. When I reached Eccleston Road, near the Job Centre, I misjudged the corner. The car skidded across the road and smashed into a garden wall. We scrambled out unhurt and legged it.

For some reason I was wearing this long, pink coat. I don't know where the hell I got it from – I must have had a distorted sense of fashion that week. I ran 400 yards up the road, ditched the coat in a garden so the police wouldn't recognise me (or so I thought) and then brazenly walked back towards the car.

But the police were not fooled. It was 11 p.m. and the officers thought: hello, hello, what's a kid his age doing out at this time of night? They arrested me and I subsequently made my second appearance at juvenile court. I was convicted of driving under age, having no insurance and for taking and driving away a vehicle. The magistrate banned me from driving for six months. This would come into effect when I reached the age of seventeen, which meant that I wouldn't be able to drive legally until I was seventeen and a half.

This had no effect on me and I continued taking cars. I didn't always drive the cars myself – often I ended up as a passenger. In the end, I had so many joyriding convictions that I wasn't allowed to drive until I was twenty.

I was not a good criminal. I couldn't get it into my thick head that a schoolboy driving a car at midnight is likely to get caught. I was just a silly little boy who got into trouble with the police through my own stupidity. I mean, taking a bike from a neighbour's garden is hardly the work of a criminal mind, is it? If I'd had any sense I'd have taken the bike to Acton and sold it. The answer was that I just didn't think and I just didn't care.

So did I go off the rails because my father beat me? I don't think so. He used to beat my brothers as well and they didn't turn out like me. I just had a naturally rebellious personality and being a rebel was fun.

I don't recommend joyriding and I regret all the trouble I caused.

There's not much I can do about it except set as good an example as I can today. I know now how it feels to have a car stolen. I've had several vehicles taken from outside my house and it feels horrible. A stolen car ruins your life for days. You leave your house expecting to find your car and then it's like a bad dream, a terrible shock when you can't find it. You've left it to the last minute to go to work and now you have to walk or take the train. Then there's all that hassle involved in informing the police. They go through the motions of trying to find it but the reality is that they don't stand a chance.

3

THE FIRST TIME . . .

The first girl I fancied was called Gillian Polding. She was white and she was in Miss Sadler's class with me at school.

I'll never forget the first time I saw Gillian. She was dressed in black shoes, red tights, red tartan skirt and a red cardigan. Her style was typical of the 1960s and her mum had dressed her up so that she looked a proper little madam. To me she was lovely and she was the only girl at Rothschild's who caught my eye.

Unfortunately, she also hated my guts.

She was a year older than me and I spent the first week at school staring at her. Her first words to me were: 'Why do you keep looking at me?' I felt so stupid. It took a year before I had the courage to speak to her.

When I felt braver I harassed her dreadfully. 'Can I sit next to you?' I begged. 'Please let me sit next to you. Please, please, please.' I was always on her case. 'I think you're very pretty. Can I walk you home?'

Gillian used to tilt her upturned nose and walk away, leaving me squirming. I gave up after that. No point in wasting too much time on a girl.

My interest in girls progressed through the pulling-knickers-down-and-running-like-hell stage. When I reached the age of fourteen I was ready to take on the entire female population. And so I began a string of relationships that, for the most part, were to lead to nothing but trouble.

My first girlfriend was called Jennifer Brown. We were both at

Twyford Secondary and she was the prettiest girl in the school. I'd first noticed her when I was twelve and she was eleven. But it was only when I turned fourteen, and my hormones started racing, that I became really interested in her.

Jennifer was Jamaican. She had dimples, beautiful, long legs and neat little breasts. She was so petite, about five foot two with tiny feet. (I've always insisted on girls with small feet. I hate big feet on a girl, they're a big turn-off.)

She wasn't a typical, rowdy black girl. She was quiet and well spoken and I decided that I liked her even more than my Crombie and Ben Shermans. I fell utterly in love.

Like Gillian before her, Jennifer took absolutely no notice of me. I'd hang around the gates after school waiting for a glimpse of her. She'd stride past me without even a glance. She probably had bad memories of what I'd been like a year before when my friends and I had teased the girls terribly. We would run past them flicking up their skirts and pinching their breasts. The girls used to shout at us and say that we were horrible.

But now I didn't want to be horrible. I only wanted to be nice to Jennifer. But the moment I showed interest in her she didn't want to know.

However, I was convinced that she secretly liked me. During the teatime break one afternoon I cornered her behind the prefab classrooms at the back of the playground. I pushed her against the building and kissed her. My clumsy fumbling was not a success. She tried to push me away.

'Nah, Oliver, don't do that. That's 'orrible.' But she wasn't as cross as she should have been. She wasn't trying hard enough to get rid of me. Underneath all her protests I was sure she was enjoying herself.

Our clinch lasted about thirty seconds. Then she ran back to her friends. I leaned against the classroom wall and shut my eyes. I couldn't keep the grin off my face. I'd kissed a girl for the first time and it felt like I'd had total sex.

Jennifer began treating me differently after that. She must have thought I wasn't so bad after all. That first kiss led to another and soon I was walking her home from school.

We became close but we never got further than kissing. I'd drop her at the bottom of her road, we'd have a quick snog and then she'd go home. I used to wait until I saw her wave and disappear into her house. Then I went home and Mum would be mad me because I was late. Dad realised quickly that I had a girlfriend, but Mum didn't click. Dad started asking me about girls and I told him about Jennifer.

I brought her home one evening to meet my parents. They were delighted I had a girlfriend. They thought she would help keep me out of trouble. Mum said to her, 'What's a nice girl like you doin' with a boy like Oliver?' All the family laughed. The first time Mum said this it was a joke. But as I grew older she was to repeat that question over and over again, and there was to come a time when she no longer meant it to be funny.

Jennifer and I had an idyllic time together. At weekends she would meet me at my house and we would go to the park where we sat on a bench and proclaimed our love for each other. She was my girlfriend and I was convinced that we would love each other forever.

The feelings were too good to last. About three months into our relationship I went one evening with some rude boy friends to a youth club disco in Wembley. It was on a council estate called Chalk Hill which these days is a bad place to grow up.

The music was blaring as we arrived. We swaggered in. Everybody was hanging around the edge of the dance floor. I cast my eyes around the room to see who was there. To my astonishment I saw Jennifer on the opposite side of the room. What was she doing in Wembley? She'd never told me she was coming here.

She was standing with a group of heavily built black guys who looked about sixteen or seventeen. I knew a couple of them. They came from Harlesden. To a suburban Ealing boy like me, Harlesden was the ghetto. Joyriding was tame compared to what Harlesden boys got up to. Harlesden was the inner city. They were into mugging and hard drugs.

So what was nice, sweet Jennifer doing with boys from Harlesden?

One of Jennifer's friends noticed that I was eyeballing her. He nudged the others. They looked over in my direction. They seemed to be talking about me. Jennifer looked up and saw me. She put her hands to her mouth in horror.

I thought to myself: why won't she come and talk to me? One of the boys put an arm around her shoulder. He was dressed in rude boy gear like me. He and his friends glared at me challengingly.

My whole body tensed. The awful realisation of what was happening began to dawn on me. I didn't want to believe it but I think I had it sussed. I made a move to cross the dance floor.

One of the boys at Jennifer's side left the pack and hurried across to me. He was only a little guy, about five foot five. I'd never met him before and he had a wise and friendly look about him.

He stopped in front of me, blocking my way. 'Think we'd better talk,' he said.

'And who are you?' I replied angrily.

'Name's Popeye.' His eyes seemed to explode out of his fat, round face. I could see how he'd got his moniker.

He gently put his hand on my arm and steered me back to the door. I turned round and glanced back at Jennifer. She looked terrified.

Popeye spoke to me in an urgent whisper. 'Listen my man,' he said. 'These guys are going to fuck you over. They're talking about cutting you up and stuff because they know you're mucking about with Jennifer.'

'Why shouldn't I muck about with her?' I retorted. 'She's my girlfriend.'

Popeye looked at me piteously. 'No, she's not, my man. She's with Rocky.'

'And who the fuck's Rocky?'

'Her boyfriend.'

'But I'm her boyfriend.'

'Nah. Been seeing Rocky for weeks.'

Feelings of panic rose in my stomach. I had been deceived. Badly. OK, it's the sort of emotional turmoil that most adolescents go through, but knowing that now didn't make things any better at the time.

'Which one's he?' I asked.

Popeye pointed at the boy with his arm around Jennifer's shoulder. He had a lopsided face and sticking-out teeth. A little of my hurt pride went when I realised that I was far better looking than him. I clocked him with my eyes. We stared each other out.

'So, let them come and do me over,' I said. I put my hand to my back pocket and felt my knife.

I didn't let Popeye know I had a weapon but I think he realised. He looked at me sadly and returned to his friends. He had a funny, rather delicate walk.

My friends gathered round me. They knew what was going on. One of them said nervously, 'Think we'll go now, Oliver.' He didn't want trouble and I couldn't blame him. It wasn't his fight.

I adopted my meanest rude boy pose. I put my hand on my hips and beckoned Jennifer over. She looked at Rocky. He nodded curtly as if to give her his permission. She walked over to me.

'What the fuck's going on?' I said to her.

'That's my boyfriend, Rocky,' she said brazenly.

'Aw, c'mon Jennifer. It's me, for fuck's sake.'

She looked at me as if she'd never seen me before. I felt a pain in the pit of my stomach. She turned round and walked away. Her rejection brought tears to my eyes. I couldn't believe what was happening. And to make matters worse, I hadn't even slept with her yet.

Popeye hurried back over. 'Look man, you might have your tool on you, but they've all got their tools so don' be stupid. You're goin' to get hurt. Leave now.'

It's funny how you can go off a girl so quickly. Within a few seconds I decided that common sense was the order of the day. I left the youth club and went home. Popeye had saved my life. We became good friends after that and I still see him today. And Rocky? Well, we got to know each other over the next few years. We're friends now, but if it hadn't been for Popeye, one of us could have ended up doing a life sentence.

That was the end of any ideas I might have had about monogamy. I decided I might as well have several girlfriends on the go rather than run the risk of being hurt by someone special. I still saw Jennifer at school and spoke to her but it wasn't the same. There was a barrier between us.

I thought I'd try an older woman. Carol was sixteen and a friend of my sister's. She was a gorgeous Guyanese Indian and the day after meeting her I was infatuated. Then I met another girl called Marita, who was even prettier. And then another, and another.

I became an expert snogger. I was still very innocent. It was all five-minute clinches under a tree in the park. There was no hands-down-the-knickers stuff, although at the time it seemed like I was having loads of sex. The problem was that I was kissing all these girls yet they all seemed to be interested in other boys. Well-developed girls like Carol had dozens of boys chasing her. And they were usually much older than immature Oliver. I suppose I had that teenage tendency of going for girls who were unavailable, out of reach.

A few weeks after the Wembley youth club fiasco I heard some good news: Jennifer had broken up with Rocky. And so one teatime I approached her in the playground. 'Can I walk you home?' I asked.

She smiled at me and I was infatuated again. 'Yeah, Oliver. Why not?'

We were both fifteen and we started getting serious. In a quiet moment in the park she admitted she had been sleeping with Rocky. I was gutted. Why couldn't I have been the first?

She took me home to meet her parents and they liked me. I wanted to go further with her but I didn't know how. My sex education had been minimal. Dad hadn't talked to me about sex and we never learned about it at school.

One afternoon I walked Jennifer home as usual. We walked in silence, but there was a feeling of anticipation between us. We both knew what was about to happen but neither of us said anything. When we got to her house her father was out and her mother was busy in the kitchen. It was about 5 p.m. She took my hand and led me upstairs.

Girls' bedrooms were sacred places where things went on that I could not even imagine. My sisters never let me near their room. So when I saw Jennifer's bedroom for the first time I was shaking with fear. I can't remember the furniture or if there were any pictures on the walls. Such was my sexual tension that all I could see was a bed. I noticed a faint aroma of make-up and perfume. I think a pair of tights was draped over a chair.

Until now my sexual meandering had been restricted to kissing and lifting up girls' skirts and playing Jack the Lad. Now it was my first time and I was scared.

(*Above left*) Dad aged forty. You can see why some people nicknamed him Lee Van Cleef

(*Above right*) Mum aged thirty-five. I can always remember her in glasses with great wings that seemed to point towards the sky

Mum and Grandma Rosalie at a cousin's wedding in 1970

Glenda's last day at school outside our house in The Whim, Barbados

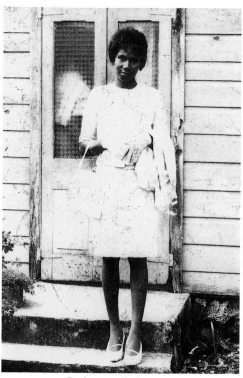

Judy, aged sixteen

My sister Jennifer in 1966, aged twelve. I nicknamed her 'Boneyard' because she was so skinny. She was the best girl footballer I've ever met

(*Left to right*) Sandra, me (aged twelve) and Jennifer in Graham Road, Acton.

Bentley (*far left, front row*), aged eighteen, at his RAF passing out parade – and to think that he and Mum wanted *me* to join up!

Kennedy outside the flat at Graham Road. He's standing by Jack's mini, the first car I learned to drive when I was eleven

Kennedy's wedding in Hanwell, 1970. I'm the moody-looking massive fourteen-year-old on the bride's left. I don't think I wanted to be there

The fourth birthday party of Judy's son, David. (*From left to right*) Dad, Judy, David, Celia (Judy's best friend from Barbados), Ricky, Mum and Noel

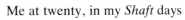
Me at twenty, in my *Shaft* days

My little brother Elvis and me in the mid-seventies

As a car sprayer in 1979. You can see my dreadlocks beginning to sprout

As a bouncer in 1990, with one of my colleagues, Paul

In 1993 I appeared as a bouncer in *The Bill*. Here I am with Jaye Griffiths, who plays D.I. Johnson

The kids: (*left to right*) Oliver, Michelle (Anne's eldest daughter), Zarra and Chanelle

Grandma Rosalie, not long before she died

Aunt Emelyn (*left*) and Aunt Pearl at Pearl's house in The Whim, 1994
(*Peter Holt*)

Mum and Dad at their house in Ashton Hall, Barbados, 1994 (*Peter Holt*)

We stood by the bed. We embraced awkwardly before breaking apart and undressing. Then we got under the cold sheets. I roughly pulled Jennifer to me.

It lasted all of fifteen seconds. I don't know what Jennifer was used to but obviously it wasn't much. She didn't seem to be disappointed. She curled her body against mine and said I was the best thing ever.

I fell hopelessly in love. Because you do, don't you, the first time? You go stupid. It's like you don't have any other friends. You have this one girl who you want to be with the whole time.

I stopped hanging out with my old friends. They'd say, 'Are you coming out tonight?' And I'd say, 'No, I'm going round to my girlfriend's house.' Jennifer and I kept a regular date, sleeping together after school each day. My parents were relieved I was back with her. At least they knew where I was in the evenings.

Jennifer also came to our house on evenings when my parents were working. I would kick my brothers out of the bedroom and lock the door so that we could go to bed.

But it was too good to last and the novelty of first love began to wear off. I started to stray back to my old friends and haunts. I'd go to Jennifer's house at 5 p.m., spend an hour in her bed and then leave her to meet my friends in the park.

I began going to blues again. Jennifer never came with me because her parents forbade her to stay out that late. I began to detect a frostiness from her mum whenever I arrived at their house. I think she was beginning to see the less charming side of me.

I couldn't stay with one girl for long. I started seeing Carol and Marita again. My mother could see I was getting bored with Jennifer and she tried a spot of matchmaking. She was keen for me to go out with a Bajan girl called Cissy whom she invited round for Sunday lunch. Cissy was mad about me, but I wasn't interested.

I was still only fifteen when I bought my first car, an Austin Riley 30 with fat, go-faster wheels. I gave £30 for it. I used to park it outside our house. Amazingly, my parents never found out about it.

Sex became the high point of my adolescent life. I got into some bizarre situations. I was driving through Ealing Common one day when I spotted a girl walking along the road. I was barely fifteen and a half at the time. I stopped the car and honked the horn.

'Oi, come over here,' I called. Not the most subtle of approaches, but it worked. She was about twenty and really pretty. My age must have blown her away, because she got in the car, no argument. I drove her to her house in Ealing and we went to bed.

Afterwards she told me she was married to a musician who was on tour in Europe. I saw her regularly for about two months. Then one day I arrived at her house and she opened the door and said that her husband was at home. Not surprisingly, I made a move to leave. 'No,' she said. 'Come in and meet him.' So I did, and we had a drink and a chat. He must have known that I was sleeping with his wife but he didn't seem to care. He was as cool as anything. I suppose he didn't consider a fifteen-year-old much of a threat.

I was still going out with Jennifer and the rest of them when I met Sue, the girl with whom I was to settle down ten years later. We met at Elthorne Youth Centre in Ealing. I used to go there with my friends when we played truant from school. We hung out there gambling at dominoes and cards.

On Tuesday nights there was a little disco and all these young white girls would turn up. They were so easy for us black boys. We'd take them out round the back of the building and have sex on the grass.

Susan started coming on Tuesday nights with her sister and her two cousins. They were unbelievably attractive girls, but Susan was the prettiest of them all. She was Sri Lankan with Portuguese and Dutch blood. She had light olive skin and delicately defined features. All the boys chased her from the moment she arrived.

Susan was eighteen months younger than me and very innocent. She was from a quiet little family and she didn't know anything about boys. On the first few occasions she came to the disco I said nothing to her. Then one evening I pounced on her in the corridor. I walked up to her, put my arms behind my back, leaned forward and gently kissed her.

It was my stock-in-trade: a sudden kiss, take 'em by surprise. Exactly the same method I'd used on Jennifer a year earlier.

Then I walked off without saying anything. Sue stood there, open-mouthed in astonishment.

I found out where she lived and the next day I went to her house.

I knocked on the door. She answered it. She took one look at me and slammed the door in my face.

The following day I tried again. The same thing happened. And the next day. And the day after that.

But I refused to give up. At the end of the week I strode up to her house and tried one final time. The door opened. 'Stop that knocking,' she said. 'Don't ever come here again.' And she slammed the door in my face.

Sue told me later that her father would have gone mad if he'd known a black boy was calling for his daughter. Her family did not trust West Indians.

A plan was called for. I made it my business to get to know Susan's youngest brother, Monty, who was fourteen. I used to meet him in the park near their house. Then one day Susan came along with him and we started getting to know each other. Within a month we were going out together.

Even then she didn't allow me near her house. I would meet her in the park and we'd sit for thirty minutes chatting before she had to go home. There was only so much of this I could take, particularly since it meant there was little chance of going to bed with her. I soon began to get bored and the infatuation wore off.

I continued to play the field, going out with any good-looking girl I could find. I didn't see anything wrong in that. I was just having a good time.

While I was learning all I needed to know about sex and partying, my school work was a disaster. I paid no attention in maths or English and I came last in the French exams because I fancied the teacher. She was about twenty-three, with long, brown legs, the stuff of Parisian fantasies. I found it impossible to concentrate in her classes.

My favourite subjects were history and geography. I enjoyed hearing about kings who invaded places and killed people. I was a bit like that, always invading blues in north London. And I saw myself as something of an explorer, discovering new clubs and London's underworld.

My behaviour at school was consistently bad. Almost every day I was caught smoking in class – when I wasn't playing truant, that is.

Skeete's desk was recognisable by the fuggy haze over it.

About the only thing in my favour was that I wasn't in the lowest class. This was down to Kennedy's influence. As deputy head boy, it would have been a severe blow to his pride to see me in the same room with all the dunces. And I managed to prevent myself from scoring zero by cheating, copying the work of my Indian friends.

Miss Sadler must have known that I cheated. She says today that I was quite bright but lazy. She was one of the most restrained, patient people I have ever met. But finally her patience would snap and she would lose her temper. 'Get out of this room, Skeete!' she would roar. 'And don't come back until you've learned some manners!'

I spent half my days outside the headmaster's office waiting to be dealt with. I had no respect for the headmaster. Until I was fourteen and a half he caned me, but the beatings stopped after that. I was growing up fast and he didn't want to mess with me in case I retaliated. He knew that I didn't care about school and that I was longing to be expelled.

The question from the teachers was always the same: 'What do you want to be when you leave school, Skeete?' Answer: 'I want to be grown up like you, sir.' Result: long-suffering look on teacher's face.

I had no ambitions. I didn't want to do anything. I wanted to hang around in the park and play dominoes. My teachers knew this and they were resigned to the fact that I was just another West Indian boy who was going to end up in trouble and on the streets.

The careers master called me into his office and gave me his usual lecture. Once we'd sorted out that I wasn't going to be a doctor or a lawyer (and that didn't take long) he said, 'Right, Skeete. Have you given any thought to your future at all?'

'Yeah. I'd like to be a professional footballer, or a racing driver.' Replies like this tend to exasperate careers masters. What he really wanted me to say was, 'I've always wanted to be a bus-driver.' Then he could say, 'Excellent choice! We'll contact London Transport right away.'

They didn't expect the black pupils to be anything more than bus-drivers. It was easier to push a black boy into a manual occupation than to go to the bother of explaining that he was never going to make it as a white-collar worker. And if black children refused to learn at school they were simply pushed aside on the grounds that it was easier to ignore them. They only caused trouble and they were harder to control than white children.

Football was my happiest memory of school. It remained all I enjoyed doing. But I was no good as a team player – I just wanted to score lots of goals. The football master, Mr Parker, was a strict Welshman with no lips. He was short, bow-legged and looked about forty, although he was only in his mid-twenties. He used to tell me off after every game: 'Trouble with you, Skeete, is you've got loads of talent but you just don't use it.'

Mr Parker had no time for boys who messed around. After one important match which the school had lost, he lined us up and whacked each of us with a bedroom slipper. If we said anything or laughed we had to go to the front of the queue and be slippered again. He must have beaten me seven or eight times.

The teachers at Twyford must have become thoroughly fed up with me. I saw myself as a lovable rogue, but in truth I was a pain in the arse. I never did little-boy things like play marbles because big-boy things like fighting and flirting with girls were more fun.

When I was fourteen, West Ham Football Club sent scouts down to Twyford to check out the school's young players. I was given a trial but I didn't play well that day. I tried to be a super-hero and refused to let anyone else near the ball. The club turned me down. Gordon Bartlett got a trial with Portsmouth and ended up training with them for a few months. But he didn't make it either. They said we were good, but not that good.

I was disappointed because I fancied making thousands of pounds as a professional footballer. But it was the same old story – I wasn't prepared to put in the effort. It was hard getting up on Saturday mornings to go to matches after having been out all night.

In retrospect, I wish I'd done better at school and I'd like to have gone to university. I think I'd have had a better chance if there had been more of an incentive to pass exams. Schools should give cash prizes to people who come top in class. Imagine that you're fifteen and you know that if you come first in an exam you'll be given £500. Everybody would go for it. You'd have a much higher academic standard throughout the country and it would quickly pay off. Top marks, Skeete. Good idea, that one.

My night-time activities were getting worse. I was part of a gang that went to blues all over London. We drank and smoked marijuana and sometimes we walked home several miles at five in the morning – if we couldn't find a car to steal. It got to the point where I was hardly ever at school and when I was I was usually fighting. Eventually it all came to a head. I was involved in yet another fight and the deputy headmaster, Mr Sparks, hauled me into his office.

Mr Sparks got out my school file and put it on his desk. He was very tall, about six foot seven. He wore glasses, brown brogues, corduroys and a dusty tweed jacket covered in patches. His black hair was slicked back with Brylcreem. He looked like something out of the 1950s. He was long-suffering and his thin, bony shoulders were stooped from years of trying to cope with pupils like me.

'Know what you're doing at this school, Skeete?' he asked.

'Nah. Whassat?'

'You're taking up space.' He took off his glasses and towered over me. 'You don't want to learn, you don't want to do as you're told . . .'

I puffed out my cheeks and sighed. So what else was new? This was so boring.

He went on, 'You know, of all the children I have ever encountered at Twyford you are one of the most difficult. In the circumstances I think it would be as well if you left and tried life on the outside, because that's what you seem to be doing anyway.'

I said nothing. I tried to stare him out but Mr Sparks was unmoved by my bravado. 'I've had words with your mother,' he continued, 'and she says she sends you to school every day but you don't turn up. It's not her fault, it's you.' He then launched into a lecture about how a generation of Skeetes had been at Twyford. Kennedy and Bentley had turned out to be model students. Why wasn't I the same?

'Don't wanna be like my brothers.'

Mr Sparks looked at me unhappily. 'Well, in that case you might as well leave. Today.'

'Great,' I answered. 'I'm going now.'

And that was the end of my schooldays. I wasn't actually expelled but it was the closest thing to it.

The physical act of leaving school was harder than I had expected. I began waking up in the morning with no school, no job and nowhere to go. Most days I ended up back at Twyford hanging around the gates waiting for my friends to come out. In a funny way I missed school. It had been my life for so long and it was difficult to let go.

My parents were not pleased to have me in the house all day. I might have been fifteen but Dad made sure that he was the only man of the house. If I refused to fix the fence or wash the windows, he said, 'Who pays the bills around here, boy? I'm in charge here, boy, and you do as I say.'

Mum and Bentley tried to make me join the RAF. They thought the military might sort me out, give me some direction. They took me down to the careers office and I signed some papers. I hadn't a clue what I was doing but the next thing I knew was that I had passed the medical and had orders to go to a training station. It occurred to me that the RAF were going to tell me what to do and I couldn't face that. I resigned before I even started. I'd seen what the services had done to Bentley and didn't want the same thing to happen to me. He had a ridiculous haircut and a serious uniform with a white belt. It was all too much for me.

The next idea was a mechanical engineering course at Hammersmith College. The teachers were lucky if they saw me; I think I went to one lesson. I couldn't see the point of more studying. Sitting behind a desk all day was so boring.

I was now getting into trouble regularly. Go into Ealing Police Station today and you'll probably find my name carved in the walls of several cells. My brothers and sisters constantly complained about me. Bentley had the greatest reason to hate me. He used to come home from the RAF and curse me for upsetting my mother. He hated me for speaking Jamaican and because every weekend he had to drag me out of a police station. It was always the same story. My Dad would go into Bentley's room at 7 a.m. on a Sunday morning and shake him awake. 'Oliver's in the police station again. Been stealing cars again. Can you give me a lift down there to get him out?' Bentley would be furious that his sleep had been disturbed. I never heard the end of it.

The arguments got worse. They were six kids in the house and we all had to do chores such as gardening, vacuuming, putting the bin out. I never contributed. I either hid or went to the park.

Eventually my mother could stand it no longer. 'If you don' do your share of the work, Oliver, then you're not welcome here.'

I don't think she expected me to leave but the arguments had become so heavy that I had no alternative. One morning I walked out. My sister Judy was married by then. I went round to her house and asked if I could stay. Her husband Noel opened the door. Judy stood behind him.

Noel told me to get lost. He didn't want me near the place.

'But Judy. Me is homeless,' I pleaded.

She walked away, embarrassed. Noel slammed the door in my face. 'And you can shut that fuckin' Jamaican up,' he yelled. Years later Judy told me that she wouldn't have minded me staying but Noel had been violently against it. I hated her for years after that.

So I had nowhere to go and no idea what I was going to do. I had not bothered to pack a bag and I had only the clothes I was wearing.

I walked to the park, where I met one of my friends, an Anglo-African boy called Adi whom I'd met at Hammersmith College. He was a littler older than me and I was impressed by him. He was the most streetwise boy I have ever known. He came from Hammersmith, and boys like him who lived closer to central London were always more worldly than the likes of me, who lived in Ealing. Our families lived in big, suburban three-bedroomed houses, while Hammersmith and Ladbroke Grove were a ghetto of council flats. I liked the ghetto. The boys were more hip and they had better clothes – even if they did have to steal to get them.

Adi dressed like a pukka rude boy: Farrah slacks, Gabicci tops, gold-tipped shoes. Despite a large head, he was good looking and popular with the girls. In the few weeks I'd known him he'd taught me how to dodge bus fares. We'd get on one bus and then jump off on to another when the conductor asked for our tickets.

We hung around outside the record shop in Shepherd's Bush Market listening to music. West Indians were getting a hard time from the police then thanks to the infamous 'sus' laws which the government had introduced in the 1970s as a way of picking up people merely 'suspected' of having committed a crime for no concrete reason. The sus laws were a bastard. Armed with this new weapon, the police were constantly arresting my friends and me on suspicion of theft. I admit that I sometimes stole the occasional piece of clothing but I never nicked money from the shopkeepers like the other boys did. Something always stopped me from doing that. I was not cut out to be a serious criminal.

When I met Adi in the park he told me that he too had been kicked out of home. 'Fuckin' parents,' he growled. 'Don' need 'em.'

He suggested that we went up to the West End. And so we began living rough on the streets of Soho. It was one of the lowest points of my life.

The first night we slept in a doorway in Brewer Street. It was an area of pimps, hookers and the occasional foot-slogging policeman. We were moved several times during the night. In the morning I felt cold and dirty. Adi seemed to be enjoying himself, relishing the freedom. He pulled me to my feet and began teaching me how to be a bum.

Adi was a proficient scavenger. We always had money. Sometimes he went through the amusement arcades breaking the machines and stealing the cash. I never found out how he did it. Or we ordered tea and sandwiches in coffee bars and did a runner without paying. We grabbed sweets from corner-shop counters and ran off. I was always a few yards behind my friend. I never knew what he was going to do next. I was permanently on my guard, keeping an eye out for policemen. We stopped short of begging. My pride would not allow me to sit on the pavement, cap in hand, asking for small change.

We met many other kids on the streets. We'd get together in alleyways off Leicester Square and brag about what we'd stolen that day. Most of them were from up north. They had run away from home and had come down to see the bright lights of London. I'd never met boys as rough as this before. They were all accomplished handbag-snatchers and I felt green in comparison.

To this day I can't work out why I lived rough like that. Even as a small child I was a neat person, almost obsessed with cleanliness. And you only have to see my house today to realise that I like things tidy. I must have been having a brainstorm to put up with so much squalor.

I was always tired and smelly. And I had a permanent stomach ache from a diet of sweets and chocolate bars. My feet stank. One day Adi walked into a shoe shop and tried on some new shoes. Then he ran off without paying, leaving his old ones behind. That afternoon I did the same thing at another shop.

The nightmare lasted two weeks. Eventually I couldn't stand the dirt any longer. Adi stayed up west, where he continued to work his scams. I think he was enjoying himself. I yearned to have a bath so I went home to Mum.

She welcomed me back but I don't think she'd been particularly worried about my absence. She was resigned to the fact that she'd lost all control of me, and anyway, I was big enough to look after myself. My parents had spent years trying to get me to behave myself and in the end they had given up.

My experience on the streets has had a lasting effect. When I walk through the West End now and I see people with northern accents begging for money, I know that they've left home and jumped on a train with nothing in their pockets. To me, that's not the right way to leave home. No good will ever come of it.

I'm not too keen on beggars, and I wonder how many of them really don't have homes to go to. I'm sure that if they begged enough money to get the train home they could go back to their old bedrooms and their mums and dads would look after them.

Except for the fact that I now had clean sheets to sleep in my life changed little. I continued to get into trouble and I lost count of the times the police caught me for joyriding. I got more driving bans but I kept on breaking the law. Cars had become such an obsession that I reckoned I might as well make my living from them. So, as I turned sixteen, I got my first job.

I had been searching for work for weeks when I went for an interview at a tiny, old-fashioned garage in Pitshanger Lane, Ealing. The place was an oily mess and looked like something out of the 1940s. I'd never seen such antiquated tools.

A mechanic told me to wait in the corridor upstairs and the boss would see me in a few minutes. Another boy was also waiting to be interviewed. 'Hello,' he said. 'Come for the job?' He was fat and looked like he had elephantiasis.

'Yeah,' I said.

'Me too.'

A smug smile crossed his sweaty face. He reckoned the position was his – no contest.

'And who do you think's going to get it?' I asked.

'We'll have to see, won't we?'

'Oh no we won't.' By this time I knew from experience how hard it was to find a job. I wasn't going to have a jerk like this buggering up my chances. I took out my flick knife and held it in front of his face. 'Tell you what,' I snarled. 'The job's mine. Now fuck off.'

I've seldom seen anyone run so fast. I know it wasn't the most pleasant way to embark on a career, but, as I said, work was difficult to find. The boss called me in and, in the absence of any competition, he hired me as an apprentice mechanic.

All I can remember about that first job was that I made tea and cleaned up behind the grease monkeys for weeks and weeks. But I really enjoyed myself. I loved learning how to unbolt engines and repair tyres. I might have made a mess of school, but cars? I couldn't learn quickly enough. Cars were already my great love and it was to stay that way until I discovered horses. But that was still a long time in the future.

I earned £5 a week. I began saving for the first time in my life and in three months I had enough to buy my first proper rude boy suit. It was a hand-made mohair number costing £42. It fitted like a dream and I pulled loads of girls when I wore it.

My parents were delighted that I had found a job. My mother was relieved that I was finally off the streets and was bringing home some much-needed extra money.

The job lasted for a year. Then my employer wrongly accused me of stealing money from the till. I was sacked, but I wasn't worried. I found work almost immediately with a garage in Hanwell. One day the paint-sprayer didn't turn up and the boss needed to have a car painted quickly. I went back to the garage that night and sprayed the vehicle while nobody was looking. My boss was delighted with my work and that's how I became a paint-sprayer, my occupation for the next eighteen years.

I enjoyed spraying and I never imagined that I would do anything else. I quickly became good at it. Spraying a car is all about rhythm, gently sweeping the spray-gun to and fro and making sure that you don't put too much paint in one place.

But even a steady job couldn't remove the temptation to steal cars. My boss had given me a key to the garage and one evening I went round and took out a car that had just been painted. It was a sparkling little Riley 1.5, perfect for low-profile joyriding. I planned to take it back later so that nobody would know it had ever left the garage.

I picked up some friends and we went on an all-night jaunt around the city, popping into a succession of blues. Inevitably, the police stopped us. They charged me with every driving offence in the book and one day in June 1973, I appeared at Ealing Juvenile Court.

The magistrate was a tired-looking man who knew me well. The charges were read out and I pleaded guilty. Well, there was not much else I could do. I'd been caught red-handed, hadn't I? The prosecution put their case and detailed my previous convictions.

The magistrate was fed up with me. 'As I see it, Skeete,' he said, 'you've had all the chances under the sun. You've had conditional discharges, probation, warnings, fines, but that still hasn't stopped you stealing cars. If I don't do something about you now you're going to become a menace to society.'

He gave me three months in a detention centre.

My jaw dropped. I'd thought they were going to let me off again. I certainly wasn't expecting to go down. The jailer took me down to the cells, where I waited until the prison van arrived to pick me up. While I was waiting I met a Jamaican guy called Vincent who had been sent to borstal for robbery.

Vincent was seventeen, the same age as me, but already he was an old lag. He had done a stretch in DC. I told him that this was my first custodial sentence and that I was terrified.

'Nah,' Vincent said. 'Don' need to worry about a fing. Shit easy, DC.'

I think he was trying to be nice. Either that or a violent, loveless childhood had given him a distorted perception of life. For 'shit easy' it was not. I was about to receive a nasty shock.

4

BUNNY-HOPS DOWN THE M1

'Eee, you, lad!' The prison officer was a small Yorkshireman with a pale face.

'Who? Me?'

'Who, me, *sir*!' His nose almost touched mine. An angry spray of saliva hit me.

Oh Christ, I thought. Here we go.

I had arrived at Send Detention Centre, a couple of miles from Dorking in Surrey. I was in a line of new inmates walking along a corridor to the reception desk, where we were to be issued with Her Majesty's clothing.

The screw's name was Mr Honeywell. I had swaggered into Send with that rude boy bounce and he did not like it one bit. He put out an arm to stop me and looked me up and down. 'Listen, boy,' he spat. 'You aren't on the streets now. You're in fooking prison now, lad. And you don't walk like that.'

'Yes . . . sir.'

Mr Honeywell gave an unpleasant smile. With that mumbled 'sir' I had made the first step towards becoming a so-called civilised member of society. But it was weeks before I completely lost the bounce. For a rude boy like me it was the only way to walk.

The most alarming aspect of Send was that it was in the country-side. Trees, fields and wide, open spaces were frightening to a city boy brought up surrounded by concrete. The closest I'd been to grass was either on a football pitch or in a large spliff. I knew my way around the streets of London, but in the depths of Surrey – hardly the most rural part of England, I admit – I might as well have been on the plains of Outer Mongolia.

The enormity of what had happened hit me when I arrived at the DC and saw the high walls and barbed wire. The complex had been built in the early 1960s. It comprised a cluster of low blockhouses in the middle of a wood and looked more like an army camp than a prison.

Mr Honeywell continued to glower at me as I surrendered what few possessions I had and collected my bundle of prison clothes. It was difficult to carry them as I had my arm in a sling following an incident two months earlier when I had tried to avenge the honour of my youngest brother, Elvis.

Elvis had been plagued by the school bully. One lunch break I waited for the bully to come out of Twyford. Eventually he emerged and walked off in the direction of the sweetshop. Before he had a chance to go inside the shop I pounced on him. I was about to punch him in the face when a friend of mine grabbed my hand and pulled me back. I lost my balance and fell backwards into the shop window. The window smashed and a foot-long shard of glass speared my arm. There was blood everywhere.

I was rushed to hospital, where they discovered a severed tendon. I was operated on and woke up in agony with my arm stuck to my chest. It had been in a sling ever since.

As I left reception, Mr Honeywell stopped me again. 'Trouble with your arm, Skeete?' he asked.

I told him what had happened. Mr Honeywell adopted an understanding look that suggested he was quite concerned. I began to cheer up. Perhaps these screws weren't so bad after all. I told him that my arm had not healed and that I was supposed to keep it in the sling for another couple of weeks.

'Oh dear, oh dear,' he said. 'That's bad luck. Won't be able to do press-ups, will you?' And with that he grabbed my arm and yanked it down.

The pain was excruciating. The blood rushed to my head and I nearly fainted. Mr Honeywell roared with laughter. Then his face changed back to a scowl. 'That'll teach you to look like fooking Napoleon,' he said before stalking off to plague someone else.

I realise now that it was the best thing he could have done. The other boys would have taken the piss if they'd seen me with my arm in a sling. And, of course, I wouldn't have been able to fight back.

I was examined by the doctor and taken to the barber to have my head shaved. Then a screw marched me to my cell. The door shut behind me. I looked at the lumpy bunk and the bars on the window. The smell of stale sweat was overpowering. I collapsed on the bunk and burst into tears. I pushed my head into the pillow and cried like a baby.

All my rude boy pride had left me. I lay in terror thinking that somebody might hear my sobs. The fact that I had carried a flick knife and worn mohair suits didn't mean a thing now. I felt so alone and homesick. I was like a small boy again, desperately wanting my mother's comfort. But I was locked up and there was nothing I could do about it.

Things didn't look any less bleak in the morning. At 6 a.m. a screw stormed into the cell and pulled me out of bed. He ordered me to dress in one minute. Then he marched me out into the exercise yard where I joined the other new arrivals.

Mr Honeywell was waiting for us. The screws prodded us into a line in front of their boss. 'Got a few things for you to remember,' he barked. 'First thing is that you're fooking scoom. Second thing is that fooking scoom get treated like fooking scoom. Third thing is what we call short, sharp, shock treatment. The idea is that it's going to be so unpleasant that you'll never want to come back.'

Later, at breakfast in the canteen, I met some of the inmates. A tall white guy with blond hair and watery blue eyes brought his tray and sat down beside me. 'You're new,' he said.

'Yeah.' I turned away. I didn't want to talk.

'I'm Rimmer.' He put out his hand. I reluctantly shook it. I was puzzled by this show of friendliness from a white prisoner. But I discovered that friendliness among the inmates in Send was the norm, regardless of colour. The attitude was that we were all in this shit-hole together, so we might as well make the most of it.

Rimmer had a good sense of humour, but he didn't mince his words. 'You don't look like the rest of these niggers, do ya?' he said bluntly. 'You ain't got them thick lips and them flared nostrils, 'ave ya?'

It wasn't the sort of introduction that would have appealed to every black person. But I thought he was funny. I looked at him and said, 'No, I haven't. I just happen to be fucking handsome. And a fucking sight better looking than you.' Rimmer exploded with laughter. We became good friends after that.

I'd like to say that some of the screws were reasonable people, but I can't remember any of them having a sense of humour. I think they were picked on the basis of the bigger the bastard, the quicker they got the job. Some of them were blatantly violent and rapped our knuckles if we did wrong. They all mourned the 'good old days' of the birch.

I had never been under such pressure. None of the hours of the day belonged to you and each day was planned with military precision. We had to walk in a certain way and talk in a certain way, and we all dressed the same. We had to make our beds in a certain way and there was no breakfast until we had done it. Pyjamas had to be folded a special way with the HM Government motif in a particular place. At night we had to fold our clothes in regulation-sized piles. If the piles weren't right, an officer would throw them on the floor and we'd have to do it again.

We spent the whole day on the go and the only respite was mealtimes. After breakfast we were marched to the gym where we did circuits for two hours with medicine balls and weights. There was always a screw breathing down our necks and we weren't allowed to stand for a minute. If you flaked out during your fifty press-ups, the instructor kept you behind to do fifty more.

After lunch there was football, volleyball and manual work. I had to work on the farm. It was probably easier than being in a Siberian labour camp, but not much. At least it was summer and the weather was warm. The DC grew its own food and we spent all day digging potatoes and picking cabbages. I hated it. I wasn't even allowed to drive the tractor. I resisted the temptation to take it for a spin when nobody was looking, even though I'd always fancied the idea of joyriding on a tractor.

One day I was scrubbing the floor of the barn when another boy let off the tractor's handbrake. The machine rolled over my hand and took off the top of my right knuckle. It hurt like hell but I was delighted. My injury got me out of work on the farm. I was transferred to the workshops, where I helped pack knives and forks into plastic bags for British Caledonian Airways – a tedious job, but a welcome change from digging.

Sundays were as hard as any other day. We had to run seven miles in the morning and the last one back got no pudding for lunch. This was deprivation of the cruellest kind. The only good thing about the food at Send – indeed the only good thing, full stop – was the pudding. You'd see inmates close to tears when they were forbidden their spotted dick and custard.

There was a variety of punishments for misbehaviour. If you failed to call an officer 'sir' he made you do bunny-hops up and down the M1 – the nickname for the longest corridor in the place. Then you had to sweep and polish the M1. One boy was caught with drugs. He thought he might get sent to a nice, cosy borstal. No chance. They put him on an exercise bike in the gym and made him pedal – for eight hours. He could hardly walk for a week. I got into trouble once for giving a screw too much lip. They gave me forty-eight hours' solitary confinement in a cell furnished only with a mattress.

The regime at Send was based on army life and designed to make men out of no-hopers. The motto was: if you want to behave like a man we will turn you into a man. There were no gangs and the screws had it all well sewn up. We were numbers, not people, and we had to learn to take orders.

Mr Honeywell's puritanical Yorkshire background made him particularly fussy about table manners. At mealtimes he would snap, 'Don't put elbows on't table, lad.' Despite using bad language himself, he hated it from us and enforced a strict no-swearing rule. The tamest expletive called for yet more bunny-hops. We weren't allowed to smoke, either. You couldn't buy cigarettes and the only black market was for sweets and magazines. Drugs, which are now commonplace in most prisons, were virtually unheard of.

DC opened my eyes. I'd seen myself as pretty tough out on the streets, but in DC there were guys far worse than me. There were seventeen-year-olds who looked twenty-three. You certainly didn't want to mess with them.

When you first walk into a place like that you think everybody's against you, particularly if you're black. But I soon made friends.

There were only fourteen black boys among the 300 inmates and we stuck together. The white boys never gave us problems. There were no fights because after all the physical work, nobody had the energy to cause trouble.

After a fortnight in the cell I was moved to a dormitory with rows and rows of beds. Lights-out was at 7 p.m. I'd been so used to sharing a room with my brothers that the presence of the other boys didn't worry me. Besides, it was less lonely than being cooped up on my own.

My mother was deeply upset that I had received a custodial sentence. She was distraught that one of her sons had gone off the rails so badly. I had no contact, no letters from her, while I was inside. She stuck stubbornly to the promise she had made three years earlier when I had first appeared in court aged fourteen. I was hurt but I couldn't blame her.

I felt guilty about what I had put my family through. The week I was locked up, my eldest sister Glenda had arrived for a holiday in London from America, where she was living. She came to court and I felt so ashamed of myself. Because Glenda was the eldest I had a respect for her that I did not have for my other brothers and sisters.

My father took it surprisingly well. For the first time in my life I saw another side to him. Although his patience had been tested to the limit, his son was in serious trouble and he would do anything he could to help. He came to visit me once. I was pleased to see that he cared. The Sunday he arrived I had been cutting grass with a scythe on the DC farm. I complained to Dad about the blisters on my hands. 'This will never happen again,' I promised him.

'You'll hurt me if it does, boy,' he replied sadly.

We sat on a bench in the grounds. I told Dad what I did each day and what I was learning. He listened to me thoughtfully and said, 'I hope this is going to teach you a lesson. I can see you're repentin' and that's probably the best news I can have.'

Dad and I talked about the family. I wanted to know what everyone was up to. We joked about my brother Bentley. 'Tell you one thing, Oliver,' Dad said. 'You're better off than him. RAF training would have been a lot harder than this place.' It was some consolation that Bentley, not my favourite person, had endured an even tougher time than I had. And he hadn't even done anything wrong.

I enjoyed Dad's visit but I was hurt that none of the boys who had been with me when I was caught had bothered to come and visit me – especially as they'd all got off with cautions as first-time offenders. Dad said, 'Well, now you know who your friends are, don't you, boy?' But there was more to it than that. I couldn't expect anything else. My friends were only following the rule of the streets: you do your bird and you do it on your own.

I got used to the discipline in DC and, except for a few shouting matches with the screws, I behaved myself. I enjoyed the sport and tried to be friendly to everybody. I gradually turned from a youth into a man. I had arrived in DC with virtually no hair on my face, but they made me shave every day and I came out with a full growth of stubble.

DC taught me that I must never get into trouble again. I could see that it had done me some good if only because I never wanted to go back. My sentence also helped to improve my sense of humour, which had been badly lacking. As a child and adolescent I had never been able to take the mickey out of myself. I couldn't stand criticism and if people looked at me too hard I flipped. But in DC I began to stop taking myself so seriously.

I came out after two months with remission for good behaviour. They gave me a few quid and set me free at 7 a.m. one August morning. I stood outside the gates, looked at the trees and rising sun, and thought: I can't wait to get out of this countryside and back to normal living. I walked two miles to Dorking station, stopping at a village shop on the way. I bought a packet of crisps, a chocolate bar, a Coke, ten Embassy and a box of matches. I ate everything within minutes and smoked most of the cigarettes on the train back to London. They made me sick.

The journey took forever. I was seventeen and this was the first time I had been on a train on my own. The toughness had been knocked out of me and I felt lonely and homesick. I couldn't wait to see my family.

When I got home to Adelaide Road my brothers and sisters jumped all over me. They were delighted to see me again. I can't say the same for Mum. She was extremely wary of me and it was a long time before we were speaking normally again.

Dad made it plain that he would not stand any more nonsense from me. 'I'm not going through this with you again,' he said. 'Any more trouble and you're out of this house and I don't want to see you again. If you do believe you're a man, you can behave yourself.'

I tried to fit in at home, but I was restless. I got a job making remould tyres but I walked out after fifteen minutes because it was too dirty. Then I joined London Transport as a trainee mechanic on the underground. That was really boring. I was a small cog in a huge company and a nine-to-five day was not for me.

Dad's authoritarian attitude eventually drove me out. I moved to Luton, north of London, where I worked on a building site. I had started seeing a girl called Carla and she came up to Luton to live with me. She was also seventeen and she hadn't told her mother where she was going. Her mother knew about me and thought I was the worst thing for her daughter. Carla and I were together for two weeks before her mother found her and dragged her back to London. I gave up on Luton – I still don't know what induced me to live in what is possibly the most boring town in Britain.

I returned to London and began seeing Jennifer again. She'd been waiting for me and was determined we would get married. I wasn't so sure about that, but I did the next best thing and got engaged to her. She had a nice, steady job in a bank and had just been given a brand-new housing association flat in Hanwell. Life looked rosy and we moved in together.

We had virtually nothing to start with, just a bed, a cooker and a fridge. There were no chairs, no carpet. Jennifer provided all the money. She bought the food and paid the bills. My role as a kept man suited me perfectly.

We spent the first week or so in bed and then the teenage romance turned sour. Thoughts of settling down couldn't have been further from my mind and I couldn't keep myself quiet. I was always out at night, coming home as dawn broke. Jennifer hoped that I would change, but I never did.

Of all the girls I've known, I treated Jennifer Brown the worst. I was consistently unfaithful to her. I began seeing a succession of different girls, all prettier than the last in my eyes. There was Marcia,

Françoise, Claudia, Marika, Caroline, Gemma . . . The list went on. My attitude then was that girls were there to have sex with; they weren't good for much else.

Jennifer knew that I was sleeping with other women. She always found out who I'd been with and we had countless rows. One weekend I went off with a girl for a weekend to Bournemouth. When I returned to the flat on Sunday night Jennifer had left a note on the mirror in the hall. She knew exactly where I'd been and who I'd been with, because one of the girl's friends had told her.

She decided to get her own back. One day I was looking for a pair of shoes in the wardrobe when I found a note with the name and address of somebody called Noel. When Jennifer returned from work I confronted her. 'What's this about?' I demanded.

'None of your business.'

'Look, I wanna know who this is.'

She broke down in tears. She told me that she had been having an affair with this man. I was tempted to hit her, but I knew there was not a lot I could say because of the way I'd been carrying on. It's OK to be wrong and strong, but you can't be wrong and strong all the time.

Jennifer promised me that she wouldn't see this Noel again. She said she was sorry she had hurt me and we made up. Three days later I came home to find a note from her. She had left the flat and gone home to her mum's. She said our relationship was not working and our engagement was over. I tried to contact her but she wouldn't take my phone calls. Thinking back on our relationship, I'm glad she left because I would only have spoiled her life. At that age I didn't care about anybody but myself and Jennifer had been taking the brunt of everything I was dishing out.

The Jennifer saga had a postscript. A few days after she'd left, I was coming out of the flat with a friend called Ronald when a Vauxhall VX4 90 roared up – I might forget my girlfriends, but I never forget a car!

Six enormous West Indians piled out. One of them snarled, 'Which one of you's Oliver?' He was an ugly brute with a vicious scowl. His friends stood around him, flexing their muscles.

I said, 'Me. Who are you?'

'Where is she?' he said. 'Where's Jennifer?'

A broad grin spread across my face. 'Oh, I see. You're Noel, ain't ya?'

'So what if I am?' he said sulkily.

I went up to him and put my arm on his shoulder. His heavies tensed, expecting trouble. Ronald sighed. He'd seen it all before; Skeete trying to be smart again. Ronald was a lanky six-footer with glasses. He wasn't a timid man but he could see these boys were long on knives and short on patience. 'For fuck's sake, Oliver,' he pleaded. 'Stop being stupid.'

I ignored him. I looked Noel in the eye. 'Look, my friend,' I soothed. 'If you're Noel, then Jennifer is your girlfriend. You'll find her at her mum's.' I added, 'You've done me a favour. You took her away from me and she's all yours. Even if she came back I wouldn't have her.'

My short speech took the wind out of Noel's sails. He looked a little sad. We talked for another ten minutes and by the time he left we were friends. The boys with him weren't so happy. Boys like them don't like being deprived of a good stabbing.

Mum was disappointed I had broken up with Jennifer. She wasn't surprised by my behaviour but she hated my disrespect for women. She was one of the old Barbadian school and she couldn't handle promiscuity. Whenever I had brought Jennifer round to the house Mum had been openly rude about me. As I said before, she was always asking Jennifer what a nice girl like her was doing with this bad boy. And she really meant it now.

The shock of DC worked for a time – but not for long. Four months after I came out, I was arrested again.

On 5 November 1973 I went with some friends to a fireworks party in Ladbroke Grove. I remember that there was a great sound system called Sufferer Hi-Fi and the party went on until 2 a.m. I had come by train and had no transport to get home. A friend of mine offered to lend me his Mini van. It had no tax, no insurance, no MOT, no nothing.

'Yeah, thanks,' I said, not thinking. I told my friends we had a car to go home in. 'Yeah, great,' they said. 'Let's go.'

As I got into the Mini I began to have second thoughts, but they didn't last for long. It's amazing how short one's memory can be.

I set off. One minute after leaving the party, we turned a corner and the passenger door flew open because it wasn't shut properly. A police car was parked around the corner. The policemen saw us and started following. I panicked and put my foot down on the accelerator. A few hundred yards down the road, I had to stop at a crossroads. My friends threw open the doors and ran off into the night. They were loaded up with marijuana and had no intention of being caught. 'Thanks a lot,' I shouted after them.

The policemen had radioed for help. I heard a wail of sirens in the distance, getting closer. It sounded like the whole of Ladbroke Grove had come alive. I abandoned the van in the middle of the road and started running.

The two policemen chased me for about a mile. I could hear them wheezing behind me. Then I looked round and saw a large blue police van approaching. I was exhausted and could go no further. I stopped by a tree. I was doubled over, trying to catch my breath, and resigned to the fact that I was going back to DC. I turned round to face my pursuers and put up my hands in surrender.

Several policemen rushed out of the van, truncheons drawn. All I could think was that they were going to give me a kicking. Remember that this was the early 1970s. You got a kicking for anything if you were black.

One of the officers dived at me. I wasn't putting up with this. As he came in for the kill I side-stepped. I tripped him up and he crashed into the tree. There was a loud crack as his head hit the stump. He slumped to the ground.

I kept my hands raised high but the police charged at me. They seemed to come from everywhere. Truncheons began raining down on my body. I put my hands over my head and lay in a foetal position as I was beaten up. I was kicked repeatedly in the face and blood cascaded down my clothes. Then I was dragged along the pavement and slung into the van.

I was taken to Harrow Road Police Station where the beating continued. They threw me into an interview room, stripped me naked and beat me with truncheons around the stomach and back of the legs. My body was covered in bruises.

The next morning I appeared at Marylebone Magistrates' Court. The police claimed that my face was swollen because I had resisted arrest. The magistrate peered at me through half-moon spectacles. He looked uneasy but refused me bail all the same. I was sent to Ashford Remand Centre in Middlesex for two weeks to await trial on charges of assault against a police officer.

Ashford was a dirty, Victorian jail. All the prisoners were in transit, either awaiting trial or on their way to start their sentences at another prison. The place should have been pulled down years before and the sanitary arrangements left a lot to be desired. The food was dreadful and when I arrived the boys were talking about how rats had been found in the stew.

I spent the first week in the hospital wing recovering from my injuries. My memories are vague. I must have been suffering from shock after the beating. I refused to talk to people and I thought my life was over. I kicked myself for driving the Mini and I felt a tinge of remorse for tripping up the copper. But then I remembered what his friends had done to me. The police attack had been so savage that I can only guess that they had been taking out their anger on me in the same way as I had done on their colleague.

I brightened up during the second week in Ashford, when I was transferred to the main block. I was walking along my landing one morning when I heard a voice behind me. 'Is that who I think it is?'

I turned round. It was one of the prison officers from Send who had recently been transferred to Ashford. He was a big, bearded Cockney.

'Oh yeah, Skeete, I knew it,' he said. 'Knew you were going to be back inside. Didn't take long, did it?'

I was mortified. I wasn't going a bundle on reunions at that moment. Here was I trying to keep a low profile and now somebody from my past had caught up with me.

The screw went on, 'You're going to spend the rest of your life in prison. This is how it starts. Won't be long before you're doing a ten.'

I've never forgotten that man. He's the one person who clued me up to the reality of what I was facing. He really made me think. And the frightening part about it was that he was right.

'Know what you are, Skeete?' he added. 'You're an idiot.' And he sniffed and walked away.

I stood there feeling like the world's biggest fool. So much for swearing that I would never break the law again. I spent the rest of the week not being allowed to forget my stupidity. Whenever I saw the screw he would look at me and giggle. 'Planning your next job, Skeete?' he would chortle. 'I'll have your bunk ready.' A prison officer with a sense of humour seemed a contradiction in terms, but I began to see the funny side. I decided that breaking the law was not for me. After all, what was the point? I was never going to make it as a great criminal.

I went back to the magistrates' court and pleaded not guilty. My father was in court. For the first time he was completely on my side. He knew that I had been beaten up and that the officers had overstepped the mark.

After the prosecution presented their case, I went into the witness box. I was not frightened of the police and I was prepared to lie if necessary. I asked the chief magistrate, ''Scuse me, your honour. I'm not being funny, but how can a seventeen-year-old boy beat up on three policemen?' Then I told him how I'd been beaten up. My police assailants gave me filthy looks. There were many racists in the Metropolitan Police in the 1970s and they hated cocky, teenaged West Indian boys. Thankfully, the Met. are a bit better these days. Some of the policemen I meet today have a sense of humour, which is more than I can say for their predecessors.

The magistrates dismissed the case against me. I was allowed to go free. The officers looked like they were ready to kill. I think they hated the lily-livered, liberal-minded magistrates even more than me.

The court was on the first floor of the building. I met my father and got into the lift to go down to the ground floor. By coincidence, the policeman who had had the argument with the tree stepped into the lift as well.

We descended. The copper and I stared at each other like dogs. He was rosy-cheeked and innocent looking and he couldn't have been much older than me. He looked very angry.

Dad nudged me as if to say, 'Behave yourself.'

Impossible. I said to the policeman, 'What you goin' to do now? You want some more of what you got last time?'

Dad grabbed me by the scruff of neck and smacked me round the head. 'Shut up, boy,' he growled. The policeman said nothing. He continued to stare at me. The lift doors opened and he walked out. Dad grabbed my arm. 'Time to pull yoursel' together, boy. If you gonna carry on like dat, don' expect any more help from me.'

That was the last time the police *rightly* charged me with anything worse than speeding. I don't know what happened, which particular experience changed my attitude, but I never got into trouble again. Sure, I ended up in prison again, but that was none of my making. More of that later.

At eighteen years old I realised that I had to conform unless I wanted to spend the rest of my life in institutions. I continued to drive without a licence but at least I wasn't nicking other people's cars, which was a step in the right direction. That was the best I could do. It simply wasn't in my nature to get any more legal.

I went back to work as a car-sprayer and began to spend most of my earnings on my obsession with the internal combustion engine. I bought an Austin 1100 for £12. I put in a new engine, tinted windows and a straight-through exhaust so that it sounded like a dragster. It only did 40 mph flat out but it looked fantastic.

My next car was a Ford Escort that I customised to go with my Jack-the-Lad image. I cut off the wings and put on flared wheel arches. I sprayed it BMW Ceylon Gold, cut a hole in the bonnet and inserted a sort of mock turbo airflow. A go-faster stripe down the side and it was perfect. Unfortunately, the engine was only 1100 cc. It was terrible to drive and smoke poured in from the airflow.

One morning an Irishman came into the garage where I was working. He'd smashed up his car, a J-registration 1600E Cortina. The 1600E Cortina was *the* car in those days. Really classy with a wooden dashboard. I said to the Irishman, 'Why don't you take this Escort? It's in good nick and I'll do a straight swap.'

He fell for it. He thought the Escort, with all its sporty bits and pieces, was the best car he'd ever seen. He drove off and I set about repairing the Cortina. A few hours later the man was back. He was coughing and spluttering from the fumes.

'Escort's rubbish,' he said. 'I want my Cortina back.'

'No chance,' I said. I had a four-year-old car worth £800 that had cost me the price of a junkyard banger. I hadn't broken the law – I'd merely indulged in a dodgy motor-trade practice.

'Go fock yerself,' he exploded. 'If you don't give my car back I'll bring my friends round.'

'In that case I'll have my friends waiting for you.'

He left empty-handed. I didn't feel sorry for him because he had been conned so easily. I never saw him again.

Of all my friends, I was the only one with a job. I was on £60 a week and my friends were scraping by on £15 dole. The flat in Hanwell was like a bus stop on Friday nights. All my friends would come round looking for a lift up to the west end clubs. About fifteen people would pile into the Cortina and I'd drive up to Soho. I had tax, insurance and an MOT but still no licence. The police stopped me a few times but I got away by pretending to be someone else and showing them a friend's licence. They never found out. All we black boys looked the same to them.

I eventually passed my test aged twenty in June 1976. It was a day of great celebration. Everything in my life was legal. I had a steady job and was on my way to becoming a responsible member of society.

Breaking the law was too much hassle. I began to pull away from my old friends. Whereas I was going straight, many of them were getting into serious trouble. They'd gone from stealing cars to stealing money and were now being caught for armed robbery.

A friend of mine called Kelvin got fifteen years for shooting a security guard during a bank robbery. He was only twenty at the time. He came out after ten years and did exactly the same thing again. I'm not sure where he is these days but I think he's out again having just finished another twelve.

When guys like Kelvin robbed a bank they would blow all the money on a new car like a Jaguar or a Triumph Stag. If they were really cool, they bought a Trans-Am Pontiac to make themselves look like a New York pimp. Then they'd smash the car up and they'd have to go and do another bank job to buy a new one.

One boy I knew stole £40,000 in cash – and promptly blew it all on a Rolls. I remember talking to his dad about it. The old man thought his son was barking mad. He said, 'I told the boy to go and buy a house with the money and get 'imself straight. But the boy not listen. He go and buy a big car and smash it up and now he got nutten'.'

These guys were way out of my league and when I talked to them it confirmed my belief that I was not a born criminal. When they began their law-breaking they would get borstal sentences. When they came out I'd say, 'How did you manage?'

'Easy,' they'd reply. 'Like standing on your head.' I couldn't understand that attitude. How anybody could say that borstal or prison was easy was beyond me. And they all thought they were big drug dealers. They'd buy a half-ounce of weed, put it into little bags and stand in a youth centre all day trying to sell it. I never got into that. I used to go to the youth centre in my lunch break and watch them. They were sad people and I wanted nothing to do with them.

The attitude of boys like that was: fuck the system. But I thought they were just plain stupid. These days they like to call themselves Yardies and claim to have underworld connections in Jamaica. How pathetic can you get? They're no more Yardies than Prince Charles. They were all born in England and brought up speaking Cockney. They know nothing about Jamaica and most of them have never been further west than Bristol.

I could hardly believe the change in myself. DC and my spell in Ashford had done the trick. I realise now that if I had hung around with my old friends I could have easily ended up doing fifteen years. But it was my fear of prison that stopped me breaking the law. In prison there's no point in banging your head on the door because nobody's going to open it. I couldn't get that feeling out of my mind. I had felt like a caged animal in DC and I did not want to go back.

While my respect for the law improved, my attitude to women was as bad as ever. And with Jennifer out of my life, I set about being young, free and single with a vengeance.

My best friend was another rude boy called Donald Cole. I met him in my late teens at a dance at Acton Town Hall. Donald was half Jamaican, half Indian and very good looking. He dressed beautifully and was a brilliant dancer. He was always surrounded by girls.

He moved into the flat with me and each night we brought home different women. Donald would usually do the chatting up and then I'd take whoever he discarded. I was in awe of him. Girls wouldn't leave him alone and I quickly learned that he was a good person to hang around with. Stick around attractive people long enough and their success will rub off on you. A simple philosophy, but it has always worked for me.

I celebrated my twenty-first birthday with a party at the flat. At the time I was seeing four different girls: Caroline, Angel, Claudia and Susan, with whom I had recently met up again. They all came to the party and I made up my mind that Susan would be the one who stayed at the end.

How wrong can you be? Susan took one look at me flirting with all these different girls and decided I was a jerk. She left after thirty minutes.

'Why are you going?' I asked.

'What do you think I am, Oliver?' she said. 'Stupid? I can see what's going on and I'm not putting up with it.'

One down, three to go. Surely if you have three girlfriends in one place you're going to end up with one of them by the end of the evening? Wrong again. One by one they left. They were tired of my games. They had all found out about each other and wanted nothing to do with me.

Donald went off with his girlfriend of the day and by midnight I was on my own. I couldn't believe it. I sat down and unwrapped my birthday presents. Jennifer had sent me a record. It was called 'Playboy.' I put it on the turntable and the words went, 'Who told you so/That I'm a playboy/And girls are my toys.' I felt like an idiot. It was one of the worst nights of my life.

I gave up the flat and moved back home. I'd started seeing a round-faced Grenadian girl called Anne. She had straightened hair, dyed a soft henna-red. Anne and I were not good for each other. I couldn't keep my eyes, or hands, off other women and she needed someone more down to earth. I couldn't give her the love she deserved.

She had a flat in Fulham and I used to stay with her for a night or two. During the week I made half-hearted attempts to settle down and earned good money spraying cars. But at weekends, when all this domestic bliss became too much for me, I returned to my old partygoing ways. I travelled the country with Donald, visiting blues in Manchester and Liverpool. I enjoyed going up north. The girls were even easier than in London. All Donald and I had to do was open our mouths and talk like London boys and they were all over us.

Anne hated my wandering ways. She was a lovely girl and she couldn't understand why I wanted to stray.

My easygoing approach to life suddenly got a shock with the news that she was pregnant. I remember the day she told me about it. Rather than worry about the practicalities of the situation, I felt great. I was proud that I was to become a father for the first time.

Anne was not so happy. She already had a four-year-old daughter called Michelle by a previous boyfriend who had walked out on her. She thought, not unreasonably, that I would do the same. Which, of course, I did.

I took no notice of Anne when she was pregnant and I feel bad about that now. I moved into her flat but I couldn't settle. I liked girls who partied hard and dressed trendily. Anne was homely and gentle – not my type at all. One evening we had a row. I made her so angry that she ended up pouring a pot of gravy on my head. I could see it wasn't working and I didn't want to cause her any more pain, so I packed my bags and left.

My love life became even more complicated. I started seeing a girl called Pat. Pat was the opposite of Anne. She was really pleased with herself, a rowdy Grenadian with sexy, straight hair. She was a tearaway who covered herself in Gucci accessories and all my friends fancied her.

Pat was going out with someone else but I soon put a stop to that. I went round to her place one night and told her, 'Oi, you're coming out with me.' Not the sophisticated approach, I admit, but that was how I dealt with girls then. I'm pleased to say that I'm a little more refined these days.

I put Pat in my car and took her to my sister Jennifer's flat in Northolt. After that evening we began seeing a lot of each other.

It wasn't long before Pat got pregnant. I couldn't believe it. The timing could not have been worse. In the space of a few months I was to become a father twice by two different women.

Three months into Pat's pregnancy, in April 1979, Anne gave birth to our daughter Chanelle. She was a lovely baby but it felt weird when she arrived. I felt like a kid having a kid. I certainly wasn't ready for nappies and bottles.

I didn't tell Anne about Pat or vice-versa. Using as much cunning as I could muster, I managed to put up a pretence of living with each of them. I had clothes at Anne's, clothes at Pat's and clothes at my mum's. My mother knew what was going on, but she had given up lecturing me. 'If these women want to get themselves pregnant for you, Oliver, then that's their business.'

Of course, the girls found out in the end and all hell broke loose. Anne discovered where Pat lived and she went round one day with Chanelle. Unfortunately, I happened to be there at the same time.

They both rounded on me. Anne yelled at me. She held Chanelle up to my face and screamed that I was a two-timing bastard. Her outburst was completely out of character and I was stung by her words.

Pat joined in. She growled, 'Is this true, Oliver?' Her voice could have frozen ice.

'Can't deny it,' I said.

Pat went berserk. She stormed around the flat picking up my belongings. She stuffed them into a bin-liner and threw them out of the window. I went downstairs to retrieve them.

By the time I came back the girls were talking to each other. To this day I don't know what plots they were hatching. Anne demanded I take her home. Back at her flat, she took the same action as Pat. Despite my feeble protestation – 'Aw c'mon, darling, where's your sense of humour?' – she too bunged my clothes into a bin-liner and chucked them into the street.

I've learned that it doesn't mean a thing when a woman throws your clothes out in a bin-liner. You don't want to hang around if she comes at you with a carving knife, but bin-liners are no problem.

Within three weeks, using every manipulative technique I could muster, I had moved back in with both of them. I was spending two nights with Anne, two nights with Pat, and the rest of the week at my mum's. But the rows didn't stop. And when I returned from yet another riotous weekend up north, Anne chucked milk bottles at my car and sent me packing. Pat was not much happier with the situation.

One day I bumped into Susan in Ealing High Street. I hadn't seen her for a while and she had a job driving a delivery van. I had already decided to move out of Pat's and I asked Sue if she would take me round in the van and help me move my things.

We arrived at the flat. Pat let me in and I pushed past her. I began packing my clothes. Sue stood by the door. Pat took one look at her, put two and two together and made five, and began swearing at her. 'Get out of here the both of you,' she snapped.

Sue wasn't too pleased. But she knew me well enough to know that whatever Pat was cross about it was almost certainly my fault.

'Oliver, can you tell me what's going on?' Sue asked. 'What have you got me into?'

'Er, nothing really,' I blustered. 'Just a little domestic dispute.'

'Huh! Domestic dispute!' Pat said. She looked at Sue with pity. 'You'd do well to steer clear of him.'

I grabbed the rest of my belongings and ran from the flat. Sue drove me to my parents' house.

'Would you like to come in?' I asked. 'Talk about old times, and all that?'

She eyed me coldly. 'No thank you, Oliver. Got to be going now.' I got the message. She wanted nothing to do with me. My life was too tangled for a nice, uncomplicated girl like her.

5

FALSE DREAD

Bob Marley was the reason I started growing dreadlocks.

The reggae superstar had been my hero for a long time. One moment he wore winkle-picker shoes and had cropped hair like all us rude boys. Then he suddenly grew this massive afro. In 1972 he stopped combing his hair and the locks appeared. I was so impressed. He looked so strong, like a lion. I wanted to be like him.

When I was twenty-three I stopped doing anything to my hair and let it grow naturally. After a few months it became matted and the locks began to form. A black person's hair doesn't grow in a straight line like a white's. It spirals when you stop combing it. If you leave it alone, the spirals interlock with each other like rope.

After all my troubles with the police and women, the dreadlocks finally did it as far as my parents were concerned. My hairstyle only confirmed what they already knew: that I was a rebel and a troublemaker. When my mum first saw my dreadlocks she went mad. She said, 'If you don't cut dem tings off you ain't comin' back here, you hear?'

Dad thought they were an affront to my Bajan upbringing. My Jamaican accent had been bad enough but my locks were the last straw. I remember sitting on the wall outside our house one evening with my brothers. I was holding court, telling jokes and laughing loudly. My dad flung open the front door and yelled at me: 'Bloody rasta, shut up dat bloody noise. It ain't bad enough you come in here with dem fuckin' tings upon yer head, but you makin' all dis noise an' givin' my house a bad name.'

Like Bob, I wanted to become a devout Rastafarian. My troubles
with women had made me depressed and I felt a hole in the pit of my
stomach. I was looking for a spiritual release.

Some of my friends were turning towards Haile Selassie, Emperor
of Ethiopia from 1930 to 1974, upon whose preachings Rastafarianism is based. Followers of this messianic movement, which dates
back to 1930s Jamaica, believe that Haile Selassie is the only true
God and that Ethiopia is the true Zion. They claim that white Christian preachers and missionaries perverted the scriptures to conceal
the fact that Adam and Eve were black. And they say that Haile
Selassie, who assumed the title Ras Tafari, will return from the dead
to create a new black world.

I saw some old schoolfriends, who had been getting into trouble
like me, finding peace in Rastafarianism. They lived in a squat called
the Dread House in Uxbridge Road, Ealing. It was a large Victorian
terraced property which hadn't been lived in for years. The boys
fixed up the rooms and moved their families in.

I went to the Dread House each day. There were Bible readings
and people sat around chanting and playing the bongos amid clouds
of marijuana smoke. I sat on the floor and listened to people preach.
Perhaps this would bring some harmony into my chaotic domestic
life.

About ten people lived in the Dread House full-time and the place
was always full of visitors. There were people coming and going
all night. Suddenly all my friends were reformed characters. They
pontificated about the evils of crime and how they were now at
peace. There was one problem, though: marijuana was illegal. And
they found this impossible to accept.

To the Rastafarian marijuana is the 'holy weed' given by Jah to his
disciples. How can something that comes from the earth be wrong?
Unlike opium poppies or coca leaves, marijuana is not mixed with
chemicals and processed. You just pick it off the earth and smoke it.
Or you boil it and drink it as medicine. It is Jah's gift to his people.

Unfortunately, the police and the judges didn't see it like that. It
was a Class B drug and the white man was terrified of it.

The Rastafarian movement of the mid-1970s was a good thing.
Many people cleaned up their act by joining communes like Dread

House. It took them out of trouble, off the streets and into spirituality. The only thing that spoilt that movement was the dope. The police were always on their case; always busting them. If Rastafarians had never smoked marijuana, they could have earned the greatest respect. They might even have had their own churches by now. They could have been like the Jehovah's Witnesses or the Pentecostals, because they were just as strict about their religion. But because they smoked weed they weren't shown any respect at all.

After eight months I could stand the harassment no longer. The place was being raided every other day and I stopped going there. My criminal record made me a marked man and I didn't fancy being busted for drugs.

My Rastafarian friends despaired of me. 'Read de Bible, Oliver,' they would urge while puffing on enormous spliffs. 'You will find peace in Jah.'

But I didn't have the patience for it. I had spent my childhood avoiding Sunday School and I wasn't going to start on the Bible now. I was more interested in girls and clubbing and my Rastafarian friends didn't do any of that. All these books and all that chanting was as bad as two women giving me hell.

They called me 'False Dread'. I had the locks but I used to shave – Rastafarians never shave. I liked dressing smartly and going out in my car; these boys had nothing and they walked everywhere.

They never had any money. And they wore those tea cosies on their heads. You know, the red, green and gold hats. You never caught me wearing anything like that. How unfashionable could you get? They looked so stupid. Who needed a tea cosy when you could wear a £100 suit?

The boys' accents changed. They went funny. They talked about 'Haile Selassie, Jah.' It was all Jah this and Jah that. They even talked to the magistrate like that when they were arrested for possession of marijuana. You can imagine the beak's reaction when the clerk said, 'How do you plead?' and this dreadlocked Rasta replied, 'Jah will guide me.' The beak must have thought he had a madman in the dock.

It happened to one of my friends. He turned up in court one day charged with possession of cannabis. The magistrate asked him if he had anything to say. He went on about Babylon this and Babylon that and the magistrate put him on a section – sent him to a nut house. They pumped him full of drugs to keep him quiet and he was never the same again. He came out, hacked off his dreadlocks and ended up on the crack pipe. He was a nice guy before he started locking his hair. Sad, really.

No, I was never tempted by it all. I'd go and listen to the Bible meetings but I always had my doubts. I felt that pure Rastafarianism would take me away from what I enjoyed. Like raving all night and having a good time. And to me these boys were not having a good time. They weren't doing anything bad or wrong, but it just wasn't me. And in a way I felt sorry for them because they were so badly victimised.

You don't see many Rastafarians like that in London any more. Most of them are trying to make careers for themselves, like social work. A lot of them run youth centres for under-privileged kids and they tend to look after their own.

Too many Rastafarians today work for the white man to be true to their religion. I know guys who still talk about Jah and Haile Selassie and they still have it in their hearts. But it doesn't have the same spiritual meaning. Today they drive big BMWs and have mobile phones. But at least working for the white man is more realistic, otherwise they'd end up in squats.

I've been described in newspapers as a Rastafarian but that's the white man's confusion. I'm not a true Rastafarian and I'm not ashamed to admit it. I'd rather people call me a false Dread, which is what I am. I might not be a Rasta in my actions but I'm a Rasta in my heart.

Dreadlocks have become a fashion for me. I mean, what's the alternative? A ponytail? No way. Black guys with ponytails look silly. And I hate the way they iron their hair. The curly perm is just as bad. People put all these American cosmetics and gadgets in their hair and it goes shiny like Barry White's. That's even sillier than the afro. Unless you're prepared to cut your hair short, dreadlocks are the only way.

Any spirituality I might have gained from the Dread House rapidly evaporated as my problems with women became acute. My attempt to find some peace hadn't worked. I was digging myself into more and more of a mess.

Pat's daughter, Zarra, was born in October 1979 and it became increasingly stressful juggling my time between my two families. Anne gave up her flat and moved into a bed-and-breakfast. I used to go round to see her and Chanelle and take them money. I slept with Anne again. Once. Yet again she got pregnant. I told her that I didn't want any more children and asked her to have an abortion. She refused and I had to accept her wishes. She gave birth to our son, also named Oliver, in October 1980.

Anne's second pregnancy was the last straw. I couldn't cope with all this pressure from two women at the same time. The children were beginning to cost me serious money and the stress of trying to provide for so many people was becoming enormous. I wasn't ready for all this responsibility. But it was my own fault for putting myself in that position in the first place. Perhaps Rastafarianism had opened my eyes after all. I finally saw that everything that was happening to me was self-inflicted. Women throwing bottles at me, my belongings being chucked out of windows, the constant demands for money – this was my punishment for what I had been doing all these years. There was only one answer. I said to myself, 'Let's get out of here, Oliver.' Or in the words of Bob Marley: 'No woman, no cry . . .'

I booked an air ticket to Barbados. There was one snag: how was I going to pay for my exodus?

I had no money because I blew most of it on parties and clothes. The rest had gone to Pat and Anne. I needed to work a scam if I was going to get away from it all.

My beloved BMW had to go. I sold it for £600 to a garage-owner called Luigi for whom I was working at the time. I went and bought the ticket. But now I needed spending money for the trip. I returned to Luigi and said, 'Look, I know somebody who wants to buy the BMW for £1500. Let me have it, I'll go and sell it and I'll make a few hundred quid for both of us.' Luigi agreed. I went off, sold the car again for £600, took all the money and got ready to leave. Totally dishonest, but a desperate situation called for desperate measures.

My grandmother gave me a few wise words before I left. Grandma had come over to London a couple of years earlier. She didn't look a day older than she had when I'd left. I guess that when you're young, old people look old no matter what their age. And she dressed exactly the same as back in Barbados, a faded pinafore and scarf around her head.

She wasn't as lively as she'd been and she'd given up beating the grandchildren. Her energy was concentrated elsewhere. She had unofficially adopted my sister Jennifer's son Darius and she was bringing him up as her own. Jennifer was at work all day and was happy with this arrangement. Darius was far better behaved than any of us and Grandma loved him dearly. She never struck him and gave him all the attention he wanted. I think she worked hard on bringing him up as best she could because she had failed so badly with me. Little Darius went mad with grief when she died in 1986.

I went round to my parents' house. I told Grandma, 'I can't take any more hassle from these women. It's costing me too much money. I'm going home to Barbados.'

Grandma disapproved strongly of my illegitimate children. She believed God was punishing me for my sins. 'Cock tax, Joon-yaar,' she told me sternly. 'Dat's what yer payin'.'

She said I could use her house while I was in Barbados. It had been empty since she had come to Britain. All I had to do was paint it and make it habitable.

She couldn't resist lecturing me. 'Listen, boy,' she went on. 'You can't go over to Barbados and do what you do here 'cos dem people shoot you. You can't go messin' with dem girls like you do here 'cos dem daddies don' stand for it.'

'Yeah, OK, Grandma.' I didn't believe the old woman. She was living back in the 1950s.

The day before my flight, Grandma took me aside again. She pointed at my dreadlocks. 'You'll have to cut dem tings off yer head before you go. Dem locks make yer a marked man.'

'I'm not cutting them for nobody,' I retorted.

She wagged a finger at me. 'You wait an' see. You won' get a job looking like dat.'

'Oh yes I will, Gran.'

'No, Joon-yaar. You mad. They don' like dem tings in Barbados.'

I thought she was talking nonsense. What did she know? I could have my hair how I wanted. I could do what I wanted. Couldn't I?

It would have been expecting too much for my trip to be completely free of female complications. Sure enough, I made another mistake. I'd started seeing a girl called Rose who worked at a West End nightclub. She later became famous as a member of the all-girl reggae group Amazulu, but when I knew her she was a barmaid. She was always telling me about this group she was trying to get together but I never believed it would happen.

Rose was half African, half Irish and very pretty. She was four years older than me and very experienced. She taught me mind-blowing things about sex. She seemed to be the perfect girlfriend. So I invited her to Barbados.

I planned to quit England and settle for good in the country of my birth. I packed all my clothes and went round the family saying farewell. Nobody seemed particularly sad to see me go.

Rose gave up her flat and joined me on the plane. We arrived on the island and settled into Grandma's house. After a few days in the sunshine my sense of humour returned and I was enjoying myself for the first time in months. The colours overwhelmed me. Everybody seemed to be smiling and it was a relief to leave grey old England behind.

I thought naively that Barbados would be exactly the same as it was when I left. But everything had changed. Houses and hotels had sprung up everywhere. One big hotel called Heyward's had taken up much of the land I used to play on.

The road up Whim Hill had been concreted. The village layout was still the same but the houses had been modernised. My parents' shack had been pulled down years earlier and only the weed-covered foundations remained. Grandma's wooden shanty had been replaced by a concrete bungalow. Electricity poles now lined the streets but there was still no proper plumbing. Water still came from a public standpipe.

There were only one or two boys I remembered left in the village. My schoolfriends had nearly all gone, mostly to America or Canada. But the new generation were suffering an upbringing similar to mine. Without exception, all the kids were still sent off to Sunday School and corporal punishment remained in vogue. The most significant change was that the island's increased prosperity through tourism meant parents could now afford to buy shoes for their children.

After a week in The Whim I was bored stupid. I hired a motorbike and Rose and I spent a month exploring the island. We stayed with a colony of Rastafarians in the hills in the parish of St Andrews. These people were very different from my friends in the Dread House. They wore no clothes and brushed their teeth with bits of sugar-cane fibre dipped in mud. Everyone had dreadlocks, even the babies. They were alarmingly holy.

Their diet consisted of nothing but rice and tomatoes, and roasted peanuts for pudding. They loved peanuts: I have never seen people eat so many. They didn't even allow you to put salt on your food and meat and fish were strictly banned. 'You must not eat any of God's animals,' I was told. This was all very well, but they looked so skinny. I was this big, strapping man while their bones protruded from their bodies. I found it difficult to understand how they could live like this – even if they did have access to some of the world's finest marijuana, shipped in regularly from Jamaica.

It confirmed to me what I already thought about Rastafarianism: that Jah wasn't for me. I could no more be a true Rastafarian in the West Indies than I could in England. And these Rastas had the same hassles with the police that we had suffered in Britain. The cops were always harassing them with marijuana raids.

Back at The Whim I had brought a slice of much-needed excitement to the sleepy village. I was the local boy made good and I entertained everybody with my tales of life in London. As a result I got a great welcome from everybody – except my great-aunt Emelyn.

While Barbados might have undergone enormous development in the tourist areas, the rest of the island was stuck in a 1950s time-warp. And my feud with Emelyn, my grandmother's sister, illustrates this well.

Emelyn is one of the last of a dying breed of Bajans who believe that the only point in life is to work the land. Her upbringing was hard. Both her parents were dead by the time she was six and she was raised by 'everybody and anybody', as she put it. As a child she earned her keep by raking up cowpats from the fields and putting them in baskets. The local plantation manager would come and weigh the dung and pay her a few cents for it to use as manure. In her teens she became a labourer, going 'up the ladder', as it was known, stacking bundles of cane on to the horse-drawn carts before they were taken to the windmill for processing into sugar.

Emelyn never went to school but she has a natural intelligence. 'She can't read or write, but you can't steal a penny from her,' is how my mother describes her. And on my last visit to Barbados, in 1994, Emelyn was still working her 'grounds'.

At the age of nearly ninety she farms two acres of land on her own. She has a small government pension – ''bout two cents is all dey give us' – and claims she has to work in order to survive. She grows cane and maize and her clothes and body are permanently splattered with mud. She remains completely unaffected by the massive changes that have occurred in Barbados during her lifetime and insists that manual labour is the only thing that keeps her alive. 'When I don' work de fields I get sick and can't move,' she says. 'Doctor tells me keep workin' till I die. An' dat's what ahm goin' to do. Me daughter used to send me money from America, but I told her stop. Got all de vegetables and 'erbs I need.'

Emelyn was seventy-five when I arrived back on the island in 1981. She lived in the house next to my grandmother's. She was a small, fiery lady, highly gossipy and viciously vindictive to anybody who crossed her. Domestic squabbles were her speciality and she had fallen out with all her neighbours at one time or another.

She hadn't liked me as a boy and she wasn't going to start now. The rest of the family had primed her that I was a bad lad and that she should keep her eye on me. From the moment I arrived in The Whim, I could see her lace curtains twitching as she watched my every move. What infuriated her more than anything was that I got on so well with the rest of the village.

Our fight started over a stick of sugar cane. Chewing sugar cane had been one of my favourite childhood treats and the sickly sweetness brought back fond memories for me. One morning I went into Emelyn's small patch of field and cut down a couple of stalks. My great-aunt spotted me from behind her window nets. She was jealously protective of her cane and decided that I had committed the crime of the century.

She rang the police. Two officers arrived just as I returned to my grandmother's house.

Emelyn came on to her verandah. 'Arrest dat boy, arrest 'im,' she screeched.

The policemen were tired, hot and bothered and looked like they would rather be back in the rum shop. They were slightly embarrassed by Emelyn's outburst.

'Is dis true?' one of them asked me.

'Yes,' I said. 'But I didn't think there'd be this fuss over two bits of sugar cane.'

The officer looked at me unhappily. He had better things to do than interview somebody about the suspected theft of two stalks of sugar cane. 'Well, don' do it again,' he warned.

This did not placate my great-aunt. 'Arrest 'im, take 'im away! Dat boy be here, bad.'

The officer turned to her and said, 'Don' you tink you over-reacting?'

'You police as bad as 'im. Dat boy no good.' The shrieks continued. The policemen gently steered my great-aunt inside her house and attempted to calm her down. Ah, Barbados. What a dear old place! I reflected that being cautioned for stealing sugar cane was fairly tame after stealing cars.

But the battle was not over. When Emelyn was in a better mood she grudgingly allowed me to use her telephone so that I could call Anne and Pat to see how my children were. But after the sugar cane incident my great-aunt was out for blood. Her opportunity for revenge came when she heard me talking to Pat one day. I was telling Pat how I missed her and how I was coming home soon. Bullshit, of course, but that was how I treated women in those days.

At last Emelyn had some effective ammunition to use against me. Over the weeks she had become very friendly with Rose. When we had arrived in Barbados Emelyn had asked us over for dinner. I had refused because her kitchen was filthy and I didn't fancy being poisoned. Rose had gone on her own and Emelyn felt that I had snubbed her. What right did I have to be so high and mighty?

Emelyn and Rose had cosy little chats each evening. And it was during one of their conversations that Emelyn told Rose about my conversation with Pat. Rose went berserk. She stormed into the house and called me a two-timing bastard. The next morning she packed her bags and I never saw her again.

I think she went to stay with a European man she had met on the beach. I'd spotted them together a few mornings earlier while she'd been on the beach on her own. I don't know if she'd slept with him already but I strongly suspected it. He had a fit body and long blond hair and she was into that look. I felt like beating him up but he was a nice guy and I had no proof that he'd done anything wrong.

I was furious with Emelyn for causing so much trouble. After Rose walked out I got on my motorbike and went out looking for revenge. I saw my great-aunt in the corner of a field tying up bundles of cane. I revved the bike and raced towards her.

Emelyn looked up at the noise of the bike. She saw me coming and she knew immediately what she had done wrong. She dropped her bundle of cane and took off across the field. Her pinafore flapped in the wind and her little legs went as fast as they could. She paused and turned. 'What you doin', boy?' she screamed. 'You stop your runnin' me 'bout.' And then she was off again.

Other people in the fields looked up to see what was going on. They interrupted their work to gaze at the bizarre sight of an elderly woman being chased by her outraged great-nephew.

I circled the field and cut off Emelyn's retreat. Her eyes popped in fright as I skidded to a halt by her. She stopped running and attempted to compose herself. 'What for you chasin' me in de grounds?' She gulped for air and smoothed her pinny. Sweat poured down her face. 'You come here to kill me, boy?'

'Jah sent me,' I snarled sarcastically above the din of the engine.

'You gonna kill me. Oh man, I call de po-lice for you.'

'You had no right to tell Rose about my private conversation,' I said. 'I expect you to apologise.'

'You kill me and den you be sorry.'

I waited for an apology but none came. My great-aunt was full of stubborn pride and she was certainly not going to admit to me that she had done wrong. I shot her a malevolent stare and gave up.

I wheeled the bike around and left her standing alone in the field.

After Rose left I went on the prowl for another girlfriend. But Grandma's warning that Bajan girls meant trouble could not have been more true. I met a girl called Sandra. She was only sixteen and her father owned a bar built around a tree on the edge of the beach at the north of the island.

Sandra was a white Bajan. She had pale skin and looked like Susan. She was very beautiful. I used to swim in the sea below her father's bar. I noticed her glancing at me coyly when she thought I wasn't looking. It was obvious she fancied me. After a few days I was infatuated. I approached her one afternoon and said, 'Listen, your dad says it's OK for me to take you for a ride on my motorbike.'

'Really?' she gasped. She was very excited.

'No, not really,' I said. But now I knew that she was keen.

Her dad must have seen us talking, because when I went for a drink in his bar later that afternoon he took me aside.

He was a large, heavy man with a bulbous nose. He had a friendly air about him but I reckoned he could be useful in a fight.

'Now, look here,' he told me quietly. 'I like you. You're a nice boy. You come from England and you've got some manners.'

'Very nice of you to say so,' I interrupted.

He went on, 'There's just one thing I ought to tell you, boy. You must not fuck with my daughter.'

He smiled broadly – and brought out a huge revolver from behind the bar. He pointed the gun at my forehead.

I put up my hands in surrender, 'Er, I don't know what you're talking about,' I spluttered. 'Mess with your daughter? No chance. Far too young for me.'

He lowered the gun. 'Glad to see we understand each other,' he said.

We become friends after that. He allowed me to talk to Sandra but only if we remained in view of the bar. In a way I was quite impressed with the man's good, old-fashioned approach to moral guidance. There's nothing like a firearm for ensuring your daughter's virginity.

Grandma's warnings continued to prove accurate. My hairstyle was the next problem and she would have collapsed with laughter had she known the trouble my locks were causing.

I began looking for work. Before long I realised that it was not only white people who were wary of dreadlocks. My own black brothers were just as prejudiced.

The Bajan authorities hated dreadlocks as much as the London police did. To the Bajans, Rastafarians were either drug dealers or murderers or both. This unfortunate image of the Rastaman was mainly thanks to the large number of Rastafarians coming in from Trinidad and Jamaica, most of whom were involved with organised crime syndicates like the Yardies. These Rastafarians were giving dreadlocks a bad name. The Bajans were terrified. Far from looking on Rastafarians as peaceful people, they treated anyone with dreadlocks as a troublemaker.

I was no exception. When I looked for a job in several of the hotels I was turned away without even being interviewed. At first I couldn't work out why. I spoke good English, I dressed well, I was polite. Surely I'd get on wonderfully with the European holiday-makers?

But the hotel managers were convinced that dreadlocks would frighten the tourists. If you wore locks, you were going to rob or kill somebody. Simple as that.

My hairstyle had already caused a problem when I had tried to go for a drink at one of the five-star hotels one evening. I was with some friends. The security guard stopped me as I walked through the gates.

'You can't come inside,' he barked.

'Why not?'

'No Rastamen allowed.'

I pointed out that I was with a friend of the hotel manager.

'I don't care who you're with,' the guard said. 'You can't come in.'

'Fuck you, then.' I started walking past him towards the hotel.

'Stop right there!' I turned round and saw that the guard had drawn his gun out. He cocked the pistol and sank into a shooting position.

My friend called the manager. Thankfully, he had a more broad-minded attitude to the question of dreadlocks. He sacked the guard on the spot. Locks or no locks, it was not good for business if his staff pulled guns on the customers.

Other Rastafarians I met in Barbados were doing menial jobs like

99

selling peanuts on the beach or making sandals in Bridgetown. I didn't want to do anything like that. I wanted to use my driving and mechanical skills.

I walked into the bus depot in Speightstown and asked for a job. The supervisor was a small man in his fifties with grey hair. He sat in a ramshackle office containing broken furniture and a creaking fan.

I explained what I was doing in Barbados and that I needed work. I told him I was a good driver and the sort of person who would get on well with the passengers. I also gave him a nice line in bullshit about having left school with O-Levels, A-Levels and just about every other qualification I could think of. 'So can you give me a job, please?' I concluded.

He gave a low chuckle. 'You want a job?' he laughed. 'With dem tings on yer head?'

'What's wrong with my dreadlocks?'

'Dem tings. You want a job with dem tings?' He was tickled that anyone with dreadlocks should even think of getting a job. 'Boy, you can't work here with dem tings on yer head.'

I was quite cross. 'What are you talking about? I'm from England, I'm educated, I can drive these buses. What's your problem?'

'I don' care if you come from Timbuktu. You ain't drivin' me buses.'

I stormed out of the office. I returned to The Whim, where I was consoled by my great-aunt Pearl. She also objected to 'dem tings'.

'Yer a nice boy, Oliver,' she said, 'but yer hair look like de rats been at it.'

Pearl is one of my favourite relations. She is a slim, elegant lady with a superb sense of humour and an uproarious laugh, a Godfearing churchgoer. She must have been stunning as a girl, but she never married, despite being one of the kindest people in the village. We have always got on well and each time I return to Barbados she is one of the first people I visit. I spend hours with her chatting over glasses of Mauby in her cosy board 'n' shingles cottage. Her house, painted cream and pastel blue and barely bigger than a Wendy house, sits on the brow of Whim Hill.

Pearl was born in 1915. She spent her life in domestic service as a lady's maid and later as a children's nanny. She was one of the old colonial school and always referred to her employer as her 'mistress'.

Unlike many of her generation who have travelled abroad in search of work, she has never left 'the Rock', as Barbados is sometimes known. 'Closest ah've been to overseas is puttin' me foot in de sea at Heyward's beach,' is her favourite joke.

Like her sister Emelyn, she laments the death of the pre-tourism days when everyone worked on the land. 'If you didn't work de land, you didn't eat. I remember in the war, all we had was sweet potaters, morning, noon and night. Could get a basket for nutten'. Long-grained rice, we called 'em.

'Now all young people wanna do is get quick dollars from tourists. People's fingernails too clean and dat's not good for Barbados.'

Pearl believes that the fate of the sweet potato illustrates the decline of agriculture in Barbados. 'Forty years ago we had so many different kinds of potater. We had "minuets" that were small and sweet, and "brass cannons" that were huge and long. An' "six weeks" that only took a little time to grow. Now they grow only one kind of potater. Lord help me! One kind of potater! What is the world comin' to?'

Pearl was unable to help me in my search for a job. With my dreadlocks I had a better chance of becoming prime minister of Cuba than finding work in Barbados. But she suggested that I talk to her neighbour, Sybil, another of my great-aunts.

Sybil is a formidable lady. She runs her own private school for three- to eleven-year-olds in Speightstown. Her pupils hold her in great awe. She commands such respect that they fall totally silent whenever they see her.

She has a reputation for being the wisest person in The Whim, a sort of village elder to whom everyone comes with their problems. If you need help filling in a government form, Sybil will explain it for you. She is also an unofficial marriage counsellor and is often to be found sorting out people's domestic troubles.

Sybil was keen to help me. She decided to go to the top. She telephoned an old friend of hers, Speightstown's Commissioner of Police, Mr Marshall. She told him that her sister's grandson had arrived from England and was looking for a job. The only drawback was that he had dreadlocks, but he was a nice boy really – not at all like these other nasty Rastas here.

I could almost hear the Commissioner's frostiness down the telephone line. But he respected my great-aunt. After much persuasion from her he agreed to see me.

I went to the police station. The officer on the front desk was determined to be unhelpful. 'Whadya want, boy?' He eyed my locks suspiciously.

'I've come to see the Commissioner.'

'He got no time for you, boy.' The officer turned away and busied himself with paperwork.

I leaned over the desk. 'Look, man, I've just come from England and I've got an appointment with the Commissioner. Will you please tell him I am here.'

The policeman perked up at the word 'appointment'. Scowling, he dialled the Commissioner's secretary. A few minutes later I was shown into Mr Marshall's office.

The Commissioner wearily asked me to sit down. He was a big, stocky man, at least six foot two, with light-coloured skin. He ordered a servant to fetch tea for both of us and got straight to the point.

'I don't like Rastafarians and I don't like dreadlocks. You Rastas are always causing trouble. What you got to say, boy?'

I spent two hours convincing the Commissioner that I was not in Barbados to cause trouble. I told him I had every qualification known to man – all lies, of course, but what can you do when you're unemployed? – and that I had not come to the island to live off the state. Far from it. I wanted to contribute to the economy of my homeland. Furthermore, I was an excellent driver and would be a credit to the island's transport system. And, of course, I was totally against drugs.

'So you don' smoke ganja?' he said.

'Me? Smoke? Good Lord, no. That stuff makes me ill.'

He bought it all. I managed to convince him that I was little short of an angel and by the end of our chat we were the best of friends. He wrote out a letter for me, signed and stamped it and told me to take it to the bus depot supervisor. The job was mine as soon as I could start.

I returned to the depot. The supervisor was not pleased to see me. 'Tol' you first time, boy. No job with dem tings.'

I showed him the letter. He read it slowly, occasionally raising his eyebrows. He sat down heavily in his chair and sighed. I felt a little sorry for him.

'Boy, why you give me all this trouble?'

'Look,' I said. 'I haven't come here to upset your little runnings. I'll make a really good driver. Just you see.'

He sighed again. 'Well, if Mr Marshall tell me I gotta give you a job, I gotta give you a job. But,' he added, 'I tell you before and I tell you now. You gotta cut off dem tings.'

'No I am not. Mr Marshall didn't mind my locks so there's no reason why you should, either.' I suggested a compromise. 'Tell you what. I'll make a hat so that my locks can fit in it and you'll never see them while I'm on the bus. That's the best I can do.' He sighed again. All right, a hat it was. I could start work the following week.

The buses were brand-new Leylands with crash gearboxes. They were beautiful to drive and were painted a glaring blue and yellow, the colours of Barbados. The drivers pushed their vehicles to the limit. Everywhere you went you would see smashed buses littering the roadside, their wheels somewhere out in a field.

The main road from the airport along the beaches to the north end of the island was particularly dangerous. Every inch of roadside was taken up with businesses, hotels, fruit-sellers and shacks. There was no pavement and the tarmac crawled with pedestrians, cyclists and stray animals. Buses frequently ripped through the crowds, killing people on their way to work.

For the first two weeks I was on probation. I was assigned to a driver who was supposed to teach me the routes. I had to sit next to him and memorise the maze of roads and lanes around the island. My driver-instructor was having an affair with the female conductor. On our first morning he left me to drive the bus on my own. Instead of sitting up front with me, he retreated to the rear of the vehicle, where he and the conductor spent the day snogging on the back seat.

I hadn't a clue where I was going, but the passengers soon put me right. They knew the routes well and told me which turns to take. Soon everybody was shouting: 'Left here! No, right! Straight on!'

Bodies pressed around me, yelling directions. I was soaked with sweat from the heat of the sun through the windscreen. There did not seem to be any bus stops in Barbados. When somebody wanted to get off they simply ordered me to stop the bus. I must have stopped a thousand times.

There were none of those dreary, miserable faces you see on London buses. Everybody was singing, laughing and joking. Sometimes a big mama got up and did a little jig in the aisle. People got on with chickens in cages and baskets of fruit on their heads.

The hills provided an entertaining diversion. I learned how to double-clutch the gearbox. As I approached each hill I would change down and rev the engine to a roar. The passengers all cheered. 'Yeah, Rastaman. Go fast, Rastaman.' The bus would charge into the incline, engine screaming, and then it would slowly lose momentum as we headed upwards. Sometimes we barely made it to the top.

By the end of my first day I was exhausted. As we pulled up back at the depot, the driver returned to the front of the bus, buttoning up his shirt. The conductor patted her hair, hitched up her skirt and left by the rear door. The driver slapped me on the back and congratulated me on my navigation.

Bus-driving in Barbados was considered a fun occupation for extrovert people. The passengers each had their favourite driver. They liked someone perhaps because he drove especially fast or played loud music during the journey. People sometimes waited for several buses to go by until their special driver arrived.

I became the favourite of the schoolgirls. They all wanted to get on my bus. I'd stop outside a school and dozens of giggling teenaged girls would clamour to get on board. They all tried to sit behind me. And when we set off, they shouted, 'Rastaman, take off yer hat, let's see yer dreadlocks.' Sometimes I took off my cap and they would run their hands through my hair.

I stayed in Barbados until I got bored. The novelty of bus-driving wore off and it didn't take long to see the whole island. Barbados is only twenty-three miles by sixteen and Ealing alone felt bigger than that. My dreadlocks were attracting funny looks and the Little England atmosphere was getting me down. It was too expensive hanging out with the tourists in the five-star hotels and a social life centred around the rum shops was not my idea of fun.

I spent a brief period as a beach bum, picking up single foreign women as they sunbathed on the white sands. There were – and still are – numerous beach bums all along the island's west-coast tourist resorts. Their dream was to meet a rich white woman who would take them away from Barbados to a life of wealth in Europe or America. Sometimes their dreams come true. A friend of mine ended up marrying a Swedish millionairess and another guy now lives in luxury in Switzerland.

I couldn't take beach-bumming seriously. It was easy pulling these women because they were into fit, young bodies like mine. Unlike the other boys, I also had a reasonably intelligible English accent so the women could understand me. But I wasn't looking for beer money, let alone marriage. I just wanted to have a good time and lots of sex.

The other beach bums couldn't understand me. And they didn't appreciate it when I moved in on their women. There was lots of competition and I got in a few fights.

The women never told me to go away. I would sit down on the edge of their beach towel and pay them a few compliments, like they had a nice hairdo, beautiful eyes, the usual rubbish. I soon knew whether I was in with a chance. The ideal target was a woman on holiday with a couple of friends. Her friends could protect her and she didn't feel threatened. I learned how to steer myself gently towards the one I fancied.

Sometimes I slept with three women in a day. But even the sex got boring after a while. The novelty of Barbados began to wear off. The island is lovely for a holiday but it's a tedious place to live if you're young. I was bored wasting my time on the beach, bored with seeing the same people every day. After three months I'd had enough and I returned to Britain.

I didn't tell anybody I was coming home. I arrived back in London and went to Pat's flat. She was astonished to see me but she said I could stay. It was two weeks before I let my mother know I was back. She was upset I hadn't rung her.

Life returned to the normal London drudgery. I began car-spraying again and attempted to settle down to a life of domestic harmony with Pat and my beautiful daughter Zarra. But after only a few weeks with Pat I was tearing my locks out. I felt trapped in her tiny council flat. Zarra had asthma and wouldn't stop crying. I was short on patience and tolerance and couldn't stand the hassle. After just a few weeks with mother and child I shovelled my belongings back into a bin-liner and returned to my parents. My mother had no sympathy for me. 'You're not going to find any happiness with women, Oliver, until you stop being so selfish,' she said.

My life changed after a friend invited me to a party in Kensington given by the pop star Toyah Wilcox. Toyah was right at the top of her career but I wasn't interested in her music. All that punk stuff was so dumb.

I was standing in a corner talking to my friend when I saw Sue across the room. I hadn't seen her for ages but I'd thought about her a lot. I went over and said hello. She had put on a lot of weight and she didn't look as attractive as I remembered her. But there must have been something there, because by the end of the evening I'd asked her out. She didn't seem too keen. She said she would think about it and we left it at that.

A few days later she called in at the garage where I was working. We made a date to meet at a bar in Ealing later in the week.

I didn't turn up. I only remembered our date the next day. I knew Sue was living at her sister's so I went round to apologise. Sue's sister let me in. There was a man hanging around by the front door. He looked like he was waiting for someone. I ignored him and went upstairs to Sue's room.

She was getting dressed. She wasn't surprised to see me. She was used to me turning up out of nowhere.

'Where are you going?' I asked.

'None of your business,' she said. 'More to the point, why did you stand me up?'

'Forgot. Sorry. Were you angry?'

'I didn't hold my breath.' She turned her back to me and zipped up her dress. 'Never change, do you, Oliver?'

'Who's the man downstairs?'

Sue fixed her earrings. 'A friend. He's taking me out.'

'Better be going, then.' It was all or nothing. I left the room and went down to the hall. I put a hand on my rival's shoulder. 'Time for you to leave,' I told him. 'I'm going out with her now.' He was gobsmacked. I opened the door for him and showed him out. He was much smaller than me and he didn't want trouble. The next moment he was running down the garden path.

I went back upstairs to Sue. ''Fraid your date's changed his mind. Couldn't wait any longer.' And I added, 'Do you always take so long to get dressed?'

She smiled. 'So where are you taking me?'

And that was the beginning of the rest of my life. Sue had been given a one-bedroomed council flat in Ealing. I moved in with her the following week. A month later she was pregnant. I was twenty-six and she was twenty-five. She told me later that she was ready to have a baby and she reckoned that my good looks made me the perfect father. But she never expected me to stay.

It was OK for a couple of months. I painted the flat and made it cosy. Friends popped round all the time and I was enjoying myself. But as time went on things became difficult. Sue's friends told her that she shouldn't be going out with me. They said I was unreliable and had loads of children everywhere. I really resented them for that, although I had to admit they had a point.

Sue's parents were no better. Her mother and father were living in Australia at the time. I remember the day she rang Sydney to tell them she was pregnant. It was a Sunday morning and we were lying in bed. Her parents went mad when they heard the news. They knew all about me and they didn't like me. 'A good-looking girl like you could have had anybody she wanted,' her mum said down the phone line. 'Why does it have to be him?'

Sue didn't answer. She passed the phone over to me. I had a word with her mother. Her voice sounded deep, as though she was sad. I understood why. Sue's elder sister was going out with a Jamaican, her other sister had married a half-caste guy and I had children with other women. Her parents were worried about her relationship with me.

When I put the phone down I told Sue that I didn't care what they thought about me, but if she felt she was doing the wrong thing we should split up. Sue cradled my head in her arms. 'They're only being like that because they want what's best for me,' she said gently. 'But

I'm a big girl now and I'll do what I like. If it means falling out with Mum and Dad then that's what will happen.' The rift lasted a few years until her parents returned from Australia. Then, I couldn't do enough to help them; I was the one who put them up and looked after them until they found their feet. They fell in love with me eventually.

Sue and I fought constantly throughout her pregnancy. I struggled to accept my new responsibilities but I clung on to my old life. I continued to go out clubbing, leaving Sue behind. I bought a wreck of a BMW. When I'd done it up I went off for weekends, visiting clubs all over Britain: Liverpool, Rotherham, Manchester – I did the lot. I would come home on Sunday night to find that Sue had been crying her eyes out. She had no idea where I'd been and I wouldn't tell her.

Sue eventually got fed up with my gallivanting. She told me that if I didn't start behaving myself she would leave me. I came down to earth with a heavy bump. I realised that I cared for Sue very much and I didn't want that to happen.

I made a determined effort to settle down and I changed slowly as the birth approached. I was overjoyed when Aloma was born, in February 1983. Quite simply, I fell in love with both Sue and the baby.

I can't remember much about the mid-1980s. The days passed quietly without incident. I now had a family that I genuinely cared about and I was earning money to support them. I got back into spraying cars and in the evenings I played quiet games of snooker with other married friends. I lost contact with my friends from the blues and shebeens. I was just a regular west London family man, keeping out of trouble and growing up.

We bought our first house in 1985. I had saved £2,000 as a down-payment on a mortgage. While our solicitor sorted out the paperwork Sue and I went on holiday to Majorca. We blew all the money on having a good time – well, you can't expect a man to grow up that quickly. We returned with nothing and I had to work all hours to raise the down-payment again. I was running up and down the streets of Acton and Ealing asking people if they wanted to have their cars sprayed.

We finally managed it and became the owners of a two-bedroomed terraced house in Currie Road, north Greenford. I did a total DIY job on it, teaching myself how to knock down walls and lay bricks. I worked hard for the nice things in life. My mum and dad's house had always been the best house in our road and I wanted mine to be the same.

After our second daughter, Keilly, was born in January 1987 I had a vasectomy. By now we were living in suburban Hanwell. Susan had her two-point-four kids and she didn't want any more. It was the perfect solution, but I didn't see it that way.

Sue didn't want to be sterilised because of the emotional trauma involved. She kept on at me about having the operation. I reacted like most men do: 'No way. Why can't you take the pill?'

After a year, she'd had enough and began ringing up clinics behind my back. A form arrived one day from the Marie Stopes Clinic in Harley Street. Sue filled in my details, forged my signature and sent it back.

I got a letter out of the blue telling me I had an appointment in ten days' time. 'What's this?' I said as I opened the mail.

'Your vasectomy,' Sue said. 'No getting out of it this time, Oliver.'

And that was that. When the day came I really didn't want to go through with it. But I went meekly to the station and took the train into central London. I sat in the carriage thinking miserably that my manhood was about to be cut to pieces. How would it feel to be a gelding?

They were charming at the clinic. They gave me a cup of tea and a biscuit and told me to wait. Another guy came out of the surgery. He looked perfectly normal, as if nothing had happened to him. 'It's all right,' he consoled me. 'It doesn't hurt.' It wasn't the pain I was worried about. And I didn't mind about not having any more children – I had enough kids already. No, what really concerned me was would I be able to get an erection again?

The doctor called me in. I got on to the operating table and waited with clenched teeth. He gave me a little injection. Then there was a smell of burning skin as he applied a heat electrode to my penis.

It was all over in minutes. I cautiously examined my groin. There was no mark and it was just as if nothing had happened. The doctor put a bit of cotton wool in my underpants and sent me home. Sue gave me a great welcome. My fear was that I wouldn't be able to shag again. But that didn't turn out to be a problem, believe me.

I was the butt of tasteless jokes for months. My brothers called me Jaffa after the seedless oranges. But I was relieved to know there would be no more children. Kids are the downfall of many people. They can be stressful. There are bound to be problems if the shopping bill is £120 a week and you're only earning £200. I'd recommend a vasectomy to anyone. Incredibly, in January 1995 the *News of the World* ran a story about some woman who claimed I'd fathered her child, even after I'd had the snip. Nonsense, of course – I know I'm good, but I'm not *that* good!

My life had changed so much. The West End boy and club hero was dead. I was now going on camping holidays with the family in Selsey and doing the gardening. It's funny how you can change in such a short time from one lifestyle to another. But I felt content and happy. I was living with a woman and enjoying it, which was something I never thought I'd achieve. And it was nice having little children around the house.

Even better, I was now getting on well with the mothers of my other children. Sue and I tried to help out Pat and Anne as much as we could. Sue often looked after Zarra, Chanelle and Oliver in order to give their mothers a break. At first Pat and Anne weren't keen on their children being cared for by my new girlfriend but they soon realised that Sue was good with children. I'm glad that Zarra, Chanelle and Oliver spent so much time with me as kids. It makes it much easier for me to talk to them now and to give them fatherly advice if they have any problems. My mother lavished affection on all my children and often looked after them round at her house. My parents were delighted I had settled down at last.

It was a sad day for everybody when Mum and Dad decided to go home to Barbados in 1987. They had both retired by then and, not surprisingly, had realised that life back in the old country would be cheaper and warmer. The goodbye parties went on for weeks. Night after night every friend they had ever met in England came round to Adelaide Road armed with a farewell bottle of rum.

My only setback was when I started my own spraying and panel-beating company. I opened a garage in Park Royal. I couldn't afford to kit it out properly and everything was really crude: instead of a proper jig to fix the cars, there were four posts stuck in the ground. Various friends came to work for me, but it was a disaster. They skived off whenever my back was turned and the work was never finished. The business soon went bust.

I reckoned that I'd probably be a freelance car-sprayer for the rest of my life and I was quite content with this. I was a working-class black boy making reasonably good and my days of crime were behind me. I had a lovely family, a nice house and a good, regular income. I never imagined that I would have more.

6

WORKING THE DOOR

Spraying cars had been a relatively safe job when I started as a teenager. The paint was cellulose and acrylic-based. By the end of the day I'd be covered in a fine dust but I could brush it off without any ill-effects.

In the 1980s a new type of paint called Two-Pack was brought out. It contained cyanide and had a built-in hardener to make it more efficient. But it was dangerous stuff. When it landed on you, it stuck solid. It clogged up my eyebrows and my hair. I would lie in the bath scrubbing myself but it still wouldn't come off.

I couldn't afford the proper safety equipment you were supposed to use with this paint. Most of my sprayer colleagues had their own garages with special paint booths, but as a freelance I moved around, working in makeshift sheds. It was not a safe environment.

Without the correct mask, I developed bad chest infections and it felt like I had a permanent cold. In addition, my right hand ached from holding the spray-gun all day. The tendons in the arm still weren't right from the time I'd fallen through the sweetshop window all those years earlier. In winter my fingers would seize up from the cold. Spraying was having a serious effect on my health and I began to think about finding a new job.

My new career began after a barbecue at my house in the summer of 1987. Sue took some photographs of me dressed in a pair of khaki shorts. When the snaps came out I was appalled. The top half of my body wasn't too bad but my legs were the skinniest things I'd ever seen. My physique was deteriorating. I was becoming a typical, unfit suburban father.

I decided to do something about it. I joined a local gym and began working on my legs. Six months later I had put two inches on them. I felt good about myself. Then I started on the rest of me. I trained three times a week and the muscle piled on.

Meanwhile, Sue's sister Florence and her husband Bob had opened a nightclub in Southall. The Mona Lisa was a proper black club, packed with all these bad boys from the Stonebridge Estate in Harlesden.

Gangs of teenaged black boys can be a club-owner's nightmare, especially when the reggae is so loud you can't hear and there are so many people that you can't move. They don't want to pay to come in, they argue about every little thing and they want to smoke drugs at the bar. The kids at the Mona Lisa were just like that. Of course, I had behaved like them at their age but that was a long time ago now. I said to myself: 'You must have been a right pain in the arse, Oliver.' God knows how much grief I must have caused my parents.

We were short of money at the time and Sue took a job as a barmaid at the Mona Lisa. Then they started getting so busy that they needed someone to work the door. Since I was pretty fit, Bob said I'd be ideal for the job.

And so I became the first 'Rastafarian' bouncer in London.

When I was young and going to clubs in the West End I regarded bouncers as scum. They were horrible people, fat and sweaty with little bow-ties stuck under double chins. Worst of all, they always gave you those nasty, suspicious looks. They were the bad face of authority and they stood for everything I hated.

I was determined I wasn't going to be like that. If I was going to be a bouncer I would be nice and friendly and show the same respect to everybody. It was difficult being friendly on the door of the Mona Lisa. Most of the trouble stemmed from Bob, a quarrelsome Jamaican, who enjoyed winding people up. There was nothing he liked better than a good argument – and that was when he wasn't being just plain rude. I still don't know how he managed to keep that club. He never stopped shouting at the customers yet it was packed every night for three years.

People would arrive outside and say something like, 'How much is it to come in?' And Bob would say, 'You deaf or some'in'? You 'eard de man in front of you, y'know 'ow much 'e paid. You fuckin' pay de same.' And everyone would scream at him and tell him to fuck off and these kids would barge through the door and storm the place and I'd feel like giving up.

Bob imposed impossible rules such as no jeans in the club – pretty stupid considering the clientele. I doubt many of them owned much more than a pair of jeans.

I received my introduction to doorman diplomacy (if that's what you can call it) one Saturday night at the end of my first week on the door. Inside it was chaos as usual. Halfway through the evening Bob pushed his way through the crowd and came outside to see me. His face, dripping sweat, bore that look of self-righteous indignation that club-owners wear when they think an employee is taking the piss.

'Whadda fuck you doing, Oliver?' he spat. 'Man by de bar wearing jeans.'

I'd suffered the dross of the Stonebridge Estate all evening and I wasn't going to take any more abuse.

'Oh yeah?' I said, peering into the club. I spotted the offender in the gloom. He looked about eighteen and was knocking back a tumbler of rum. 'Yeah, I see him. Nice pair of Levis.'

'Shuddup, Oliver. Get de boy outta here.'

I elbowed my way through the club and to the bar. I put my arm around the customer's shoulder and talked to him, nice and friendly. 'How come you're wearing those?' I said, pointing at his denims. 'I certainly didn't let you in with them.'

The man smiled nastily. 'Changed, didn't I?' he laughed. He waved a pair of scuffed corduroys in my face. 'Went to the toilet and changed.'

Well, the whole exercise seemed pretty pointless to me. 'The owner says no jeans,' I explained. 'Time to go.'

He refused to leave. I asked again. He put down his glass, swivelled his body and threw a punch at me. I ducked and his fist missed my face. I caught his arm and yanked it behind his back in a half-nelson. I pulled him away from the bar and shoved him past the other customers through the door and into the street. Outside the club we had that usual, boring slanging match that doormen so often have to put up with. He finally gave up and disappeared up the street. I began to feel sorry for all those bouncers I'd known when I was a teenager just like him.

The Mona Lisa stretched my patience to the limit. One evening I saw a guy touch Sue's bottom as she walked past with a bowl of ice. I lost my temper. I was going to kill the bastard. I grabbed a baseball bat from behind the bar and swung it at him. Luckily somebody caught it, otherwise I would have hurt him. Far from feeling protected by her loving partner, Sue was furious. She called me an animal and had a right go at me. She said I was being silly because I was jealous. That hurt but it taught me a lesson: the most skilled part of door work is keeping out of trouble.

Bob had another rule: no hats. No jeans was bad enough, but no hats? That was really stupid. Black people have this thing with hats. They love them. Baseball caps, trilbys, fedoras – they adore any sort of hat. But Bob wasn't having it. He wanted only 'well-dressed' people in his club, and, according to him, you couldn't be well dressed in a hat.

One night two big Rastafarians turned up. They were wearing their 'crowns', those tall leather caps so beloved of Rastamen, into which they had stacked their dreadlocks. At first sight, they seemed quite reasonable people. They arrived at the entrance and smiled when they saw another Dread on the door. It was the first time they'd seen a Rastafarian bouncer.

They greeted me with cries of 'Jah be wid you, man.'

'Yeah, great,' I said, eyeing their hats and thinking of Bob's half-baked rule.

I steered the boys away from the door and adopted a serious expression. 'Look, I know this sounds really stupid and I don't want to cause any trouble, but the man doesn't allow you to wear your crowns in there.'

They looked at each other, puzzled.

'Whadya mean?' one of them asked.

'No hats in the club.' I clenched my teeth and waited for the reaction.

'Hey, man,' his friend said. 'As a Dread y'sel', d'you expeck us to take off our crowns?'

'Well, that's what the man says.'

'Nah,' said the first Dread. 'Not taking off mine.'

'And I'm not taking off mine, neither,' said the second Dread.

This called for tact. Something about these boys told me they were not the sort of peace-loving Rastafarians I'd known back in the days of Dread House. I said 'Hang on a mo'' and retreated into the club to find Bob.

He was playing big bossman at the bar. 'There are these two Dreads outside who won't take off their hats,' I reported.

'Well, tell them to fuck off, then.'

'I don't think that's a good idea, Bob.' I gave him a brief lecture on Rastafarianism. 'Those hats are part of them, it's like their religion. You know that.'

'They can still fuck off.'

I shook my head in disbelief and returned to the door. The Rastas looked impatient. 'Listen, the man says you've got to take off your crowns. Otherwise you can't come in.' The men glanced at each other again. Something unspoken went between them. It was not a nice vibe. Then the first one said, 'You listen to me, brother. Mebbe we do this New York-style.' And with that he slipped his right hand into his jacket. He pulled it halfway out to reveal the grip of an automatic pistol.

See what I mean? That was the type of clientele I was dealing with at the Mona Lisa.

'Er, wait a minute,' I said. 'You mean you're going to shoot me over a *hat*? If I was dealing with people like the owner of this club I wouldn't even bother coming here. I'd go to another club.'

'Wanna come into this club,' the second Rastafarian said sulkily. His mate fingered the pistol butt.

I decided that verbal finesse was called for. My nerves were jangling so much that I couldn't stop talking. 'Well, be my guest,' I said. 'If you're going to draw a gun over a hat, I'm going to stand aside and let you do what the hell you like. I'm not getting shot, I can tell you. I've been in a lot of bad clubs in my life and the moment anyone has even said "gun" I've been off. You want to wear your hats, you go right ahead. Just talk to the owner. His name's Bob. I'm sure he'll be understanding . . .'

I was still blocking the door, but guns or no guns, these gangsters were not going to tangle with a fellow Dread. Even hoodlums like them could see it was not in the spirit of brotherly love. I went on and on about how the owner of this club was the biggest ras'hole they were ever likely to meet and why couldn't they go over to Ladbroke Grove where they'd find much better night-time fun. My monologue was beginning to sound like a John Cleese impression and I think I bored them stupid. When I finally finished they raised their eyebrows as if to say 'Thank Jah this guy has finally shut up.'

'Respeck, man,' the first Rastafarian said.

'Yeah, respeck,' repeated the second. And with that they took off their hats and walked into the club without trouble.

That was how I tried to work the door. Be polite to people and, Jah willing, they'll be polite back.

My bouncing career progressed. Back in the gym I had got to know a group of boys who worked for an all-black security firm in Hanwell called Atlas Security. Their main work was supplying bouncers for West End clubs.

Their leader was a Jamaican called Sydney. He was the smallest person in the gym but everybody held him in the highest esteem. I liked him despite the fact that he had a mean glint in his eye. He weighed just over ten stone but he could lift more weight than me. I started training with him and we got on well. By this time I was fourteen stone and exploding out of my shirts.

One day Sydney said, 'Why don't you come and work the door with us?' I quickly agreed. By now it was 1989. I was still spraying cars but I was fed up with the job. I couldn't stand the Mona Lisa any longer and the rates Atlas paid meant that I could survive on professional door work alone.

Sydney took me along to my first job. It was at a place in Ealing called Haven Stables. I was introduced to the other doormen. One of them was a huge man called Chopper who had a long scar across his head. He was bald and very ugly but quite friendly.

The others were just as big and tough. They regarded me with disgust. Who was this bloke with those pansy dreadlocks down to his waist? They looked at me as if to say, 'You can't have a Rastaman working the door. This is not known. There are no Rastafarian doormen in London so why has this one turned up?'

Ex-servicemen, ex-Foreign Legionnaires, guys who have been in prison for killing people – this is the sort of person I started working with. They were not the kind of men I'd go out of my way to mix with. But at least I was no longer myself one of those kids going to the clubs and being harassed by doormen. I was almost part of the establishment.

On my first night on the Haven Stables I was teamed up with an ex-soldier called 'Bulldog' Dave. He was wide and weighed about seventeen stone. We hit it off immediately and spent all night talking and getting to know each other. Sydney ticked us off dozens of times for not doing the job properly.

Bulldog had served in the Falklands. He told me stories about what he and his comrades used to do to their Argentinian prisoners. Like shooting the Argentinians in cold blood and putting their fingers in their prisoners' eyes and digging the eyeballs out. Boys in the army are not nice. They like killing people; that's why they join up. I'd always thought they joined the forces to see the world and to learn different sports like you see on the TV commercials. Come off it. Most of them join up so they can kill people. And Bulldog was one of them.

Haven Stables was a white, middle-class wine-bar-cum-disco. The decorations consisted of naked shopfront mannequins pinned up on the walls. They had big shiny tits and were supposed to give the place a classy look.

You couldn't find a greater contrast to the Mona Lisa. Haven Stables was full of office people and most of them were drunk. Drunks are the worst people to deal with. They just want to fight everybody. But Sydney's doormen seldom had any hassle. We were so big that nobody wanted to mess with us, even if they were plastered.

That was until I came along.

I'd only been there a week when I ended up in big trouble. Bulldog and I were standing by the door, watching a party of yuppies in red braces swilling champagne. They were getting louder and louder, really obnoxious people.

One of them stood up. He was small and spotty. He gave a war-cry and ripped one of the mannequins off the wall. He hugged it to him and started dancing with it. His friends thought he was being really funny.

Bulldog and I strolled over. When the boy saw us coming he dropped the dummy on the floor. I said, 'Look, can you please put that back on the wall?'

He said, 'What are you talking about? Wasn't me.'

I tried the diplomatic approach. Perhaps negotiation would work. 'Look, if it's that much trouble, I'll put it back on the wall,' I said, 'but first you're going to leave.'

I grabbed his arm and escorted him towards the door. But the champagne had put him in a fighting mood. He pulled away, grabbed a handful of my dreadlocks and yanked them out of my head.

Dreadlocks come out surprisingly easily. I was so startled that I let go of him for a second. My locks were all over the floor and the other doormen were laughing at me. 'Hang on a moment,' I said. 'What have you done to my hairdo?'

Then the pain came. My scalp was in agony. I lost my temper. I grabbed the boy in a head-lock and jerked him forward. We rolled on to the floor. I managed to grab his arms and hauled him to his feet. I dragged him to the door and flung him into the road. He must have tripped on the pavement because the next moment he was flying head-first into a parked car.

He struck the vehicle with a loud crunch. I think he must have hit his nose. A spray of blood flew across the car's bonnet. Then the man's friends poured out and started shouting at me. They accused me of punching and kicking their colleague.

Their accusations were nonsense but somebody called the police. They didn't even bother to hear my side of the story. They listened to the customers and decided that they were respectable business people on a quiet night out. The officers took one look at me and said I was under arrest. I was flung into a squad car and taken to Southall Police Station.

After I'd said my bit in the interview room, I think that the police were beginning to sympathise with me. They'd only arrested me because I was so big. One of the officers said, 'You could have been a bit more gentle. He was only a little lad and look at the size of you.'

I replied, 'Well, if someone had you by the dreadlocks what would you do?' The policeman agreed that it couldn't have been very nice having one's locks pulled out. I added petulantly, 'I was only trying to stop him damaging my hairstyle. It wasn't my fault he hit his face.'

I spent the night in a cell. But I'd got so used to being locked up during my youth that I wasn't worried. The jailer wished me a pleasant night and the door clanked shut behind me. I took off my coat and rolled it into a ball. I lay down on the bunk, put my makeshift pillow behind my head and went to sleep.

They let me out in the morning and I was charged with causing actual bodily harm. Apparently, fourteen people had made statements saying I'd attacked the guy – it's amazing what a few bottles of Moët can do to you.

I appeared before a magistrate, pleaded not guilty and was given bail. A few weeks later I went to court for the trial. None of the witnesses turned up to give evidence. The magistrate dismissed the case and gave me £50 expenses.

But that was only the beginning. I was to learn that you spend a lot of time in court when you're a doorman. The mannequin incident was the only time I was in the dock myself, but I was often being called into the witness box to give evidence on behalf of colleagues accused of assault on customers.

Because I worked on being nice to the punters, and Sydney saw that I could be tactful, he usually employed me on the door rather than as part of the mean machine sorting out trouble inside a club. I prided myself on the fact that I didn't have to fight anyone to get a result. I became skilled at defusing situations that looked like turning nasty. If I saw anyone being a nuisance I'd say, 'Listen, Sydney's not far away. You don't want him finding you because he'll rip your head off. Why don't you leave by the back door?' Troublemakers would think I was the best friend they'd ever had and they'd leave without argument. They'd hang around nearby but they'd still leave. Sydney had a terrifying reputation. No one wanted to mess with him.

When my colleagues learned I wasn't a fighter they used to call me names like 'chicken'. Or they'd sneer, 'Ooh, he's a girl, what with his long 'air an' that.' I had grown a slightly effete Clark Gable pencil moustache and that didn't help, either.

121

They took the piss out of me constantly and called me a pansy and a girlie. I made a point of dressing smartly for work. While everybody else turned up in black tie, I'd wear a yellow tie with pink spots. I was different, and I didn't want to look like just another gorilla. 'Ooh, dear,' they would scoff, 'don't touch 'is suit. Might slap you on the wrist.'

Having spent most of the 1980s as a quiet family man, it was flattering to have the attention of women again. The girls were the best part of the door work and it was difficult to resist being chatted up. Girls were always wanting to kiss me and play with my dreadlocks. They were used to seeing fat, ugly doormen. But I wasn't fat or ugly, and the other doormen were jealous of me.

In 1991 Atlas got their first West End contract. We were hired to do the security at a one-nighter called the Krazy Klub at the Astoria Theatre, Charing Cross Road. It was at the height of the Acid House scene and London promoters were making thousands from Saturday-night raves.

This crowd were very different from the yuppies of Ealing. They were determined to cause trouble and everybody was trying to smuggle in drugs, guns and knives.

It was the first time I'd seen kids on Ecstasy. We would search everyone as they came into the Astoria and deprive them of their various stimulants, putting all the pills and powders in a box. By the end of the evening it would be full and the contents would be flushed down a toilet. The doormen might not have been the straightest people around and some of them liked the occasional spliff, but we were all violently against hard drugs.

The police had been giving the Krazy Klub's promoters hassle, so there was a strict rule that everyone was searched. The police were called if we caught anyone who looked like a dealer and had large quantities of drugs on them. I didn't agree with that. If a boy had 50 Es on him I couldn't see that it was our job to grass him up. Much better to tell him he was banned from the club.

The Astoria was almost as bad as the Mona Lisa. It was full of very pretty, very young white girls being chased by gangs of teenaged black boys. The girls were hopelessly impressionable and the boys floated around taking their pick. I would look at these boys and sigh.

I knew this type only too well because I'd been one of them.

Little girls, barely sixteen and dressed in skin-tight mini-skirts and see-through tops, would skip up to me and try to stroke my locks until I pushed them away. They were all spaced out on Ecstasy. It was as if they were talking to me but not really looking at me. Weird. And I would be thinking all the time that I wanted to send these children home to their mums and dads. They looked like they'd just come up from the home counties and had left Mummy in a cold sweat at home worrying about them. I wouldn't like to see my kids in places like that. All this Ecstasy and speed was horrible. The kids were getting old before their time – you could see the damage the drugs were causing.

So-called peace-loving drugs like Ecstasy created an atmosphere of tension and violence. One night at the Astoria a white man went mad when he saw his girlfriend chatting to a black man. The white guy pulled out a CS gas canister and sprayed it into his girlfriend's face.

There was gas all over the place. Everyone's eyes were streaming. I called the other doormen. We wrapped handkerchiefs around our faces and jumped on the white guy. We roughed him up a bit, carried him to the entrance and threw him on to the pavement.

We surrounded him. I shone a torch into his face. 'Don't you ever come near this club again,' I said.

'Yeah?' he said. He stared at me through mad eyes. He stumbled to his feet and limped away. Halfway down the street he turned back and shouted, 'Fucking Rasta. I'm gonna come back and shoot you.'

Well, everyone panicked, didn't they? My colleagues were terrified. 'Hear what the man said?' they gabbled. 'Said he's going to shoot Oliver.'

Sydney told me, 'Go and put your coat on. Go home and take two weeks off.' I did as he said, but I couldn't understand what the fuss was about. I'd been threatened before with guns and knives and nobody had ever come back. I learned years ago that if somebody goes around saying 'I'm going to cut you' or 'I'm going to shoot you', he's not really going to do it.

A fortnight later I was back inside the Astoria when I saw the man who had threatened me. Sydney and I were standing by the dance floor when suddenly he nudged me. 'Oi, there's the geezer who said he'd shoot you.'

The man spotted me. He trotted off the dance floor and walked up to me, not a care in the world. 'Nice to see you,' he said, shaking my hand. 'Sorry about the other night. I was off my head.'

I turned to Sydney. 'Told you so. If a bloke's going to shoot you, he's going to do it there and then. He's not going to give you time to think about it.'

Things became even more violent when we took over the security at a club in Covent Garden called the Rock Garden. It was a live music venue on the edge of the old flower market in the heart of London. You'd get everyone there from tourists to serious rock-music fans.

The doormen before us had been fired for taking backhanders and letting in large amounts of drugs. I got the job of fronting the door and it was up to me to decide who came in.

It was a brilliant ego trip. People would plead with me to let them in and I'd stand there, hand on my chin, pretending to make up my mind.

One night I was strutting up and down the queue outside as usual, deciding whom I'd let in. The crowd consisted mainly of trendy, well-dressed boys and girls. I walked down the line saying, 'Yeah, you're OK, come in.' If I didn't like the look of them it was, 'Why don't you go back to the suburbs?'

I was getting nicely into my stride when a man walked up to me. He was followed by what looked like three enormous bodyguards.

'All right, mate?' he said to me in a purring voice. 'Having a nice evening?'

'Yeah, lovely, thank you. How about you?'

'Yeah, not so bad.'

Oh, this one was a smoothie, no mistake. Nice Armani suit (though possibly a Hong Kong copy) and a pair of tasselled loafers. He was short and stocky with a thick neck and a thin smile. Not aggressive, but he looked like he might have a pop. Definitely a villain.

We were making small-talk when the club manageress appeared in the doorway. 'Oliver. A quick word please,' she called.

'Won't be a mo',' I told Thick Neck.

The manageress was a plump woman of about thirty. She looked worried and beckoned me inside the door. 'Look, Oliver,' she said, keeping one eye on our friend. 'I don't want that lot in here.'

'Why not?'

'Trouble.'

I returned to Thick Neck. 'Look, I'm really sorry, but for some reason my boss doesn't want you in tonight. So do us a favour, come back next week. I'll have a word with her in the meantime and then you'll be able to come in.'

The silence was deafening, the smiles all gone.

'No,' Thick Neck said. 'You don't understand. I come here every week and I'm coming in now.'

I stood my ground. ''Fraid not. She doesn't want you.'

Well, he got the hump, didn't he? Having been all posh and well mannered one moment, he suddenly changed. He went berserk and threw a punch at me. I saw it coming and dodged out of the way.

One advantage of the Astoria CS gas incident was that I had discovered what powerful stuff it was. As a result, I now carried a canister at all times. It was the perfect anti-gatecrasher device.

I fumbled in my pocket and brought out the gas. I pushed the button and gave it a good spray. He ducked and I missed him. One of the man's gorillas came from behind him. He was also waving a CS canister. He sprayed the gas right in my face.

I put my hands to my eyes. They were in agony and I couldn't see anything. Being CS-gassed is a horrible sensation and I thought I was about to go blind. I turned on my heels and rushed inside the club. I fumbled my way to the men's room and washed my eyes with water.

When I came out, the queue of clubbers had broken up. People were screaming and running everywhere. The cloud of gas had spread into the club's restaurant and diners were pouring out in panic. Sydney was pacing around like a demented tiger. His eyes were red and streaming.

Thick Neck and his heavies had escaped in the commotion. And that was the last we saw of them – for the time being. I ordered the manageress to tell me who they were. She explained that Thick Neck was the leader of a drug-dealing and extortion outfit which called itself the Inner City Firm. I discovered later that the gang did not restrict themselves to conventional crime: they were also well known for causing trouble on the terraces at West Ham football matches.

Peace returned to Covent Garden, but I had a nasty feeling that these boys would be back. Thick Neck didn't seem like the type to let an incident like this go.

They returned a couple of weeks later. It had been a busy night and I was looking forward to going home to bed. At about 1 a.m. I was leaning against the door when I saw Thick Neck and a mob of five or six cronies walking down the street. They were all smiles. Oh no, I thought, here we go again.

'Nice evening, innit?' Thick Neck couldn't have been more pleasant. 'Thought we'd pop in for a drink.'

I wasn't prepared to argue. As I said, it had been a long night and I couldn't be bothered with any more trouble. I decided to let them in. It was as if all the problems of a couple of weeks earlier had been forgotten. We shared the same attitude: no one, not even the hardest villain, wants continuous war, and it's often much easier to forgive and forget. Nobody had been hurt during the CS incident and there were no hard feelings between Thick Neck and myself. I wished them a pleasant evening and they walked past me into the club.

All would have been fine if they hadn't been spotted by one of the other doormen. He went and told Sydney. Sydney flew into one of his tempers. He started prowling the club searching for Thick Neck.

What happened next was a typical gangland cock-up. The original confrontation was over, and that should have been the end of it. But one of Thick Neck's friends decided to get stupid. He was walking past Sydney, who was drinking a cup of coffee, and gave him a hard shove with his elbow, smashing the cup into his face. Sydney yelled for help and the other doormen came running. Fists started flying but somehow Thick Neck and his thugs managed to escape. The next thing I knew, they were running out of the club past me.

Thick Neck must have called for support on a mobile phone, because within ten minutes a mob of about thirty yobs turned up armed with baseball bats and knives. I was impressed at how quickly they arrived. It made me think that Thick Neck must have planned this all along.

I took one look at the assortment of weapons and decided that I wasn't going to tangle with this lot. I dived into the club and Sydney bolted the door behind me. Baseball bats rained on the door as the mob tried to smash their way in.

Sydney was raging. He told us to gather up all the weapons we could find. We grabbed baseball bats from behind the bar. Someone had a broom handle. When we were ready, Sydney roared, 'Let's get the fucking pussies.' He opened the door and we charged out.

The piazza outside the club turned into a battleground. There must have been fifty people out there all apparently trying to kill each other. Someone screamed. I saw a man lying in a pool of blood in the street and another man standing over him with a knife. The knifeman looked at me and then ran off. I rushed over to the injured man to find he was an Atlas doorman, a man of forty called Keith. He had been stabbed in the chest. Blood seeped through his shirt. He was badly hurt and groaning for help.

The fighting continued for a few minutes until an ambulance arrived, siren wailing and lights flashing. Then the police turned up. About twenty officers, truncheons drawn, stormed up the street.

Thick Neck's mob began to run. They disappeared down the side streets leading away from Covent Garden. The Atlas doormen had the same idea and scarpered in the opposite direction. Only Sydney and myself remained. We stayed with Keith and told the ambulancemen what had happened.

The police were understanding when they realised that Keith was our friend. They could see that we were not to blame. One of the officers had caught a man who had been seen running down the road with a bloodied knife in his hand. It was all over.

Keith was taken to hospital, but despite all the blood he was not seriously injured and made a full recovery. He now has a long scar across his stomach, though.

The day after the fight, Sydney and I went along to Bow Street Police Station where the police asked us to identify Keith's attacker in a line-up. Twelve men were brought into a room and paraded in front of us. The accused man was standing to the left of the line. Sydney and I glanced at each other. We both recognised him from the fight. A silent message passed between us. We turned to the officer in charge and told him that we could not see the man who had stabbed Keith.

The policeman sighed. 'Bleedin' doormen, always the same.' He hadn't expected anything else. He knew perfectly well that getting a man locked up is not the way of the underworld. You don't grass on anyone, even the enemy. You sort out your own problems.

Despite the hazards, I was enjoying my career as a bouncer; I'd always liked the excitement of a bit of danger and the money wasn't bad. I had no great ambitions for the future and I reckoned I'd be doing door work for a few years to come.

I certainly had no sporting ambitions. Once upon a time I'd fanta-sised about becoming a professional footballer. But those dreams had died when I'd failed the West Ham trial aged fifteen back at secondary school. No, I had to admit that I was an ordinary working-class man who was going down the same plodding, wage-earning road as everybody else I knew. I was in my early thirties, my life was ticking over fairly easily and I was resigned to the fact that I was going to be a Mr Nobody for the rest of my days. That was until I discovered what was to become the great passion of my life.

7

THE LONE RASTA

The first time I rode a horse it nearly put me off riding for life.

It happened in the early summer of 1980, before I acquired my new status as a family man. One of my favourite drinking haunts was a north London shebeen called the Graveyard. It owed its name to its position next to the cemetery on the Harrow Road. The police seemed unaware of its presence – either that, or they simply turned a blind eye to the booze being sold there illegally.

I'd been visiting the Graveyard for years. The clientele was a mixture of West Indian men and single white girls. I had a fond memory of a night there many years earlier when an exceptionally pretty girl in a tight, low-cut dress had approached me while I was playing snooker. I was pondering over a difficult shot that would win me the game if I succeeded. The girl leaned over me, her breasts lightly brushing my back. She whispered that if I potted the black ball she would 'take me home and give me a right good seeing to'.

It was not the sort of offer you get every night. I lined up the cue, took the shot and the black dropped into the pocket. True to her word, the lady took me back to her West End hotel room where we celebrated my victory.

The Graveyard was that sort of place: full of sexy women and you never knew what was going to happen next.

The club hid behind an anonymous shopfront and everyone was carefully screened before they were allowed to enter. The front door opened on to a couple of snooker rooms crowded with hustlers. The place rang with the beep-beep of space-invader machines. Down a

129

narrow corridor was a tiny gambling room packed with poker players. Another room served as the dance floor and the building shook with the thump of reggae.

At about one in the morning the place began to fill up with hookers coming in for a drink after 'work'. I was in the bar at the back of the club when I spotted a beautiful Hispanic girl I had not seen before. She was dressed in a fur coat and I speculated that she had nothing on underneath.

A friend of mine began chatting her up. He had on one of those Curtis Mayfield broad-rimmed hats and looked quaintly old-fashioned. I leaned on the bar and stared in the girl's direction. Before long she was eyeing me up over my friend's shoulder. She soon got bored with him. I could see her making an excuse about needing to get to the bar or something and she pushed through the crowd to me.

I bought her a drink and we began talking. She turned out to be Spanish and had a husky, seductive accent. Close up, she was prettier than ever and I could not help fancying her. We spent the rest of the night dancing and at 6 a.m. she asked me to take her home. By this stage I had only one thing on my mind and so I took her back to her place in Bayswater.

It was an expensive address and the flat was an interior decorator's dream. She obviously had plenty of money. A high-class hooker, perhaps.

But sex was not on her mind. Far from it. While I waited in the sitting room she went into the bedroom to get changed. She emerged wearing a pair of jeans and announced that she was hungry. I managed to disguise my disappointment and trusted that maybe things would brighten up later. So instead of leaping into her bed, we went for breakfast at the Cavendish Hotel off Piccadilly in the West End.

After breakfast, I paid the bill. She piped up, 'Well, what shall we do now?'

I could think of only one thing, but my escort didn't seem to have the same idea. I thought: well, Oliver, you win some, you lose some. I prepared to make my way home to Acton.

'I know what,' she said suddenly. 'I've got a great idea. Can you ride a horse?'

'What?' This was a new one on me. 'No,' I replied. 'Never been on a horse in my life.'

'It doesn't matter. Let's go riding in Hyde Park. It's easy. You'll soon get the hang of it.'

I hadn't a clue what I was getting myself into. But though I was bleary from lack of sleep, I was well on for it. By this stage I was so obsessed by the girl that, short of joining a cavalry charge, I was prepared to do anything. Riding a horse couldn't be that difficult and the possibilities for showing off my muscles seemed endless. I figured that my new friend would be a lot keener on me after she'd seen my athletic side.

We drove to a mews a few yards from Hyde Park Corner, the home of one of the few riding schools in central London. At the end of the mews was a series of stables with horses you could rent for an hour's hack in the park. I'd never heard of the place before. It was the first time I realised there were horses in London, other than those owned by the police and the army.

It was about 7.30 a.m. and the city was barely awake. We booked our mounts and one of the stablegirls agreed to give me a riding lesson. She brought out a chestnut mare from the stables. It was a huge beast and I began to think that this was not a good idea. But I couldn't back out now, not with a pretty girl at my side.

The stablehand showed me how to get on to the horse. I put my left foot into the left stirrup, grabbed the saddle with both hands and pulled myself up. I swung my right leg over and sat down heavily in the saddle. The horse gave a grunt. The stablehand fussed around below me, adjusting the girth. I sat there uneasily, wondering what I had let myself in for.

The Spanish girl was given a horse. She climbed smoothly on to its back. She had obviously done this before. The stablegirl mounted her own horse and led us out of the mews towards the park.

I did nothing except sit in my saddle and follow the others. The mare seemed to have gone this way many times before and she needed little encouragement to move. As we plodded across Hyde Park Corner I began to get used to the gentle rocking motion. By the time we reached the park gates I was quite enjoying myself. This wasn't so bad after all. Riding seemed to be fairly straightforward.

We reached the stretch of sand-covered riding track known as

Rotten Row. I had just got the hang of walking when my teacher suggested that we try a trot. She and the Spanish girl set off in front of me. Following instructions, I gave my horse a sharp kick in the ribs and it broke into a trot.

But I didn't know what the hell I was doing. I bounced around in the saddle and my feet slipped out of the stirrups. My hands bobbed up and down uncontrollably.

And all for the sake of a woman. Pathetic, really.

All my concentration was now directed at the horse. This was the most uncomfortable thing I'd ever done. What was the pleasure in riding? My balls were bruised from banging against the saddle and any thoughts of sex had vanished. I felt frightened and I became convinced I was going to fall off and be trampled on.

The Spanish girl looked back at me across her shoulder. She smiled. I could have sworn she was enjoying my discomfort. The stablehand wheeled her horse round and came alongside me. 'How about a canter?' she asked.

'Sure. No problem.' Macho Oliver again. It was going to take more than bruised testicles to kill my bravado. I added with feeling, 'Anything's better than this trot.'

My teacher told me what to do. 'Just sit down, hold on to the front of your saddle and squeeze with your legs.'

I did exactly that. Nothing happened. I squeezed again, much harder this time.

I must have overdone it. The horse gave a whinny, pawed the ground a couple of times with a front leg – and took off like a thunderbolt.

As we sped down Rotten Row I yelled, 'What do I do now?'

'Pull the reins,' my instructor shouted.

I pulled the reins into my chest. My action had absolutely no effect. Horse and rider continued to hurtle across the park. An early-morning jogger looked up in horror as this black man, a crazed expression on his face, shot past, dreadlocks flying in the wind. I hung on to the saddle as best I could, because, as they say in the cowboy movies, I was about to disappear over the horizon.

When I'd started out from the stables I had figured that if I wasn't frightened of cars I shouldn't be frightened of a horse. But horses are not like cars; they have minds of their own. If you let the throttle off a motorbike it stops; come off the gas in a car, it stops. But a horse? If it doesn't want to stop, it simply won't. And my horse had no intention of stopping.

From somewhere behind me, the stablegirl was screaming at me. I couldn't hear what she was saying. I think that in my panic I must have been still squeezing with my legs. And the more I squeezed, the faster the animal went. The stablegirl eventually caught up with me and I managed to catch a few words. 'Get your bloody legs off the side of the horse!' she bellowed.

I did as she told me. The horse stopped. Magic.

I was trembling like a scared child. Sweat ran down my collar. My legs ached from where the stirrups had pinched them. The pain in my groin was indescribable.

The Spaniard kicked her horse up to where we stood. She threw her head back and laughed wildly at my pained expression. It was the funniest thing she'd ever seen.

My pride was severely hurt. 'Christ, I'm not doing any more of this,' I said. 'Can we go home now?'

We walked slowly back to the stables, the two girls guarding me closely in case the horse bolted again. I couldn't wait to get off. It had been the worst experience of my life.

I took the Spanish girl back to her flat, gave her a brief peck on the cheek and went home. That was the last I saw of her. I can't even remember her name. As for riding, I promised myself that I would never get on a horse again.

I broke that promise nine years later. It was 1989 and I was on holiday in Barbados with Susan, Aloma and Keilly.

We were on the beach one day when two boys on horses approached us. They asked if we'd like a ride. The children were very excited and the boys took them for a gentle walk along the sand. Then it was my turn. I don't know whether it was the sun and the relaxed holiday atmosphere, but I had forgotten the Hyde Park episode. My big head said, 'Sure, let's go for a run.' And, dressed in no more than a pair of swimming trunks, I jumped on to one of the horses.

I think the boys expected me to try a quiet, gentle trot. But the next thing I knew I was off down the beach into that cowboy sunset again. I couldn't stop the animal; it was a rerun of Hyde Park.

Sue and the children looked aghast as I disappeared in a cloud of sand. Nobody had told me that it takes great skill to stop a horse in full gallop in a wide, open space such as a beach.

My feet slipped out of the stirrups and I was bobbing up and down in the saddle. I nearly ran over a woman walking her dog on the seashore. She waved her fist at me. Bloody Rastas; always causing trouble.

The horse swerved away from the sea and we sped up the sand, ending up in the front garden of one of the beachfront houses. The horse skidded to a halt, gave a contented snort and began munching on a flowerbed. The owners of the house saw us through the windows and rushed out.

'What dat 'oss doin' in our yard? You get dat ting outta here.'

I dismounted, grabbed the reins and tried to pull the animal out of the garden. It refused to budge. The couple threatened to call the police.

'OK, OK, but this thing won't move,' I said. Eventually the horse lost interest in the flowers and I managed to manoeuvre it on to the beach.

I should have given up and walked back. But some inner madness told me I was enjoying myself. I remounted and steered the horse in the direction I'd come.

I tried to keep the animal at a walk but it was having none of it. Its ears went back and within seconds we were cantering back down the beach. After a couple of minutes I began to think that this wasn't so bad after all. I was enjoying the feeling of the wind in my face and the power of the horse beneath me.

These happy sensations did not last long. Up ahead I could see a broken coconut tree that was leaning towards the sea and blocking our path. I could either go underneath or jump it. I didn't fancy jumping. I managed to slow the horse and tried to guide it beneath the tree. But it was in a frisky mood and took no notice of my commands.

And so, for the first time in my life, I jumped. Quite unintentionally.

The horse took an almighty leap and we sailed through the air. I was losing my grip on the saddle and thought we would never land. I was terrified. Suddenly we hit the ground. I held on tight and amazingly I didn't fall off. A few yards further on the horse stopped. It was as if it knew I'd had enough.

I was out of breath and sore. I thought, OK, Oliver, one jump in your life is enough. I got off and led the horse the rest of the way along the beach.

For the next year I thought no more about riding. But the horses in Barbados had left a lasting impression on my daughters. Put a little girl on a horse and she never forgets it. Aloma and Keilly were no exception to this rule. It was their enthusiasm for riding that was to lead me eventually to showjumping.

On a spring afternoon in 1991 I was driving along with the family in the car when we saw a woman leading a group of children on ponies.

My daughters were transfixed. They stared longingly at the ponies. 'Oh Dad, can we have a go?' they implored.

I said no. Anything to do with horses was likely to be expensive and we could not afford to waste money. Riding seemed a dangerous sport for four- and eight-year-old girls – a view reinforced by my only experience of riding in London: bolting in Hyde Park. I was frightened for my daughters and tried to talk them out of it.

But they would not let it go. Every time we drove through Ealing after that we always seemed to see children on ponies. It took two weeks of badgering before Aloma and Keilly finally persuaded me. After they had pleaded, 'Daddy, Daddy, please!' for the hundredth time I could stand it no longer. I threw caution to the winds and booked lessons for them at Ealing Riding School.

The girls loved the lessons. I used to watch them trotting round the indoor ring, listening closely to what their instructor told them: how to sit, where to put your legs, how to hold the reins. It seemed really easy and I kept thinking that I could do this. After three months of watching Aloma and Keilly I realised that horses weren't as dangerous as they looked. And I wanted to have a go myself.

I had my first lesson. I don't remember much about it except that something happened to me. It is difficult to explain the feeling, but it was as if, in spite of my first two experiences, I had always been meant to ride horses. It was as if I had come home.

Even so, it took me time to get used to horses. It was several weeks before I plucked up the courage to put my hand underneath a horse's mouth and feed it a sugar lump. I suppose I was frightened of these strange creatures. I was a thirty-five-year-old man who had been brought up in the city. I had no idea of what to expect from these animals. Horses couldn't be further removed from my background, and because they were bigger than me, I had to be frightened of them.

Most people I have met on the equestrian circuit are country-born and were introduced to horses as toddlers. As soon as their legs were long enough to reach the stirrups they were thrust into the saddle. Horses are in their blood. Mummy and Daddy grew up with horses and their grandparents did so before that.

My image of horses had been that they kicked and bit at the slightest provocation. And if you got on to one, it would throw you off or bolt or step on you and mash your foot to pieces.

When I found out that this wasn't true, that horses are naturally very gentle creatures, I fell in love with them. I admit that thirty-five is an advanced age at which to develop a passion that for most people starts in childhood. But after my first lesson I knew that all I wanted to do was work with horses. I was conquering one of my fears and I loved the buzz. Riding was so different from anything I had done before. Some people get their kicks from sky-diving or bungee-jumping, but for me, cantering on a horse was the most thrilling thing I had ever done.

My parents are baffled by my love of horses. They haven't a clue where it comes from, although they remind me that I loved cowboy films as a child. Westerns were the thing then. You'd see a guy come out of a saloon, jump on to his horse, kick it, and ride off into the sunset. Now that is beautiful.

My childhood hero was the 1950s cowboy actor Audie Murphy. Audie had a white horse. It was the skinniest, boniest beast you'd ever seen. But it was so fast. All I wanted to do on horses was to go as fast as Audie.

Those old Westerns had speed. That's why they appealed to small boys like myself. Boys want to drive trains, racing cars, motorbikes, bicycles – anything as long as it's as fast as possible. I was like that. I loved speed, adventure and danger. When I saw those cowboys living rough, skidding horses down the sides of hills and ploughing through rivers in eruptions of spray, it was unbelievably exciting. I have realised that my love of horses has a lot to do with those films. And I still fantasise about being Audie Murphy when I ride today.

I became impatient after a couple of months of lessons spent going around in circles following eighteen other riders, being yelled at to keep my 'back straight, knees in, heels down'. It was boring and it was taking too long. I didn't fancy four years of tuition before I could even go for a gallop. One day I sneaked a horse out of the school and went for a canter across the local park. It was not a good move. The stables received a string of complaints about a crazed Rastafarian on a horse. My instructor gave me a strict ticking-off when I returned.

All I wanted to do was to race across a field as fast as possible. I was getting fed up with having to book lessons every time I wanted to ride and then having to do the same basic things over and over again. I wanted to be able to do what I liked whenever I wanted. But that's the trouble with me: I have never done things by halves; it has always been all or nothing. There was only one way to do this: to teach myself. So I went out and bought a horse.

I realise now that I was incredibly naive. I had no idea about what sort of horse to buy. One of the girls at Ealing Riding School offered to help me. After making a few phone calls we drove down to a yard near Windsor owned by a horsey lady in an ill-fitting wig.

She took us out for a hack in Windsor Great Park. I was put on a horse called Oddjob. We had a scary canter across an open field. At one point, the horse in front kicked out at my horse and knocked one of my feet out of its stirrup. Oddjob swerved sharply and I nearly fell off.

Oddjob was a strawberry roan Welsh cob. His coat was a funny colour, a mixture of grey and ginger hairs. He was a heavy, ungainly horse with enormous feet. When he cantered it sounded like bricks being dropped on concrete. But he seemed lively enough. I thought, this is the horse for me and handed over £1,600 in cash. I considered this a good deal, especially as one lesson a week each for Sue, the children and myself had been costing £40.

Ealing Riding School ran a scheme called the working livery whereby they kept and fed your own horse for you. We agreed that they could use Oddjob for lessons in return for looking after him. I could ride him whenever I wanted to.

Oddjob was a disaster. He might have been at home in the open fields but when I got him home to Ealing Riding School's indoor ring he didn't want to do anything. He hated going round in circles (and who can blame him?) and he would hardly walk, let alone trot. He was a dopey animal and lived in a twilight world that was close to coma. If you were polite you might have described him as placid. But actually there was only one word for him: crap. I spent weeks trying to get him to go but in the end I gave up. I sold him at a loss of £100.

I looked for another horse. I went to see an 18–hand ex-racer at a yard in St Albans, reasoning that a racehorse would satisfy my taste for speed. The owner took it into the local indoor riding school and I got on. The animal refused to budge. It was used to tiny jockeys and I was kicking it too low down on its flanks. After several attempts, I gave it an almighty blow. I obviously hit the right spot. The horse flared its nostrils, and before you could say 'Aintree' it was off round the ring at full pelt. Then it headed for a door. I hauled in the reins too briskly. It stopped sharp and I soared over its head – or rather, I came 'out of the front door', as horsey folk say.

I went to get back on it, but the owner wouldn't let me. 'I'm sorry,' he said crossly. 'But I don't think you know how to ride this horse.'

'What do you mean?'

'What I mean,' he said, eyeing my dreadlocks, 'is that you obviously haven't been riding for long and that you need a few more lessons.'

That was when I realised I couldn't ride properly. It was a sobering revelation. I had been used to a cob like Oddjob that wouldn't go even if you let off a stick of dynamite behind him. I thought I had been doing well just to make him trot, but a real horse like this one was an entirely different proposition. I was completely out of my depth.

My next horse was not much better than Oddjob. Pip was a black thoroughbred mare with white socks which I bought from a dealer in

Sussex. Again, she seemed perfect until I got her home. She turned out to have something wrong with her hooves. They were very brittle and kept splintering so that the shoes would not stay on.

But at least she responded to me. She was a well-mannered, gentle horse and Aloma and Keilly loved her. Her feet improved and I spent the summer of 1991 at a yard near Uxbridge, to the west of London, going out on long hacks on my own. I made a lot of mistakes and fell off countless times.

I thought I'd done really well to ride all by myself without having an instructor hassling me to do this and do that with my legs and feet. Actually, looking back on it, I was behaving like a complete idiot. What I was doing was very dangerous. I thought that after a few sessions in the ring at Ealing I knew how to ride. Surely once you had learned how to hang on at a canter or a gallop that was all you needed to know. Nonsense, of course.

My arrogance nearly killed me twice when I fell off while galloping across the fields near the yard at Uxbridge. I also used to take Pip to Windsor Great Park where we would go hurtling through avenues of oak trees at dangerously high speeds. I was always being caught by the park wardens for going too fast and for riding without the £75 licence. I thought that I was just having fun, but in fact I was putting myself and my family's security at great risk.

I'd strongly advise anyone against doing what I did. An inexperienced rider who rushes out and buys a horse, and then goes riding on their own, stands a good chance of being crippled for life, if not killed. Sheer ignorance will do it, that and the chance that you could be conned into buying an unsuitable, possibly dangerous horse that nobody else wants. I was lucky that my impatience and foolhardiness didn't end up causing me serious damage.

I did have one memorable hack on Pip. Bored with the countryside, I decided to take her into London one day. We travelled seven miles up the Uxbridge Road to Ealing. I caused quite a sensation. You do not expect to see a Rastafarian on a horse on the Uxbridge Road. Bus-drivers honked their horns and motorists leaned out of their windows to get a closer look. When I reached Hanwell I passed some old Rastafarian friends of mine. 'Hey, Dread,' they yelled. 'What for you be doin' on a horse?' It was a great experience but I wouldn't do it again. At the time I didn't know any better, but I realise now that it was unwise for a novice to ride alone on such a busy road.

I soon grew bored with Pip. She cantered well but I yearned for something more adventurous. At the end of 1991 I sold her and bought a 17-hand Irish cross-thoroughbred called Tucker's Town, who had enjoyed some success as a showjumper.

By the time I was a year into my riding, I still had no showjumping ambitions. Apart from my unplanned jump in Barbados, I hadn't even gone over a fence yet. I'd watched showjumping a couple of times on television but I hated it. It was slow and boring; a bunch of poncily dressed, upper-class twits going over the same fences in front of an equally upper-class crowd who couldn't even be bothered to cheer. It didn't appeal at all. I just wanted to learn to ride and have some fun. I was still doing door work at night and horses were a hobby, a way of keeping fit.

To be fair, Tucker's Town wasn't a bad horse, but we were not talking Olympics here. He was a heavy brute with a habit of suddenly stopping whenever he felt like it, but he was the right size for me. Here was a horse on which I could finally learn how to ride properly.

I joined a stables near Bracknell in Berkshire. It was a scruffy little place that looked more like a gypsy encampment than a riding school – it was coated with a thick layer of mud. But it was here that my lessons started in earnest. I was beginning to realise that going out on solo hacks was not going to improve my riding. I swallowed my pride and started learning with the stables' instructor, a girl called Simone.

The first thing she did was to remove the reins and stirrups on my horse and make me ride round the ring on a lungeing rein using only my body to control the horse. This no-hands no-legs method of riding teaches you quickly about balance. It was difficult at first and I toppled off many times. But after a few lessons I managed to stay on and I learned that the horse would respond to even the slightest movements of my body. It taught me that I didn't need to haul so hard on the reins or kick so much with my feet; sometimes just a small body movement is enough to make a horse change direction or speed.

The owner of the stables was called Kevin Gardner. We got on well together, and one day he suggested that I try some jumping.

To put it mildly, I was shit scared. I kept putting it off and making excuses, saying that I was content with gentle hacks. I'd heard a rumour that showjumping was cruel to horses. Nonsense. It's the most natural thing in the world for a horse to jump.

Kevin was a small, delicate man with fine features and a gently persistent manner. He insisted that jumping was easy once you'd done it the first time. 'Go on, Oliver,' he said. 'You'll enjoy it. Honestly.'

So one wet September morning I saddled up Tucker's Town and took him into the field. Kevin put up a couple of trot poles, no more than a foot high, and I spent the morning going over them. Then he announced that it was time to try the real thing. He put up a grid of five fences, starting low and ending with a four-foot high pole.

I lined up Tucker's Town. I squeezed him lightly and we set off. He hopped easily over the first four poles. The final fence was a different story. I had forgotten that when you jump you're supposed to lean forward. Tucker's Town leaped into the air and I lost control. There was an almighty blow to my balls as the horse took off and my feet left the stirrups.

I flew backwards, toppled off the saddle and crashed to the ground. I landed badly, twisting my knee. Then I made my second mistake. For some reason, perhaps due to stubbornness and hurt pride, I refused to let go of the reins.

Tucker's Town kicked and bucked his way across the field. After I had been dragged for about fifty feet I finally let go. I was bruised and muddy. Kevin chased after the horse and brought it back. A big grin covered his face.

'Right, we'll try that again,' he said.

'You've got to be joking.'

'I'm absolutely serious. If you don't get back on immediately you'll be too frightened to do it again.'

I could see his point. It was like driving for the first time after a car smash. I reluctantly climbed back on to Tucker's Town and returned to the jumps. This time I cleared the final fence perfectly. Kevin cheered. I'd been riding barely a year and, despite a painful leg, my first day's jumping had gone well. I couldn't wait to try again. The thrill of going over a fence had replaced my desire for speed. For the first time in my life I felt totally committed to something.

After a month's jumping lessons I decided it was time for some competitive riding. Kevin wasn't keen. He said it was too early to enter competitions since I still couldn't ride properly. I was determined to prove him wrong. In June 1992 Tucker's Town and I went to our first show.

I borrowed a horsebox from a friend. It was old and falling to bits and the bodywork was chipped and rusty. When I led Tucker's Town up the ramp I'm sure I noticed a rather snotty look about him. He was used to better transport.

The party consisted of Susan, the children and a friend of mine called George the Mexican. After me, George was the last person you'd expect to see at an English horse show. We had first met in the street in west Ealing. I was getting some money out of a bank cashpoint machine when he walked up to me and announced, 'Scusi, joo tell me fuck off eef joo like, but I'se don' know nobody een London and joo look like goo' guy to know.'

His English was terrible and I had to concentrate hard to understand him. He looked completely out of place in Ealing. He was in his early thirties, about six foot tall with frizzy hair and a droopy Zapata moustache. He wore cowboy boots and a poncho and might have just walked off the set of a Lee van Cleef movie. He seemed a genuine sort of person so I invited him to have a beer with me.

George told me he'd just arrived in London from his home in a village near Acapulco, Mexico. He knew nobody, was staying in a bedsit in Ealing, and had been walking the streets all day. Back in Mexico he had earned a living as an Acapulco beach bum, preying on American women of a certain age. 'Reech ladees on 'oliday 'ave goo' time with guy like me. Buy me 'spenseef presents.'

We became good friends. I found him a job as a cloakroom attendant at the Haven Stables nightclub and he later did a bit of door work with me.

As I said, George was not the sort of person you'd expect to find at a horsey event in rural England, but then, neither was I. George was keen to see me in action after all I'd told him about my riding.

Many times during quieter moments on the doors of clubs I had droned on about horses. Most of the doormen had been bored stiff by it all, but George seemed to enjoy my tales of vaulting fences and falling off.

He leaped at the chance to go to a real, old-world English horse show. He'd done a bit of riding cowboy-style in Mexico and he fancied a nice day out in the country. So we all piled into my old Ford Escort, hitched up the horsebox with Tucker's Town inside, and set off for a tiny show in Feltham in Middlesex.

Feltham was a low-key event known as an unaffiliated show – you did not have to be a member of the British Show Jumping Association to take part. Apart from being the only black person there, I was also one of the oldest. Most of the other riders were ten- and eleven-year-old Pony Club girls who were far more experienced than me – good for my humility if nothing else. I couldn't believe how they raced their horses at full gallop over the jumps with no fear at all. They must have terrified their mums and dads. I made a mental note never to let my daughters ride like that.

We parked the horsebox and slung a hay-net on the side. It looked miserably tatty alongside the other competitors' thirty-foot lorries complete with showers and toilets.

Nonetheless, I was in a buoyant mood as I got Tucker's Town ready. He kept doing little dances with his feet as I saddled him up. George had to practically hold him down as I screwed the non-slip jumping studs into his shoes. The horse seemed more enthusiastic than I'd ever seen him before. Perhaps he had picked up some of my excitement.

I noticed that everyone seemed to be staring at me. It was at this moment that I fully realised for the first time that I was something of a novelty in the horse world. Country people who go to horse shows rarely see black people. And a six-foot-one black man with dread-locks taking part in competitive showjumping? Well, the idea was simply preposterous.

For the first of what was to become many occasions my dreadlocks created a problem. Kevin had advised me that the stuffy buggers on the circuit considered it slovenly and unprofessional to let your hair run free. Whether you were male or female, long hair should be tied in a bun. Note to the British Show Jumping Association: it is almost impossible to put dreadlocks into a bun. I had bought the biggest riding hat I could find and I stuffed in my locks the best I could.

I've since given up trying to do this. However tight I tie my hair it still tumbles out while I'm riding. I've taken to letting the locks hang down and I've had no complaints. Maybe in twenty years' time, when showjumping is overrun by Rastafarian riders, the BSJA will introduce a special rule for dreadlocks. But until then I'm letting them run free 'n' wild.

The other competitors went through their paces. Then it was my turn to be called into the ring. I steered Tucker's Town to the starting cones, the bell rang and we set off.

Tucker's Town decided to behave himself. I was amazed. He had recently revealed a disturbing habit of stopping suddenly whenever he felt like it. But today he was in a winning frame of mind and he went beautifully, effortlessly jumping everything in his path.

We had a nasty moment at the last fence, however. Tucker's Town took it sideways and we hurtled over at a thirty-degree angle. I lost my balance and was nearly jumped out of the saddle. My feet left the stirrups and I was hanging on halfway down Tucker Town's left flank. It would have been a great circus act but it wasn't the sort of thing you do on the showjumping circuit.

But I wasn't giving up now. I clung on to Tucker's Town's neck to stop myself sliding off and somehow I managed to keep my feet off the ground. The finish line was only yards away and I clung on grimly. At last we passed through the final row of cones – and I fell off right in front of the judges. Not an elegant finish, but that didn't matter. I was grinning like an idiot. My very first time in the ring and I had scored a clear round.

I could hear the family and George the Mexican all cheering as if they were at a football match. They were the only spectators making any noise. I have learned since, of course, that the showjumping crowd tends to be genteel and restrained. It is certainly not the done thing to cheer. About the only encouragement you'll get is when you leave the ring. Somebody might say in a dignified tone, 'That was absolutely marvellous.' (Or, if you rode badly, 'That was absolute shit.') They certainly don't yell, 'Yes! Whoo!'

My family had been yelling Yes!-Whoo! very loudly indeed. I got off Tucker's Town and lightly ticked off Sue. Showjumping is a gentlemanly sport, I explained, and there are certain rules of etiquette. Could she please keep the noise down in future. She looked at me coldly. 'What a boring lot,' she said.

Afterwards, complete strangers came up to congratulate me. They were amazed when I told them that it was my first competition and that I had only been riding for just over a year. It is still remarked upon today. I go to shows and people tell me they were at Feltham. They say they will never forget the day when the Rasta showjumper turned up for his first outing.

My success at Feltham convinced me that showjumping was easy and that I was brilliant at it. How wrong can you be! A couple of months later I entered a show at Henley in Oxfordshire. It was another family outing and George the Mexican came along again.

I was all hyped up after Feltham, expecting another easy round. I walked the course at Henley and did well during the practice ride. Then I went into the ring and there began one of the most humiliating experiences of my life.

I was so desperate to do well that I was suffering from terrible nerves. I jumped the first two fences, but then my mind just went blank. I completely forgot where I was going. I went round and round in circles in a panic. The horse was going one way and I was looking the other. My hands were clammy and sweat dripped down my forehead.

I could vaguely hear Sue shouting at me. 'Over there, stupid!' she yelled.

Toffee-nosed voices in the crowd remarked, 'I say, that's against the rules. She's not allowed to tell him where to go.'

Sue would not let up. 'You're supposed to go for the red fence. Not the blue one. Arggh!'

A crackle came over the tannoy. The judge told me I was eliminated. I came out of the ring, my head bowed in shame. Tucker's Town gave a contemptuous snort. Even he seemed disgusted by it all.

Sue was furious with me. 'Made a right prat of yourself, didn't you? What on earth were you thinking of?'

George was not much more encouraging. 'Ees shit, Oleever. Joo no do it like udder people.'

'What do you mean?' I asked belligerently.

'Joo seet on 'oss like joo riding cow.' George had watched every mistake I had made. He knew nothing about showjumping but he could see that I was doing it differently from everybody else. I must have looked really silly that day. What was worse was that he had videoed my round and insisted on a post-mortem when we got home. We studied every jump and he pointed out where he thought I was going wrong. 'Joo like crazee gaucho. Oughtta relax and be more Engleesh.' George might have known nothing about the sport but he dispelled any illusions I might have had about my talents. I still cringe when I watch that film.

I stepped up the lessons with Kevin. He taught me as best he could but I was getting hurt a lot. I realised that I wasn't very good at what I was doing. I had virtually no experience of jumping and I didn't know what to do when the horse was going into the fence, let alone when it went over it. I found it hard learning to go with the horse and lean forward over a jump. I kept falling off.

During one spectacular tumble I twisted the ligaments in my knee. I could hardly walk for a month. Whenever I fall off I tend to land on my feet. I was always jarring my ankles and they constantly ached.

I went to several more unaffiliated shows and my riding improved. I still had no thoughts of professional showjumping but I wanted more. And despite Kevin's help, I realised that if I wanted to compete properly I needed lessons from a professional trainer. I asked around the circuit and discovered that a former professional showjumper called Barry Fox was running three-day showjumping clinics at his stables at Riseley, near Reading. This sounded like what I needed.

I rang Barry's yard, spoke to his wife, Annette, and booked my lessons. I think she must have thought she was talking to a white person, because when I turned up the next weekend I could see the amazement in her face. When I got to know her a bit better she said to me, 'Jesus Christ, you frightened the life out of me.' She'd never seen a dreadlocked black man as big as me before. And certainly not in rural Berkshire.

Barry was a broad-shouldered, rugged man with neat blond hair. He was a brilliant coach. A former member of the British show-jumping team, he had worked with horses for twenty-five years. He travelled all over Europe teaching people to ride and people from as far away as Brazil and Hong Kong came to train at his yard.

After my first lesson, Barry told me that he thought I could be pretty good. I was physically extremely fit but I needed to improve my balance. Barry could tell whether someone was going to make a professional rider just by the way they sat in the saddle. He said that I had a natural position and looked as if I belonged on a horse.

But he warned that I was entering an exceptionally tough sport. 'It looks so easy yet one mistake and the whole round becomes a disaster,' he said. 'Even to think of attempting this sport at your age is incredibly courageous, especially since most of us have been riding since we were knee-high. But your bravery could give you the confidence that is vital in showjumping.'

Barry had seldom met an inexperienced rider with so little fear of horses. He launched me on a uncompromising training pro-gramme. We started at the beginning. He showed me how to sit properly on a horse and how to stop my legs and hands flopping about. I thought I'd learned all this back at Ealing Riding School, but Barry's tuition was a revelation. I realised how much I had to learn.

I still knew only the basics of riding. In other words, I had learned to jump before I could ride. But I loved the sport and I secretly began to think that maybe there could be a career in this. I watched Barry go around the ring and it looked so sweet. The way he glided over the fences, horse and rider as one, was like ballet. It was beauti-ful to watch and I desperately wanted to do it like him.

People say that showjumping is the most difficult sport at which to succeed. It is so exacting. Imagine a pole four inches in diameter resting on cups. You have to get your horse to the spot where it can consistently clear that pole on all types of ground. You may be going up or downhill; there could be tight turns and long runs over several different kinds of fences.

The horse must want to jump more than you do. It's not enough for you to remain cool. You must be cold. And the horse must be able to cope with that cold temperament.

At the end of the three-day clinic, Barry made me an offer that was to change the course of my life. He usually charged £25 a lesson, but because I was short of money he would do a special deal. He would give me free tuition if I helped out at his yard. I could keep my horse there and work off the livery. I couldn't agree quickly enough. The arrangement saved me about £80 a week and Barry a lot of hard work.

I travelled down to the yard every day. It was incredibly hard work as I was still working the door at clubs around London. I would come home at 4 a.m., snatch a couple of hours' sleep and then drive to Berkshire where I mucked out the stables and humped bales of hay. In the afternoon, Barry gave me lessons. I greedily absorbed everything he taught me and within a month he had me jumping a course of fences properly.

In September 1992 he announced it was time for my next show. The Reading and Wokingham Agricultural Show was the first time I was to be seen on the professional circuit. I arrived with a danger-ously unhealthy attitude: I reckoned that because I was being trained by a professional, I *was* a professional. Wrong again.

Barry and Annette came with me to make sure everything went smoothly. I felt particularly cocky. Everyone stared at me as I walked through the showground and it felt good. They were all talking about Barry Fox's Rastaman.

I did a practice warm-up and waited for my class to be called. Annette said she had something to do and told me not to do my round until she came back. She was going to tell me what pace to use going into the ring, where to go, how to take the first fence and so on.

Her back had been turned for only five minutes when my number was announced over the tannoy. Big-head Oliver thought he knew best. I conveniently forgot that I had a trainer with me and sashayed into the ring.

I don't know what got into him but Tucker's Town was back on his usual obstinate form. He stopped just a few yards over the start line and wouldn't go near the first fence. I can only imagine that before I owned him he had been jumped too hard. The fact that he was back on the professional circuit, with an array of jumps stretching out before him, must have brought back unpleasant memories. This lot looked too much like hard work and he wasn't going near them. I tried to coax him into life but he refused to budge. It was as if he was trying to tell me, 'Bugger off. I've had enough of this jumping lark.'

The judges eliminated me. I came out of the ring to face Annette's anger.

She whacked me around the thighs with her riding crop. 'What the hell were you doing?' she yelled. 'Why did you go in there without my permission?'

I cowered away. A horsey lady in a temper can be more frightening than the worst screw in DC. 'Because my number came up,' I mumbled.

'So bloody what? Never go in a ring until you've talked to your trainer first. Christ, Oliver, you think you bloody know it all.' I was severely humbled and the incident highlighted my inexperience. I had no idea that even if your number is called you don't have to do your round if you are not ready.

The lessons continued. Some days I was riding really well; other days I performed like a total novice. I got angry with myself but Barry coached me with soft words of encouragement. He said I was doing all right considering the amount of time I'd been riding. 'Don't get upset if you fall off and congratulate yourself when you do well. Learn from your mistakes.' I began to see that my mistakes would be more frequent than my triumphs and I learned to keep my cool.

The Reading and Wokingham debacle spelled the end of Tucker's Town. 'That horse has got to go,' Barry declared. A week later I had sold him. I set about the hard task of searching for a new animal.

I'm not saying for a moment that any of the horse dealers I've done business with have indulged in dodgy practices, but buying a horse can be as risky as buying a used car. Some of Britain's bloodstock men are no better than equestrian Arfur Daleys. They can't put the clock back, but they'll use every trick in the book to convince you that you've found the perfect showjumper when in fact you've just purchased a year's supply of dog food. It's all too easy to sit on a horse that gives you a nice feel and jumps so splendidly that you say all wide-eyed, 'Ooh, this is nice. I'll have it.'

I'd already experienced the 'trust-me-I'm-so-knowledgeable-about-horses' middle-man – he tells you that the price of a horse is £4,000 but when you go direct to the dealer it's only £2,000. And some of the other horse world con tricks are so cunning that professional riders with years of experience fall for them.

Dealers can be very clever. They can produce a jump from a horse in all kinds of different ways. For example, they'll set up a double fence with a low front rail, and keep raising the height of the front rail to impress you. This makes the jump look huge and seems to test the horse's ability. In fact, it's an optical illusion. The horse appears to jump beautifully, but get it home and it keeps knocking down the fences.

The other favourite con is to set a fence at a measured distance. The horse has been round that fence thirty times a day for the past week. You think you've found the best jumper ever but actually it's got no more talent than a clockwork mouse. I've heard of one character who has had one fence in exactly the same place for five years and his horses jump in exactly the same way, at the same stride and on the same rein, every time. But get your purchase home, put him in your own ring, and he hasn't a clue.

Barry took me to Ireland to find the right animal. I was glad he was with me to make sure I wasn't ripped off. Ireland was quite an experience. I was still at the stage where I had to get used to a horse before I could ride it, and suddenly I was being put on all these different horses and trying them out over high fences.

We went from farm to farm looking at endless animals and I eventually found the right one at a yard near Waterford. Betsy was a chestnut mare, only 15.2 hands high. I didn't realise it at the time but she was far too small for me. Barry didn't think that mattered because she easily carried my weight.

I took her home and quickly became very fond of her. She was a real character. Of all types of horses, chestnut mares are supposed to be the most trouble and have minds of their own. Betsy was no exception. One weekend she'd go out and win every rosette in sight; the next she'd buck at everything I told her to do and wouldn't win a thing. But she was very gentle in the stable. She never pushed me and would stand patiently, gently nuzzling my hair, while I saddled her up.

Me looking the country gent, all togged up in my riding gear (*Action-Plus*)

On White Cloud, with police escort, during the Brixton Road publicity stunt in 1993

My second horse, Pip, before I fattened her up

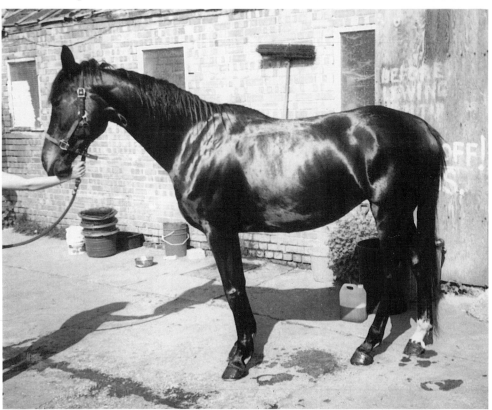

Sara, the world's most difficult horse, at Tracey Hedges' yard in Berkshire

On Betsy at Langford Farm Show in 1992 at the start of my career. Any professional will see that she is too small for me (*Keith Curtis Photography*)

On Timmy at Langford Farm,
1994

Timmy and I collect the rosette
for fifth place at Langford Farm;
Timmy looks comatose as usual

Me on No Problems at Royal Windsor . . .

. . . No Problems not living up to his name – I fell off!

Me with John Whitaker, the world's greatest showjumper, at Hickstead, 1994 (*Elizabeth Furth*)

Jumping during one of my endless training sessions with Nigel Goddard (*Action-Plus/ Glyn Kirk*)

Me being naughty and riding without a hard hat (*Katz Pictures/Martin Black*)

Riding is not as easy as it looks – this is the sort of behaviour I have to put up with from my horses (*Rex Features*)

(*Right to left*) Me, Keilly, Aloma and Sue at home in Hanwell (*Katz Pictures/ Martin Black*)

As well as going to shows myself, I tagged along with Barry when he rode at big events. I learned a lot through watching him and I began to meet some of the famous names in showjumping.

One night I drove to Manchester to see Barry compete. Afterwards, he invited me into the competitors' canteen. It was about midnight and the riders were in the bar drinking. When I walked in some of them made remarks directed at me. They weren't so much unpleasant as cheeky, but it was the first time I had encountered racism on the circuit.

One guy started singing a reggae song from behind his pint of beer. I thought to myself, oh dear, oh dear. There were two ways of dealing with this. Either I could go over and beat shit out of him, or I could ignore him. I decided that I was not going to be ignorant and start a fight. I gave the man my most charming smile. He soon shut up.

I decided then that I was going to the top whether these people liked it or not. I was going right to the heart of the old aristocratic, landed world of showjumping and again, there were two ways of going about it. Either I could tread on everybody's toes and get a reputation for trouble, or I could behave like a gentleman and get everybody on my side. The second way seemed the obvious choice.

In fact that show at Manchester is about the only time anyone on the circuit has been directly rude to me, but the stares didn't stop. I was going to all these little country shows and people would nudge each other as I walked past. It happened all the time at the beginning and I was aware of it immediately. One person would nudge another, and that person would nudge his or her neighbour and all of a sudden there would be thirty people gaping at me. They'd never been so close to a Rastaman before. In a weird sort of way I got a feeling of satisfaction from it. I had always known that this sort of person existed but I had never had anything to do with them before. Culturally, they were a million miles away from me. I came from a world of stolen Ford Cortinas; this was fully taxed and insured Volvo country.

I thought at first that they might not take to me however much of a gentleman I was; that they would be automatically prejudiced against anyone remotely resembling a Rastafarian. Perhaps they had seen videos of Bob Marley going 'iree marn' and talking about Babylon and they expected me to do the same.

I pretended not to notice the funny looks. I certainly wasn't going to turn round and say, 'What the fuck are you staring at?' like I would have done in London. I could see they were genuinely inquisitive. They were more intrigued than anything else.

When I became a little better known on the circuit, people would come up and talk to me. I think that at first they thought I was a rich musician who was into horses. After all, isn't every black man with dreadlocks a reggae singer? And I don't think anyone took me seriously. But when they realised that I loved horses as much as they did, they began to treat me as just another member of the horse-show set.

At least the horses didn't seem to notice that I was different. Horses will differentiate between weight and strength, but not colour. Horses don't notice dreadlocks, although dogs sense them. I'm always getting trouble from dogs growling at me.

The shows furthest from London were the strangest. You certainly never see dreadlocks in the depths of Hampshire or Wiltshire. Little gymkhana princesses would pull my hair and ask me my name. I'd notice Mummy standing a few yards away pretending not to be interested. Yet I would suspect that she was the one who'd sent her daughter over to see what I was doing there.

Sometimes Mummy herself would come over and pull my hair. The reaction was usually, 'Christ, it's like rope.' I'd answer, 'Yeah, that's what happens when you don't comb your hair. Do you know that your hundred-times great-grandpappy probably had hair like this when he was living back in the cave?' Or, 'It's no different from judges' wigs, and I've seen a few of those in my time.' I can't tell you some of the odd looks I got.

The elderly country gents were the funniest. Retired colonels in patched tweed jackets would stop and tell me what a splendid job I was doing. They only just stopped short of asking which corner of the Empire I was from. I think they were amazed that I was not some sort of Yardie and could actually speak English. I'd talk to these people and attempt to explain that the only difference between black people and them was that our skins were darker.

Sometimes teenagers would try to talk about drugs. They'd try to impress me by saying, 'Yeah, man, I had some great Durban Poison last night.' And I'd say, 'Durban Poison? What the hell's that? What you going on about, man?' Or they'd ask if I'd give them a spliff on the assumption that just because you have dreadlocks you must go round in a permanent haze of marijuana. That really irritated me.

But most of the showjumping crowd were very polite. People would invite me to their yards for lunch and to look at their horses. I began to feel accepted.

Real racism in sport tends to be confined to working-class whites on the football terraces. I've been to matches where I've seen people shouting abuse and throwing bananas at the black players. But the showjumping crowd were not slobs, yobs or hooligans – they were well educated and, as far as I could see, they were not into colour.

Meeting these people also dispelled any prejudices I might have had about them. The horsey set have a reputation for being snobby and rich, but that's not always true. They're not all multi-millionaires. It was more often a case of a nice farmhouse, a couple of three-year-old cars, a few hundred acres and a decent portfolio of stocks and shares.

What really fascinated me was that most of these people still had their bicycles and toys from when they were kids. My toys lasted five minutes because my brothers wrecked them. I have nothing from the past, no mementoes at all.

Some of the houses I visited were filthy. Why is it that so many comfortably off country people insist on living in squalor? I suppose it's inverted snobbery; that it's considered smart to live like that. You'd be constantly tripping over Wellington boots and there were dogs' hairs everywhere. I was having supper in kitchens that were cluttered up with pots, pans and riding tackle, last year's birthday cards on the mantlepiece and the whiff of cat's piss – yet there would be thousands of pounds' worth of inherited furniture in the drawing room. All very different from my immaculately kept semi-detached in Hanwell. Sue and I might not be able to afford eighteenth-century furniture but at least we know how to keep a house clean.

But I found my new friends to be very affable people and they took me for exactly what I was – a struggling showjumper. I was polite back to them and I hope that helped to change their minds about Rastafarians. I can understand that it was a big shock for the horsey world to find a 'Rastafarian' in their midst. But I can tell you it was very strange for me, too.

As I went to more shows, falling off became my trademark. In an odd sort of way, my falls helped to break the ice with the other riders. They nicknamed me 'The Lone Rasta' and they took the piss in the nicest possible way as they got to know me better. I'd walk past some of the guys and someone would get down on the ground and lie on his back kicking his legs in the air and say, 'Guess who this is?' And everyone else would chorus: 'Oliver Skeete.' And I'd laugh and say, 'Oh yeah, very funny.' It made it easier for me that my colleagues felt relaxed enough around me to take the mickey; it made me feel accepted.

I learned a lot about horses in a short space of time. I carefully watched the other riders and then I copied them. At the age of thirty-six I was tackling horses with the same enthusiasm I had shown for cars at fifteen. I knew everything about cars but horses were far harder. A car comes with a manual to tell you what's wrong with it, but you can't buy a manual for a horse. Each Ford Escort is the same but a horse is an individual. Horses were much more interesting.

To start with I found the horsey expressions pretty strange. It was a whole new language. Before I started riding I knew the tail, the mane and the legs, and that was about it. But if you're around equestrian people all the time you have to learn the difference between a fetlock and a wither. I took my copy of the *Horsemanship Manual* to work in the evenings. Whenever there was a quiet moment on the door of the club I was working I'd go and lock myself in the toilet and memorise the different parts of the horse.

My love of riding took me abroad. I joined a horse dealer friend called John Moss on a buying expedition to Poland. We spent a week looking at horses all over the country. Most of them were dirt cheap and we met many German dealers snapping up bargain bloodstock. We'd stop at tiny villages in the middle of nowhere and visit broken-down farmhouses where the bedroom, kitchen and bathroom were one and the same room. It was like going back to the early 1900s – they had enamel cups and open cooking ranges. You'd find the horses in a muddy paddock at the back among the chickens and pigs.

The weirdest thing about Poland was how people reacted to my dreadlocks. Villagers would pour out of their homes to look at this black man with the strange things on his head. They presented me with jars of raw pickled pig. In one village, the whole school turned out to look at me. When I tried to get close to the children they screamed and ran in terror. Perhaps they thought I came from outer space.

One night we stayed in Posnan. I popped into a bar for a drink, a tatty little place with a ripped pool table, and ended up meeting one of the few black people in Poland. He was a half-caste called George and he spoke a few words of English. He had a thick Jamaican accent that he'd picked up from Bob Marley records. His father was African and his mother Polish. He had been in and out of jail all his life and we shared our experiences of being on the wrong side of the law. Before I left he put his arms around me and hugged me. He cried and cried. He'd hardly seen another black man in his whole life and he was overwhelmed by emotion. It was a touching moment and I shed a few tears myself.

In December 1992 I had my big break on the professional circuit. Barry took me up to Scotland to take part in a competition at Captain Mark Phillips' equestrian centre at Gleneagles.

I rode sloppily and fell off at the first fence. I could have kicked myself. I stormed out of the ring in a foul temper. But when I quietened down it dawned on me that the reaction from the crowd had been amazing. Everyone seemed to be on my side. People were coming up to me and asking me how I had got into riding, how did I get my hair like that. I thought that if these people were so intrigued by a showjumping Rastafarian, maybe I could do something with this. The buzz in the arena was exhilarating beyond belief and it felt like where I wanted to be. I remembered Barry's advice: don't give up just because you fall off. When I got back to London I decided to take the plunge and become a full-time showjumper.

I gave up my job with Atlas Security. Door work was getting me down. It was too violent and I was always anticipating a confrontation with drunken clubgoers. Bulldog Dave had been smashed in the head with glass and George the Mexican had been stabbed in the eye. It was happening to everybody. I reckoned it wasn't going to be long before I ended up in hospital too.

The risk was too high to justify the money. Fifty quid a night is not much set against people drawing knives, throwing bricks and ripping out your dreadlocks. I was putting my life on the line. And my freedom. I was aware that if trouble started and I hurt somebody, I could end up in prison.

The door was also getting me into trouble with Sue. I was drifting back to my old ways: staying out all night drinking, chatting up girls. Sometimes it was daylight when I got home. Sue would stand there in her dressing-gown throwing plates at me.

It was no better if I behaved myself and hurried home as soon as I finished work. The other doormen took the piss out of me when I refused their offers to go drinking. 'Look at Oliver,' they jeered. 'Woman's got 'im under manners.' No, the clubs were a danger area. It was horses full-time from now on. They were a way out of my old life and gave me a chance to make a name for myself.

Even in the 1990s showjumping remains one of the world's most elitist sports. It takes substantial capital to buy decent horses. It's like motor racing back in the 1920s, when tracks like Brooklands were dominated by the Bentley Boys and if you didn't have a trust fund you didn't stand a chance.

I realised that I was not in a position to go professional overnight. Most of the top riders had plenty of money, their own horses and acres of land to keep them on. There was no way a West Indian former car-sprayer and nightclub bouncer from Acton could do it like them.

But I had something else to offer as well as my natural talent. I was different. I was the only black person in the sport in Britain and the world's only Rastafarian showjumper, lapsed or otherwise. I knew a couple of black South African riders but they were competing at the lowest amateur level. I was aware that I might be accused of exploiting my colour but I didn't care. I was looking out for myself and my family's security first. And if I could make it as a top showjumper, then maybe I could help other black people to do it.

I needed money, so I set out to find some. When I got back to London from Gleneagles I rang the *Sun* newspaper. The *Sun* was the biggest-selling paper in Britain and surely they could find a few quid to sponsor me.

I spoke to a man on the newsdesk. He laughed. Loudly. He said that he didn't think most *Sun* readers had even heard of showjumping so sponsorship was out of the question. But he was fascinated to find out what a Rastafarian was doing in such a nobs' sport. He said he would certainly write something about me.

I couldn't wait for the *Sun* article to come out. A couple of days later, when it was due to be published, I ran out and bought five copies.

I found the article. The headline read, 'Rasta Gets a Pony Tail'. It made me look really stupid. I was serious about what I was doing but the *Sun* had made a big joke out of it. I certainly didn't expect anyone to take the piece seriously. I reckoned that it would all be forgotten by the next day.

But the public reaction was amazing. I began to get some idea of what it felt like to be famous. Whenever I walked down the street motorists would hoot their car horns and give me thumbs-up signs. Other Rastafarians would stop me and say, 'Yeah, Dread, respeck. I seen ya' in de noospaper.' They were immensely impressed, although I don't think they had a clue what it was I was actually doing.

A week later I was down at Barry's yard when one of the stable lads came to find me to tell me there was a telephone call for me. He said it was Carlton Television. I told him to go away and stop taking the piss. No, he said, it really was Carlton Television. I took the call and the woman at Carlton said she'd seen the *Sun* article and could they come down and film me at the yard? It took me five seconds to say yes.

Carlton brought down a crew and filmed me going over jumps and mucking out stables. I couldn't believe it. The publicity was snowballing and now I had a chance of attracting the sponsorship I needed to break into professional showjumping. The clip went out on the *London Tonight* programme. More people began to recognise me in the street and some of them asked for my autograph. Everything was going too well to be true. I felt that nothing could stop me.

I was Britain's only black showjumper and the public wanted to see me succeed.

And then my dream was suddenly shattered.

8

BANGED UP IN CHELMSFORD

The early hours of 26 January 1993. I am lying in bed at home in Hanwell. I'm going over the jumps perfectly . . . think I'm on Tucker's Town . . . the final fence . . . never seen such a big fence . . . the horse stumbles . . . oh no! . . . we crash to the ground with a bang.

I began to surface from a deep sleep. There was another bang. I woke up with a start. Someone was pounding on the front door. I looked at my watch. It was 7 a.m. Another bang on the door. I tottered out of bed and went to the window.

I looked out. 'Who is it?' I shouted.

A man with a clipboard appeared from under the porch. He stood in the front garden. He looked a rather grey little man and I thought he might be from the council, though what the council wanted at this time in the morning was anyone's guess.

'Mr Oliver Skeete?' he called.

'That's me.'

'Will you please open the door?'

'Who are you?'

'Customs and Excise.'

'Who?'

'Customs,' he repeated. 'Will you please let us in?'

'Only if you tell me what it's about.'

'Just open the door.'

What the hell did Customs and Excise want with me at 7 a.m.? I put on my dressing gown, went downstairs and opened the front door.

Then I was sent flying as about fifteen men stormed into the house. They came from a fleet of unmarked cars parked in the street. Some of them rushed upstairs and the others bulldozed me down the hall into the kitchen.

'What the fuck's going on?' I gasped.

One of the men pushed me on to a chair and told me to shut up. He said that they were customs officers and that they were searching my house. I asked again what I was supposed to have done. He refused to answer. He wouldn't say what they were looking for.

They searched every cupboard in the kitchen and went through the rubbish bins. They took all my personal papers and put them in plastic bags.

They kept making sarcastic comments: 'Oh, this is a nice place, Mr Skeete', 'What a smart kitchen you have, Mr Skeete', 'How come you've got such a nice house?' The typical attitude of white authority. Just because I was black they expected me to live like a pig. Did they think that only white people had the right to live in a clean house? Besides, it was just a normal semi-detached. My street in Hanwell was very nice but it was hardly Belgrave Square.

Then they brought in the sniffer dogs, two Labradors. I presumed that one was searching for drugs and I can only imagine that the other was for firearms. I pondered on this. I might have owned flick knives in my youth, but I'd never had anything to do with guns. The closest I'd got to a firearm was when I fired a shotgun during a clay-pigeon shoot at the Cheshire County Show (I did rather well considering I'd never fired a gun before. Didn't miss one).

One of the Labradors climbed on to the kitchen worktop. The dog-handler whispered words of encouragement.

'Get that dog off there,' I exploded. 'It's not hygienic.'

'Shut up, Mr Skeete.'

Upstairs the kids were crying. Three customs men had charged into Aloma and Keilly's room, waking them up with a start. The girls were terrified. They thought they were about to be murdered in their beds. Sue was shouting that no one had a right to frighten children like that.

I heard the shrieks of terror. The anger rose to my throat. I'm afraid that my years of juvenile crime had not shown me the best side of the law and I tend to get nasty with anyone who faintly resembles a policeman. Hearing my kids cry was too much. I got the hump.

One of the officers made a stupid comment about 'the nice wallpaper'.

'Don't fucking talk to me about interior decoration!' I snapped. 'You can cut the chit-chat and tell me why you're here.' I began to get up from the chair. The officer shoved me back down. He still wouldn't tell me what it was all about.

His colleagues left the kitchen and moved on to the sitting room.

'You fucking wait for me,' I said. 'If you're going to search the house I want to be there. I don't want you planting anything on me.' They did not appreciate this slur on their integrity and there were a few mumbled growls, but reluctantly they agreed to let me accompany them.

Sue came downstairs and interrupted us at the sitting-room door. 'You lot stay where you are,' she yelled. 'You're not going in there with those boots on.' We had recently bought a new carpet and she didn't fancy the officers' size 14s all over it.

The customs men were not prepared to tangle with Sue. They looked at each other, raised their eyebrows and solemnly took off their shoes. The morning took on the quality of a French farce as the officers continued the search in their stockinged feet. The sniffer Labradors wagged their tails and climbed over the furniture. Sue complained loudly about dog hairs on the settee.

The customs men searched the rest of the house. I went with them. They looked in all the obvious places but I noticed there were dozens of places that they missed. It seemed a rather half-hearted effort. It was almost as if they expected to find nothing.

After disrupting our lives for twenty minutes, the officer in charge gave me a clue as to what it was about. He said that I was under suspicion of importing drugs from Jamaica into Britain.

'What the fuck are you talking about?' I said. 'I've never been to Jamaica in my life.' I showed him my passport. Not a Jamaican stamp in sight. 'Time for you to leave, I think.'

The customs man looked at me blankly. He said that we'd have to find someone to look after the children because he was arresting both Susan and me. I was dumbfounded. I looked at Sue. The expression on her face was one of pure horror. This type of situation was old hat to me because I'd been in trouble before, but it was out of Sue's league.

We found a neighbour to take care of the kids and the customs men put us in one of their cars. We set out on a miserable ninety-mile drive to the port of Harwich on the east coast of England where the officers were based.

The weather was cold and grey. I held Sue's hand while she sobbed quietly. There have been many times in my life when I have known only too well why I was in the back of a police car. But this time I had something to moan about. When you don't know why you've been arrested you feel completely lost.

As we sped through east London I asked again what we were supposed to have done. The officers still refused to answer. They stared straight ahead, not a hint of a smile. I seethed silently. The police could be quite civilised in situations like this, but these boys were a different matter altogether. They had found nothing in my house and they appeared to have no grounds for arresting us. Yet we were being treated as if we were automatically guilty.

We arrived at Harwich Customs and Excise headquarters. They said Sue and I would be split up. I took her in my arms and she sobbed. Then a woman officer led her away. Sue kept glancing over her shoulder at me. She was so frightened. I felt totally helpless.

I was taken to an interview room where I was told to wait. After a few minutes a senior officer came in with a colleague. They sat down opposite me and told me why I was under arrest.

The story went like this: two white girls had received jail sentences after being caught at Heathrow with suitcases containing 25 kilos of cannabis. They claimed that I was the man who had sent them on the drug run.

The chief customs man told me the names of the girls. Sue and I knew them well as they lived round the corner from us. They had sometimes babysat for us. I was astonished. This was the first time I had heard of their involvement in drugs.

The customs men were taking the allegations very seriously. The senior officer was in his early forties. He wore a smart suit and thought he was pretty cool. He brimmed with as much sophistication as you can find in Harwich. I found him blown-up and pompous. He had a look in his eyes that said he was dying to lock me up. I'm sure he was a great family man and lovely to animals, but he was not very nice if you had dreadlocks.

He gave me a long, hard stare and questioned me about where I had been on a particular night. I realised I was in deep trouble. These boys were trying to pin something on me. My experience with the police has taught me that if in doubt it is best to say nothing until you see a lawyer. 'No comment,' I said. 'Absolutely no comment.' I said nothing more.

Mr Cool looked at his colleague. This was not supposed to happen. They must have expected me to break down with a full confession. I was beginning to think they weren't that clever.

In the light of all my years of dealing with the police that interview was a doddle. I'd been through it a million times before and I have to say that this was a fairly inferior interrogation. I don't disrespect what Customs and Excise do – they have a job like all of us. But if they were going to pick on me wrongfully, and with the slimmest of evidence, then I certainly wasn't going to show them my better side. I felt they were just out to screw me.

The officers saw they were getting nowhere. They didn't seem to know what to say next. At least the police try to push you a bit if you're uncooperative, but these boys had shied at the first fence. They reluctantly found a lawyer for me; but even after my brief arrived I still wouldn't talk.

There was only one weapon left in the customs men's armoury. They told me that they were holding Sue and I overnight and that we would appear in court the next morning. I felt sick. I was trying to build up a reputation as a showjumper and I'd just seen it take a huge knock. I was struggling to break into an upper-class world which even included members of the royal family, and now I was being accused of being a common drug dealer. It was the worst thing that could have happened to me.

The next day we appeared before Saffron Walden magistrates. I met up with Sue a few minutes before we went into court. I hugged her. She looked dreadful. It was all so new to her. Spending a night in the cells must have been horrible for her.

A jailer took us up the stairs into the dock. A third defendant was brought up with us. He was another Rastafarian, a man called Delroy, who had been picked up for the same alleged offence. According to Customs, this man was supposed to be my co-conspirator. I had never met him before.

I was not surprised to see that my co-defendant had dreadlocks – as far as Customs are concerned, Rastafarians are the only people who bring drugs into this country. The police also think that Rastafarians are responsible for all the crack in Britain. That's nonsense.

People who take crack are idiots and the people who sell the stuff want locking up. The newspapers say that the Yardies – Jamaican gangsters – control the British crack industry, but the truth is that the drugs are run by rich and powerful white men who use black people as distributors. All these black boys are running around claiming to be Yardies but there wouldn't be any drugs if it wasn't for those white guys with the money. They stay nice and clean in the background.

It's all very well the press getting hysterical, but what happens is that the police go into the council estates and put loads of little black drug addicts into prison. They should get to the root of the problem; find the guys with the money and the ships, planes and containers. They're the ones to catch.

We settled in the dock. Delroy and I nodded to each other. ''Nuf respeck, Dread,' he murmured. Though we were strangers, our dreadlocks created a bond between us. I shook his hand.

The prosecuting solicitor did his bit and we were charged with conspiracy to import cannabis. Sue got bail but the magistrate remanded Delroy and me in custody to give Customs and Excise time to prepare their case. I was refused bail on the grounds that I was an ex-bouncer and might intimidate witnesses. See what working the door can do for you?

The court jailers took Delroy and me down to the cells. I said another tearful goodbye to Sue. Delroy and I waited in the gloom before being taken out to a police car. I was handcuffed to Delroy and pushed into the back seat. The door and window handles had been removed to prevent us from trying to escape.

Two policemen escorted us to Chelmsford Prison. The coppers were quite pleasant – a nice change after Customs. They had seen the article in the *Sun* and knew all about me. They were fascinated to know how I'd got into showjumping. We chatted all the way to the jail and I enjoyed telling them about my horse. The depression hit me as we pulled up at the main gate. I thought, oh, Christ, here we go again. More bird. Same old story.

It had been a long time since I was last inside, but the high walls and razor-wire brought back bitter memories of my youth. I reasoned that it wasn't all bad. One of the few things in my favour was that I wasn't going to a detention centre. Furthermore, I knew I had done nothing wrong. I was innocent and they had no evidence against me. I shouldn't even be in a police cell, let alone a prison. I reckoned that in a couple of days I'd be out of there.

Delroy and I were put in the same cell. Maybe they thought we'd work out a deal between us and then confess all. Delroy was a quiet, gentle man. He kept himself to himself and turned out to be a good cellmate.

Our cell was tiny and painted the usual, HM-issue dingy green. There was a toilet, a sink and two bunks one on top of the other. The bunks were bolted to the wall to prevent Chelmsford's more lively clientele from battering the door down with them.

There was one barred window halfway up a wall. I pulled myself up by the bars and gazed out across the barren tarmac of the exercise yard. The January sky was as grey and wintry as ever. I dropped down. 'What now?' I said. Delroy shrugged. We both knew there was little to do except sit it out. He hauled himself on to the top bunk, rolled over and went to sleep.

The other inmates had seen me in the *Sun* and knew that I was in the prison. My imminent arrival had been reported on the radio earlier that day and so I was expected. My fellow prisoners were thrilled to have a minor celebrity in their company and were keen to make me welcome. I had not been in my cell long before one of the cons appeared with a mug of tea and a plate of hot, buttered scones. 'Get that down you,' he said. 'Then you can tell us about your horses.' Maybe Chelmsford wasn't going to be so bad after all. It all seemed quite civilised.

My celebrity status was confirmed the next day. News of my arrest was all over newspapers: 'Rasta Horseman Arrested on Drugs Charges' and gems like that. That's the trouble with the papers. They write the nicest piece about you one day and then a load of shit the next. In a strange way, I felt guilty. It felt as if the publicity had got Sue and me into trouble. I had wanted my face in the media so perhaps I should take some of the blame. If I hadn't been on television I wouldn't have been having all this hassle.

The other prisoners wanted to know all about my arrest. Rumours swept the jail. Had I done it? Was I really the main man in the Jamaica-Britain dope connection? Was it true that I had half a million quid tucked away? I swore that it had nothing to do with me. 'Yeah, yeah, yeah,' they mocked. 'We believe you. That's what they all say.'

'I swear to God,' I repeated. 'I know nothing about drug smuggling. I'll only be in here for three or four days and then I'll be out.' The prisoners grinned. Young Mr Skeete had a lot to learn.

A week later I was in court again. Customs and Excise said they needed more time to prepare their case. They were still pursuing their inquiries. I asked for bail. The magistrate gave me a look that said 'You must be joking, Mr Skeete' and I was refused my freedom again.

He remanded me in custody for another three weeks. I felt as low as a man can feel as I returned to prison. How was my family? Could they cope without me? The prisoners laughed at me as I trudged along the landing back to my cell. One of them cackled, 'Told you you'd be back.' Another sniggered, 'Time to cancel the milk, mate.' They all thought I was bang to rights.

My lawyer visited me in jail. He showed me the statement made by a mystery witness. The description of me was baffling to say the least. Apparently the villain of the piece was supposed to be five foot nine with an afro hairstyle. Really similar, huh?

A couple of days after I had returned from court Mr Cool Customs Man and his friend came to Chelmsford to interview me again. One of the screws fetched me from my cell. We walked across the exercise yard to the administration block, where I was shown into a cramped, grey interview room. My lawyer was waiting for me.

We sat on metal chairs across a table from the customs men.

The interview began.

Mr Cool shuffled a huge batch of papers in front of him. He looked up and gave me his hardest stare. 'Mr Skeete,' he said. 'We have heard that you have told a friend, and I quote, "If I go down, I'm taking everybody with me." '

I stood up and shoved my chair back. It clattered across the floor. I had the right hump. I said to my lawyer, 'Right. I'm out of here. Now.' And I walked out of the door.

The interview ended. It had lasted barely thirty seconds. Well, it was a right load of old bollocks; hardly the most subtle way to begin an interrogation. What did the man think he was going on about? Didn't he know that people only said those sorts of things on the telly? I reckon he had made it up to see if I was cracking under the strain of jail. I suppose he thought that if I were guilty I might talk in order to make some sort of deal.

The screw took me back to the prison block. As I walked across the exercise yard I looked back. I could see Mr Cool, hands behind his back, standing at the interview room window like the Kommandant in Colditz. He was staring down at me. I raised my right hand and gave him a one-finger salute. He looked a very angry man.

I was fuming by the time I got back to my cell. I told Delroy what had happened. He put his hand on my shoulder to calm me down. 'Easy, Dread,' he said. He shook his head sadly. 'Hey, what you expect, man? Expect any different?' I had to agree that I did not.

It was the same old story. The authorities had it in for successful black people. It's the old plantation-owner mentality: keep them down so they don't become too cocky. Except that these days they can't stop us from reading books to educate ourselves, so they try to pin fictitious criminal charges on us instead. It's not as blatant, but it works just as well. If we show any signs of getting to the top there's always somebody trying to knock us down.

I wasn't the first black person to be hounded by the law and I won't be the last. The London police are always using puny excuses to stop successful black people in nice cars for alleged driving offences. Actually, they stop anyone who's black, so much so that complaints of racial discrimination to the Police Complaints

Authority rose more than fourfold in 1994. If you're white and you want to see what I mean, borrow a Porsche or a Mercedes and get a black friend to drive you around London. Just wait and see – it won't be long before you're stopped.

The days went by. I started to accept the fact that I was in Chelmsford whether I liked it or not.

Being in prison wasn't too bad. Everybody was really good to me, even the screws. It was refreshing to deal with human beings after the gorillas all those years earlier at DC. Everyone seemed to know when I was next in court and how my case was progressing.

Chelmsford is a remand prison so there was an air of hope about the place. You'd see people dressing up in suits and going off to court every day. The lucky ones didn't return. The rest stormed back in foul tempers because they hadn't got bail.

I wouldn't say I was given special privileges, but people did show me a little respect. I wasn't a stupid little kid running around the prison making a lot of noise. I was a struggling showjumper who'd been set up. I got anything I wanted and there was always someone at hand with a teabag if I'd run out. Important things in prison, teabags.

Boredom is the big killer. It's a monotonous life being locked up for sixteen or seventeen hours a day in a small cell. I tried to brighten up my surroundings as much as possible. While the other prisoners had girlie pictures on their walls I put up pictures of horses and famous showjumpers. Barry Fox and another riding friend called Brian Knight visited me several times and brought me copies of *Horse and Hound*. I spent hours cutting out the best pictures and sticking them above my bunk. Delroy knew nothing about horses. He couldn't understand why I wanted to look at such boring pictures, or why I kept going on about how I missed Betsy. He found my obsession completely baffling.

I used to count the minutes to when the cell door was unlocked. We'd be let out in the morning for fifteen minutes to stroll along the landing. Then we were locked up again. Lunch was at midday, after which there were two free hours. You could either walk in the exercise yard, play football or work out in the gym. I spent my time in the gym. It helped keep me sane. Then there was more time in the cell before we were allowed out for the evening meal. After supper it was lock-up until the morning.

I read a lot. I spent hours studying the *British Show Jumping Association Manual*. I doubt that book has been read much in prisons (although the food was so bad that the cure for colic might have come in handy). Otherwise, it was thrillers by Alistair MacLean and Sue brought me the complete collection of Asterix books.

My family was always on my mind. I missed Sue and the children dreadfully. I couldn't sleep for worrying about them. After a week they were allowed to visit me. The raid had scared Aloma and Keilly out of their wits. They were withdrawn and restless. They kept crying and saying, 'When are you coming home, Daddy?' I felt sick. The pain when they left was indescribable.

The pent-up feelings got to me after a couple of weeks. I had permanent butterflies in my stomach and I snapped at the smallest things. One morning I was late coming down for lunch. I was last in the queue. When I got to the end, what remained of the food looked unfit for human consumption. Lumps of grey chicken resembling rat and a watery smudge of cabbage do little for one's humour.

I lost my temper. The right hump again. I began shouting and yelling at nobody in particular. The other cons looked up from their meals and stopped talking. Even the screws standing round the side of the canteen went quiet. I was known as a quiet man and I think people in prisons have a strange feeling about quiet inmates. They are likely to get very dangerous if they suddenly start making a noise. Everybody stayed out of my way for the rest of the day. The screws avoided me as well. They knew I was a sensible boy and I wasn't out to cause aggravation. They had a healthy, easy-going attitude and they weren't going to punish someone for being noisy. What harm did it do if a prisoner threw an occasional wobbly?

One day Princess Anne arrived on an official visit. The irony of the situation was not lost on me and I could see the funny side.

Anne was visiting Chelmsford to see what prison life was like but she spent most of the time talking to the governor, the screws and all the other men in suits. Poxy waste of time. If I'd have been her I'd rather have chatted with the prisoners.

Her mother's guests got a brief look-in at the end of the visit.

Some of the cons were lined up in the canteen and Anne spent about five minutes with us. I stayed in the background behind a crowd of prisoners. She looked a nice lady but she didn't talk to me. Pity, because we'd have had loads to talk about. But I suppose her advisers didn't think it would be appropriate.

The governor was aware that I was a showjumper and he obviously knew that the Princess's love of horses meant we'd have plenty in common. But HM Prison, Chelmsford is not the ideal place to meet a member of the royal family for the first time. Perhaps a horse show might be less embarrassing for all concerned.

My time in jail passed slowly. My lawyer brought in a batch of papers containing Customs' so-called case against me. There were dozens of statements but there was no firm evidence against me.

On 26 February I went to court again. It was exactly a month since I'd been arrested.

The prosecution still hadn't got their act together. I sat in the dock and heard Customs say they needed more time to find their witnesses. They demanded that I should be held in custody for another two weeks.

But the magistrate had other ideas. For the first time, someone in authority seemed to be on my side. He said that I'd been in jail for long enough already and gave me bail. I grabbed the dock rail, put my head between my knees and gave a big sigh of relief. The nightmare was over and I could go home.

I was still not totally off the hook, however. The prosecution were given one more week to find their mysterious witnesses. On 5 March I returned to court. What little murky iniquities were they going to dig up against me this time?

I need not have worried. Because, quite frankly, the prosecution were made to look like a right bunch of arseholes. Customs admitted that they still didn't have any firm evidence against me except that my children had once had two drug smugglers as babysitters. The magistrate threw the case out of court and I walked free without a blemish on my character. My co-defendant, Delroy, subsequently walked away from the same charge.

I came home to Hanwell and didn't go out of the house for a week. I was in a state of shock and had lost all interest in living, as well as the heart for riding. I made myself cups of tea and stared out of the window. Sue and the kids had given me a great welcome but after a couple of days we were arguing. We had no money and my family's reputation was in tatters. I had been arrested and jailed and everyone knew about it. I'd been trying to make a name for myself and now that name had gone up in smoke. I felt like shit.

My riding really suffered. Barry and Annette didn't want me back at their yard after what had happened. They were nice about it but they had lost customers as a result of the publicity. Some airline pilot from Hong Kong had been due to bring his children over for riding lessons but he had changed his mind after reading about my case.

A couple of days after I came out of prison I met Barry in an hotel in London's West End. He told me I would have to find another stables. I was gutted because I'd really enjoyed myself down there. He had helped my riding so much. But I couldn't be angry with him. I understood his dilemma. I couldn't hold it against him: it was his livelihood and if I was bad for business then that was just bad luck. I made arrangements to move my horse to a farm at Denham in Essex owned by a friend of mine.

I wanted to take legal action. I wanted someone to pay for my misery. But the trouble is that you can't sue Customs and Excise for wrongful arrest. They have incredible powers and make the police seem like school prefects. It doesn't seem right that they are allowed to cause people so much anguish.

My name was mud on the showjumping circuit. Before my arrest I'd lined up interviews with some horsey magazines but the moment I was banged up they didn't want to know.

I cheered up when I discovered that the national newspapers were on my side. The *Independent* described my imprisonment as 'a gross miscarriage of justice'. Then a couple of reporter friends rang up to say that they thought what had happened to me was shocking.

I thought, right, Oliver, this has got to stop. I couldn't sit in Hanwell doing nothing. If I gave up now I'd spend the rest of my life wondering if I could have made it as a top showjumper. It was time to take action, and I decided to get back out on the publicity trail. I didn't care if some people thought I was a drug dealer. I was going back out there to put them straight.

171

I sat down by the telephone and started ringing the papers. Everybody wanted to hear about my ordeal. The first publicity was in the London West Indian weekly *The Voice*. They wrote an article about how I had been wrongfully arrested. Then the London *Evening Standard* did a piece about how I was determined to return to showjumping. Now that there was a bit of controversy about me the media seemed even more interested than they had been before I was locked up.

It's a funny old world. Although Customs and Excise had deprived me of my liberty for four weeks, they ended up doing me one of the biggest favours of my life.

Good can come out of bad and I have been able to put my prison experience to good use. Sixteen months after I was released from Chelmsford I was at the opening of the flat-racing season at Doncaster, where I met the deputy governor of Pentonville Prison, Stuart Mitson.

Stuart and I hit it off immediately. We had a good laugh about how we'd been on opposite sides of the fence, so to speak. He invited me to Pentonville to talk to the prisoners. He said that my experience as a black celebrity and ex-prisoner was invaluable.

I was intrigued to see what it would be like going inside and being able to come out when I wanted. It felt very strange the first time I went into Pentonville. The screws opened the doors for me and then stepped aside saying, 'This way, sir.' I told them that it felt weird being called sir since it wasn't long ago that I'd have been just another miserable con. They laughed. They thought it was a great joke.

Pentonville is a super-clean prison. You walk in there thinking it's not so bad. But nothing can compensate for that feeling of helplessness when you're locked up. They shut me in a cell with one of the guys I was talking to. I tried to put myself into his shoes. It brought back uncomfortable memories.

So now I have a new role: Oliver, the social worker. How times have changed! I go to Pentonville each month and discuss subjects like racism in prison with the prisoners. They love it. We discuss our experiences and I get them talking.

At one meeting there were ten black men and every one had been in prison at least three times. I asked them what they were going to do when they got out. How were they going to stop themselves being sent down again?

One large man, who fancied himself as a bit of a hard case, was doing all the talking. He was blaming the system, angry with everybody. He said that prison was too easy and that was why people kept coming back. I argued with him. I said, 'Look, even if you're given ice-cream and TV in prison you're still locked up. No matter what the prison is like, losing your freedom should be enough to let you know it's not worth it.'

He looked at me as if I didn't know what I was talking about. 'It's all right for you. You're famous, you don't know what it's really like.'

I explained that I'd been through exactly the same sort of stuff he'd suffered. But I had learned as a teenager that prison wasn't for me. I didn't want to be locked up for the rest of my life. I told him that he should try joining the system and going out to find work. OK, he might only earn peanuts but if he kept dreaming about gold bracelets and fast cars he'd keep coming back to jail.

He scowled at me. People like him don't want to listen. He had that 'hard-man' attitude and I think my words went over his head. But I hope my visits to Pentonville are helpful to some of the inmates. They do me good: they remind me of where I've been and that's enough to stop me going back.

9

FAMOUS, BUT SKINT

I've said in newspaper interviews that black people don't like horses because the plantation-owners chased their slave ancestors on them. That may sound like a joke to many people but I believe there's some truth in it. The reality today is that riding is expensive and most black people can't afford horses – we have to spend our time making sure our families are eating, not bloody showjumping.

My black friends regard me with amazement when I rabbit on about hocks and stifle joints. Few of them have a clue what I am talking about. Black people are not supposed to like horses. A few rich black Americans like the chat-show host Arsenio Hall have stables but there are virtually none of us in Britain's equestrian world.

Riding is a country pursuit and you don't find many black people in British rural communities. Maybe this will change. When I was a boy my role model was Clive Best, who played for West Ham, one of a handful of black footballers in Britain. But thirty years on we have a multitude of black footballers. My hope is that the same will happen in showjumping, that many more black people will follow my example and take up riding. I was in Berkshire in the autumn of 1994, when I met a black family having jumping lessons. That made me feel good. My dream is that in ten years' time there will be many black competitors in all horse events from showjumping to dressage and eventing.

You don't have to be a rich country squire to learn the basics of horsemanship, but you do need money if you want to get to the top in showjumping. The sort of horse I needed was going to cost me around £5,000 to £10,000 – not expensive when you consider that a top jumper can set you back up to £200,000. To compete at the top level I also needed a professional trainer at around £30 an hour.

When I came out of Chelmsford I was living on £70 a week dole money. Sue was bringing in another few quid with a part-time job as a lunchtime supervisor at a primary school. We could just about afford the groceries and my petrol money to go riding, but wealthy we were certainly not. I couldn't afford to spend £200 on a horse, let alone £200,000.

I barely had a penny in the world yet I had ended up in a sport that is dominated by money. The only way I was going to find the funds I needed was through sponsorship. And if I wanted to attract big-money sponsors I needed to set myself up with plenty of publicity again. I had to make the most of the fact that I was unique in showjumping.

A large feature in the *Mail on Sunday* gave me my big break into the sporting world. After it appeared I began to get invitations to parties at West End clubs like Stringfellow's, where I met the British 'black pack'.

I got to know the boxer Nigel Benn when Sue and I went down to Stringfellow's one night. I think he fancied Sue. She was in a sexy, flared catsuit and he couldn't keep his eyes off her. We started chatting and it was the beginning of a good friendship. He's given me a lot of encouragement in my showjumping ambitions. He knows that the odds are stacked against me but he says he's seldom met anyone who's so self-assured. 'Just get out there, Oliver, and don't think about losing. If you really want to be a top showjumper you'll be one.'

Nigel has incredible charisma. He's noticeable but not loud, and he's always surrounded by people at parties. The champagne always flows when he's around.

The Wimbledon footballer John Fashanu is another genuine person who's helped me to believe in myself. I met John when I went to Birmingham for my first big television appearance, as a celebrity guest on *Gladiators*. I had admired him for a long time. He's well spoken, does a lot of charity work and to me he is 'The Man', the most educated person in soccer.

John made me feel really comfortable. We met in the bar of Birmingham's Hyatt Regency Hotel, where the pop star Prince stayed when he was touring Britain a few years ago. He took over a whole floor and ordered that it be painted black. Strange man, Prince. John introduced me to some of the other contestants, including the boxers Gary Mason and Dennis Andreas and the Wimbledon defender Vinny Jones.

I hadn't known I would be doing the show until a few days beforehand and I was nervous. This was serious television and I couldn't believe it was happening to me. I was still finding it hard to cope with the fact that a dreadlocked showjumper could cause such a national stir.

We decided over a drink that we were not going to fool around. We were going to sort out these gladiators. It wasn't in my nature to just turn up, grab the publicity and come last. As with everything I have ever done, I wanted to win.

Walking out in front of a crowd of 5,000 people in Birmingham's National Exhibition Centre was terrifying. I hadn't been onstage for nearly twenty-five years – and that was dressed in tights in the school nativity play at Twyford. John Fashanu interviewed me about how I got involved in showjumping but I can't remember much about it. For some reason he kept calling me Skeetie, which felt strange. Nobody's ever called me Skeetie before. When it came to my turn to race I came fifth. I was exhausted. Fighting against the gladiators was hard work.

The best thing about doing *Gladiators* was meeting John. He has a great business head and I go to him with my career problems. He's quiet and reserved but he's not afraid to go out and meet his fans. I remember joining him at an afro hair and beauty exhibition at Alexandra Palace. The organisers wanted us to sit behind a desk and sign autographs, but John had other ideas. We walked through the crowds, giving the girls hugs and kisses and chatting to everybody. I hate the way some stars think they're so important that they steer clear of their fans. Children especially appreciate it if you treat them as human beings and not as nuisances to be avoided.

I was invited on to more television shows. I was on *The Chrystal Rose Show* at the same time as that larger-than-life society figure Dai Llewellyn. All I knew about Dai was that he was quite old yet he had incredible success pulling girls young enough to be his daughter. Dai had heard all about my affairs years ago with different women and he seemed to warm to me.

Before we went in front of the cameras he said, 'Well, Skeete, you're a bit like me, aren't you?'

'What's that supposed to mean?'

'Know a pretty woman when you see one.' And he added, 'Here's a tip for you. You'll find there are a lot of people who don't like it if you're a bit different like us. Don't be surprised if some of the newspapers take the piss.' I like Dai. He's a bit of an upper-crust old lag but he put me at my ease immediately. His father, Sir Harry Llewellyn, was one of the most famous showjumpers this century and any son of Sir Harry's can't be bad.

I did a guest slot as a bouncer on the police TV series *The Bill*. I can't say I liked acting much. I was paid £187 for two days' and nights' work and I was so knackered afterwards that I couldn't ride for three days. Modelling is better. I did a shot jumping a horse over a sofa for a furniture company. That only took four hours.

Taking the initiative and ringing up the newspapers myself had got me a long way, but I realised I couldn't do it all on my own. I needed a manager.

A sportswriter friend, Ron Shillingford on the London West Indian newspaper *The Voice*, suggested that I contact the boxing promotor and manager Frank Maloney. He said Frank was always on the look-out for new sporting personalities. Frank manages world heavyweight boxing champion Lennox Lewis, a big hero of mine. I had my doubts about getting involved with such a heavy-duty promotor, but if Frank was good enough for Lennox, then he was good enough for me.

I telephoned Frank and he laughed when he heard who I was. He had read all about me and he sounded excited. I was doing a great job for showjumping, etc., etc., and he would be pleased to see me.

We met at Frank's office in Manor House, north London. He was a quiet man with a sharp edge to him. We talked about how to market me – 'a marketing man's dream' was how he described my image – and then he put his publicity machine into action.

He turned out to be a brilliant media manipulator, for within a week of meeting him I was in four different newspapers. Frank dreamed up the perfect publicity stunt. 'I know what,' he said. 'We'll send you down the Brixton Road on a white horse.'

Brixton Road? What was the man talking about? I might be West Indian but I'd hardly been to Brixton in my life. I used to hang out there occasionally in my rude boy days but I hated the place. Really rough, it was.

'Leave it out,' I told him. 'You joking or what? I'm a suburban Ealing boy. I'd feel as out of place riding in Brixton as you would.'

But Frank had this image of me as a south Londoner. I was black therefore I must come from Brixton. He was determined to see this one through. I seriously wondered whether he was firing on all cylinders. But I knew the man was a genius when it came to the newspapers so I didn't argue with him.

By this time I was keeping my horse at a yard in Berkshire owned by a girl called Alison Foxley who was helping to train me. I told Alison I needed to borrow a white horse and she persuaded one of her friends to lend me one.

One Thursday morning I met Frank in Brixton. Alison arrived with a horsebox containing a beautiful grey-white gelding called White Cloud.

I took one look at White Cloud and realised he was not entirely suitable for a hack through the middle of Brixton. He was very highly strung and as he skittered nervously out of his horsebox I could see that he would spook at the slightest thing. He was used to little Berkshire lanes where the noisiest sound is the cuckoo. Brixton Road, with all the cars and buses, not to mention the crowds, was another matter altogether.

As I was reflecting on this, a Rastafarian in an elderly BMW drove past. He spotted the dreadlocks and riding gear, tooted his horn and yelled, 'Respeck, Dread.' White Cloud gave a startled whinny and tried to break away from my grasp. Oh Christ, I thought, what have I landed myself with? At this rate he was going to bolt with me all the way to Brighton.

'Look Alison,' I said. 'We've got to stop this horse from hearing or he's going to freak out.' There was only one answer. Alison went to a chemist's and bought a large pack of cotton wool which we stuffed into White Cloud's ears.

I mounted the horse. He was a bit twitchy but a lot better for the cotton wool. I gave his flanks a squeeze and we set off down Brixton Road.

The reaction was amazing. Everybody stopped to watch and crowds of black people shouted encouragement from the pavement. Frank had rung the papers and TV and I was surrounded by a camera crew and a posse of photographers. Frank had also contacted the police, who provided a mounted escort. Now that *was* ironic. Twenty years ago, that police horse would have been chasing me, but now here I was with an official escort through Brixton. The police-man and I chatted about riding and we got on well. His horse was beautiful. I have great respect for those police horses. They're so agile and they're bomb-proof in crowds.

That stunt brought me loads more publicity and a week later I was invited on to Britain's most successful TV chat show, *The Michael Barrymore Show*.

Walking down those steps in front of 17 million viewers was even worse that going into DC. The nerves were churning me up inside; it was like coming into a big jump for the first time on a new horse.

But Michael put me at my ease immediately. He's a charming man and he didn't take the piss out of me like he does with some of his other guests. Nothing was rehearsed and that made it even scarier. It was easy for Michael – he had one of those idiot boards next to the camera with all the questions on it. He asked me what it was like having dreadlocks and I told him it was more a fashion thing than a religion. But I said that you had to have the walk to go with them. I got up from the sofa and did a little rude boy bounce across the stage.

My next TV appearance was on the *Big Breakfast* show. I was supposed to be showing children how to look after ponies. I demon-strated how to wrap bandages around your horse's leg and how to plait manes. Then I had to get on a horse and show the kids how to jump across poles. I was willing myself not to make a mistake.

All this publicity spread my fame – not bad for an Ealing boy who had started riding so late and wasn't even among the top 2,000

British showjumpers. Of course, some of the newspapers started taking the piss but I had to laugh – there's no point in complaining about the papers: if you don't like what they publish, the simple answer is don't read them. They described me as 'the showjumper from hell' and 'Britain's second most shameless showjumper after David Broome'. One journalist suggested that the only reason I'd started riding was so that I could get into the best parties. I'm the first to admit that horses have been a way out of my old world of stolen cars and council estates, and that I thoroughly enjoy a good party – what's wrong with that? But horses mean more to me than that.

David Broome was not happy to have his name bracketed with mine. Actually, he was furious, or so I heard on the circuit. David is not known for his partiality to a joke and his sense of humour cracked after I was interviewed in the *Daily Express*. I didn't mention Broomie once, but the newspaper cheekily wound him up by describing him as 'Britain's second most famous showjumper'.

We were invited to do a television show together, but Broome refused. When asked why, he said, 'Skeete's only getting this publicity because he's black.' He didn't think it was fair that there were all these riders competing in world championships who weren't getting any publicity. I agree. Of course I'm getting the publicity because I'm black. But when I start getting publicity because I'm doing better than Broome and his colleagues I'll bet he won't like that either. I've met him at several shows but we haven't spoken.

Most other sports that were once the preserve of the rich, such as motor racing and tennis, are open to anybody today. But if a white guy from an east London council estate showed any interest in showjumping he'd get nowhere. The only reason I've managed to work my way in is because I'm black and I can attract attention and, more importantly, potential sponsorship. And that's sad when you think about it. I have been lucky. A poor white person from an urban background like mine wouldn't have stood a chance.

But I take the rough with the smooth and I suppose that bitchiness and envy are just side-effects of being popular. Some of the other riders said, 'He's having a laugh, isn't he? He can't even ride.' That's the way some showjumpers are. The ones who thought they were superstar riders were nice to my face, but the moment my back was turned they were crabbing me. I heard jealous whispers on the circuit that I was arrogant, too big for my boots. I made a point of being charming to everybody I met. I didn't want to fall out with anybody because I'd done in months what they had been trying to do for years.

I couldn't be angry with them because they were right. After all, I had amassed nearly as much publicity as Harvey Smith and I was still entering newcomers' classes. It must have been galling to see somebody come into the sport so late in life and, within three years, receive such massive public support.

The horse world can be malicious. Not all the riders are professionals. Many simply have lots of money and they set out to destroy the opposition by buying the most expensive horses. I know who these people are and I stay out of their way.

The true professionals, like John Whitaker and his brother Michael, have been wonderful to me. I've met John many times and he always asks how I'm getting along. He thinks I'm good for the sport because I've brought some fun into it. John paid me a great compliment one day when he turned up at a yard where I was training. After watching me ride round the ring he said, 'All you've got to do is keep your hands still in front of the fence. Apart from that, your riding is excellent.'

The 1950s Olympic showjumping legend Pat Smythe, the greatest horsewoman this century, has also given me encouragement. Pat won numerous prizes as a member of the British showjumping team from 1947 to 1965. I met her at a lunch party given by another former international rider, Johnny Kidd, at his country house in Wiltshire. Pat's in her sixties now and she gave up riding ten years ago but she keeps a close eye on the sport.

When she joined the professional circuit all those years ago there were hardly any black people in the country, let alone getting on horses. She was fascinated to meet me. She'd seen me on television and said I was doing marvellous things for the sport by attracting so much interest. 'I know you've got a long way to go, but don't let anyone stop you,' she told me. 'You've got the talent to be a good rider.'

Many of my colleagues see me as somebody who is helping showjumping to get the recognition it deserves, but others say I'm an opportunist who is bringing the sport into disrepute. They claim I'm lowering the tone of what should remain the noble pastime of the landed gentry. These people never say, 'Get out of here, you black bastard, we don't like what you're doing.' Instead, they simply don't talk to me, which is fair enough, because if I don't like people I don't talk to them either. Human nature, isn't it?

It is my view that bringing showjumping to the masses would be good for the sport. I'm not a shy person and I'm not afraid to say what I think. Everyone would benefit with more publicity because the sponsors would flock to spend their money.

The British Show Jumping Association do a great job but perhaps they should pay a little more attention to what the public thinks. I bet that the people who go to Hickstead this year will be exactly the same people who went last year and the year before.

By spring 1994 I could see my career was not taking off as quickly as I wanted. I saw all these boys and girls who had been riding since the age of six and even they couldn't make it to the top. I was facing one hell of a challenge and I desperately needed new horses if I was to realise my ambitions. I also needed enough money to rent a small yard in the country.

I might have been famous, but I was skint.

Frank had told me that he'd have no problem finding me a sponsor. Yet six months after meeting him, no companies had come forward with money and the publicity was beginning to dry up. I might have spent time in jail and had troubles with the police, but my search for sponsorship was turning into the biggest battle of my life. It was developing into a long, drawn-out business and at times I felt like giving up.

People kept asking me why black companies hadn't come forward with money. I found this an embarrassing question to answer. American black millionaires like the actor Bill Cosby are only too happy to give financial assistance to struggling young blacks if it is in a good cause. But well-to-do British black people aren't like that. It's as if they don't like to see their brothers doing well. The West Indian press can be just as bad. The London black newspaper *The Voice* has devoted endless column inches to taking the piss out of my sport and the way I dress.

Lack of sponsorship didn't stop me going to horse shows, even if I usually had only enough money to enter one class. My riding would be over in half an hour and then I'd spend the rest of the day hanging around watching everybody else. It was frustrating not being able to take part properly.

The few thousand pounds I had saved from my years as a car-sprayer and bouncer had gone on furthering my career. All I had now was my dole money and Sue's tiny part-time earnings.

The children suffered greatly and riding lessons were out of the question. Keilly's shoes were falling off her feet and Aloma was growing so fast that her clothes were too small. They kept saying, 'Dad, can we go the funfair? Can we go swimming?' And I'd reply, 'No, we can't afford it.' That felt bad.

British Telecom threatened to cut off the phone because of unpaid bills and I owed hundreds for gas and electricity. The Inland Revenue was hounding me for tax from my work as a bouncer and the council had sent me a summons for non-payment of poll tax. The bank had sent round a debt collector to collect £799. My money troubles were getting me down. I took to staring at the mock crystal chandelier in our sitting room, wondering how I could hang a noose from it.

My brother Ricky was not talking to me because I hadn't paid back £1,000 he'd lent me. Like most of my friends, he thought that because I had been in the papers and on television I must be loaded. When I went down the pub everybody expected me to dip my hands in my pocket. And of course nobody believed me when I said I was probably worse off than any of them.

They only needed to see my car to appreciate that I was not a millionaire. A millionaire does not drive a thirteen-year-old Ford Escort with a leaking water pump and a body that looks like it has been through the First World War. The car kept breaking down and I had to rely on the generosity of friends to keep it running. An ex-doorman friend called Trevor owned a scrapyard in Hayes. He was really good to me, giving me free spare parts, like generators, so that I could save my money to pay for petrol for another day's riding.

The costs of going to shows can mount up frighteningly. The entry fees vary from £5 to £10 per class for each horse, so if you enter three horses in two classes each, as many riders do, it will cost around £50. With the diesel for the horsebox you could be looking at £100 for just one day's riding. You have to be rich if you want to do the job properly and appear at shows every Saturday and Sunday. The fact is that former nightclub doormen do not have that sort of cash.

My greatest strength was Sue. Although we had barely enough money to feed ourselves, she never complained once, not even when I spent our last £30 one day on taking the train to Manchester to meet a potential sponsor. She helped to keep my feet on the ground. I was beginning to get over-enthusiastic and to celebrate before things happened, but Sue was far more cautious.

She was also remarkably tolerant of the sexy, bachelor-boy image that the papers painted of me. She has always taken the attitude that we are not married and that I stay with her because I want to, not because I have to. As a result, we have a great, trusting relationship.

She knows that my career means I hang out with good-looking young women in the horse world. She never accuses me of sleeping with any of them, which is good because otherwise I wouldn't have anybody to ride with. She accepts that I get on better with women than men, which is a relief. If she didn't, I would be in big trouble.

Since I have become well known, I've had girls throwing themselves at me. When I go to nightclubs girls slip me their phone numbers. When I'm out with Sue she takes no notice. She stares at them coolly and they soon go away.

The night after I'd appeared on *Gladiators* we went to Stringfellow's. A blonde aged about twenty-two yelled, 'Oooh, there's that showjumper guy!' With that she rushed over to me and leaped on me, arms round my neck, legs round my waist. I looked nervously at Sue. She grimaced as if she'd never seen a bigger slut in her life. I pushed the girl off and said, 'Excuse me, my girlfriend's with me, you know. That's not a very nice thing to do.' Actually it was quite a stimulating experience, but I could see Sue was hurt.

On another evening we went to a restaurant in east London and a girl jumped into my lap. She was kissing me all over and shrieking, 'I think you're gorgeous.' Sue stood there with her hand over her mouth pretending to yawn as if to say, 'I should leave him alone, darling. You don't know what he's really like.'

Then another girl came up and said, 'My friend is madly in love with you. Can you go and give her a snog for me?'

'Forget it,' I said. 'I don't go around snogging strange girls.' But it blew me away. Women can be unreal, can't they?

When I come home from making a public appearance, Sue asks, 'Well, Oliver, how many phone numbers did you get today?' I pull all these scraps of paper out of my pockets. She says, 'What do you think you are, a stamp collector?' Then she rips them up and puts them in the bin. Sometimes we have a giggle over my fan mail. I get letters from women offering me sex. Some of the things they suggest can be totally baffling. In most cases, I wouldn't know where to start.

Sometimes I sit down at home and think about the sort of life I'd be living if I were a bachelor. It's a nice thought for a while: all those endless nights of torrid, casual sex. Then I think of Sue and the kids and my home. It doesn't take long to weigh up the options. Sue and the kids always win.

The trouble with a string of young, pretty girls is that after you've slept with them once it's finished. There's nothing else to look forward to. I love Sue very much. Jennifer was the first love of my life and I won't deny that. But it's been a different kind of love with Susan. I've never screwed about with her in the same way I did when I was with Jennifer. She trusts me and I try not to abuse that trust.

Sue's only condition as regards my fame is that she can stay in the background. *OK* magazine came to our house to do an 'at home' picture feature about me and photographed us lying on our bed. I could see how embarrassed she was and she told me afterwards, 'I hated that, Oliver. That's the last time we have the press in our bedroom and the last time that anybody takes my picture.'

It was even worse for her when we went to the West End premiere of the movie *Cool Runnings*. All these flashbulbs started popping as we walked into the cinema. I loved it but Sue couldn't wait to escape to the Ladies'. She says that she thinks fame is not what it's cracked up to be. She'd rather people didn't know who she was. One day at her school, one of her colleagues brought in a magazine with our picture in it. It was the last straw when she realised her workmates knew who her partner was.

Fame can have its irritating side. I often meet strangers on trains who say to me, 'Oh, ain't you the bloke I saw on the telly the other night?' My reaction is, 'Yeah, well in that case say hello.' Why do people always say 'I saw you on the telly' and then not have the courtesy to introduce themselves? I can understand why some stars become so abrupt with their fans.

My relationship with Frank Maloney began to turn sour. Where were all these sponsors he promised? Whenever I rang him he was in America organising Lennox Lewis's fight against Phil Jackson. I couldn't blame him for taking so little notice of me. He was reputedly earning £500,000 from the fight and I was small fry in comparison to Lewis. There was no way I was going to make Frank that sort of money. But I wasn't going to sit around at home while he was busy in the fight game.

I put the word about that I was still looking for sponsors. I began getting calls from various other PR men and hustlers wanting to be my agent. They all had a good line in bullshit and the ones I met in nightclubs had the best. They kept asking me to sign this and that.

My teens had taught me all I needed to know about bullshit and I refused to sign anything. My answer was always the same: you get me the sponsors and I'll give you a percentage of whatever money you raise. What is the point of promising somebody 20 per cent of my earnings when 20 per cent of fuck-all is fuck-all? I had this public relations business sussed out: if in doubt, do it yourself. I had been on my own when I rang up the *Sun* that first time and I didn't have to worry about paying percentages to anybody.

I couldn't waste any more time looking for sponsorship. Lack of money was not going to stop me from riding. I needed as much experience in the saddle as possible and if a sponsor wasn't going to cough up thousands of pounds for new horses then I had to make the best of what I had. My dad had managed to support a family of ten against all odds so there was no reason why I couldn't use the same determination.

Friends rallied round. After Barry Fox, I was trained for six months by another former international showjumper, Nigel Goddard, also based in Berkshire. I improved greatly with Nigel and he helped the technical side of my riding more than anyone.

After Nigel I moved to Alison Foxley's yard at the tiny village of

Tidmarsh, near Pangbourne in Berkshire. Like so many other people I had met on the circuit, Alison had great faith in my skills and gave me free lessons and stabling.

I still had Betsy, the mare I had bought in Ireland, but she was too small for me. I also had a three-year-old called Dolly, whom I had bought as a foal. I had given Alison a half-share in Dolly as repayment for the use of the yard and we planned to break her in and sell her.

Alison was a straight-talking blonde in her late twenties. She had spent her life around horses. She told me that with the right horses and financial backing I had every chance of making it as a top showjumper. Some riders reach a level and go no further, but I had an instinctive feel for horses that made me special. After all, it was virtually unheard of for a person to start professional showjumping in his mid-thirties. I needed to go to as many shows as possible, regardless of how minor they were. It was all very well jumping in a ring at home, but it was an entirely different matter faced with the buzz and crowds of an arena.

In May 1994 I took a risk and entered one of showjumping's most prestigious events, The Royal Windsor Horse Show. The only problem was finding a suitable horse. I spent two weeks looking for a mount. Two days before the show I rang a horse dealer friend called Nick Smith who told me that one of his horses, called No Problems, had entries for the show. But he was thinking of withdrawing the horse because he was about to be sold and he didn't want to risk damaging him in the ring.

I persuaded Nick to let me ride No Problems, and barely twenty-four hours before the show I drove to his yard at Paceham in Surrey, where the horse and I were introduced. Most people who enter shows like the Royal Windsor have been riding their horses for months. I knew that I was at a great disadvantage.

A friend of mine called Nat Heal, who had also been helping to train me, got on No Problems and hacked him down the lanes to a practice ground a mile away. I followed him in my car. It became clear that whoever had named the horse had either great optimism or a quirky sense of humour. No Problems had hardly ever been on a road before. He was jumping about, spooking and suddenly shooting out into the middle of the road for no reason. Whenever a car passed, he swerved sideways and almost disappeared through the hedge. Eventually Nat could stand no more. He dismounted and led the horse the rest of the way. I thought, what have I got myself into? I've got to ride that thing in front of everybody at Royal Windsor tomorrow and it looks like it's in serious need of psychiatric help.

No Problems' other drawback was that he was suffering from a sore mouth and could not wear a normal bit. He had to be fitted with a bitless bridle which went across the nose and worked by putting pressure on his nostrils. Horses without bits in their mouths are notoriously difficult to steer. It did cross my mind that I should not be riding a strange horse at Royal Windsor with a bridle that he wasn't used to.

At the showground, I gingerly put my foot into a stirrup and heaved myself on to No Problems' back. I could feel the tension in him. Nick put up a little cross-pole for me to try. I gently pushed No Problems forward and he clumsily negotiated the obstacle. After that, I went round a small course of fences no more than three foot six high. The horse took them badly, tearing into them and stumbling over them like a hippopotamus.

It felt uncomfortable and scruffy. Then Nick raised the fences by another foot, a height which was greater than the one for the class I was due to enter the next day. No Problems blundered through them. We knocked down five and I nearly fell off.

I returned to Nick and dismounted. 'Look, I'm not sure about this. This horse and I don't seem to get along. I'm going to make a complete fool of myself tomorrow.'

'Don't worry about a thing, old boy. You'll do splendidly.' Nick was a smooth character in his early thirties with an enormous beer gut. He brimmed with bonhomie and was remarkably jovial about my disaster. 'It might have felt awful to you but it looked super to me. I should give it a try.'

He convinced me. The next morning I got in my old Escort and drove down to Windsor for the show. I had neither a ticket nor a car-park pass and one of the elderly bowler-hatted stewards stopped me at the main gate. I apologised for being so disorganised and explained that I was riding today.

He peered at my dreadlocks and smiled. 'Oh yes, son, I know all about you. I don't think you need a ticket.'

The steward leaned on the car and added, 'I'd like to tell you that you're doing a great job for the sport. Glad to see you're breaking the mould.' His words touched me.

I parked the car and started looking for Nick Smith's groom, who was supposed to have brought the horse. By now it was 11 a.m. Nick had told me that the class would start at 12.30, but I discovered he had got the time wrong. It started at 11.30 and I had only half an hour before I was due in the ring.

I wandered past the dozens of horseboxes parked around the ground but I couldn't find No Problems anywhere. I looked and looked but there was no sign of him. I began to panic. Where the hell was he? I reflected that my return to the professional showjumping circuit was turning into a farce. What was I supposed to do? I could hardly go up to people and say, 'Er, excuse me, have you seen my horse?' So I kept walking, peering into horseboxes for a sight of the groom.

Eventually I found the horsebox in a corner of the ground. The groom was relieved to see me and I helped him to saddle up the horse. We did not have a girth long enough to go around No Problems' back so I had to borrow one from the next-door horsebox. On top of everything else, in my rush to leave London I had forgotten my spurs. I felt horribly unprepared.

As I rode across the ground everybody's eyes were on me. The other riders stared at me. I'd seen many of them at shows over the previous eighteen months and they hadn't spoken a word to me. But the atmosphere was different now. They wished me good luck when I told them that I was riding a horse I'd met the day before. They thought I was either mad or stupid or both and were waiting to see whether Skeete's big mouth was about to be silenced forever. This was my first major outing since I had become better known and I prayed silently that I wouldn't fall off.

When I reached the collecting ring I noticed the Duchess of York in the crowd. She was staring at me too. I gave her a wave and she smiled. That cheered me up a lot.

The warm-up went well. Word had travelled that I was here and a group of photographers surrounded me. It felt as if the whole world was watching. I don't usually get butterflies before a competition but people say that my nerves show in my facial expressions. God knows what my face looked like at that moment. Everything was loaded against me. This could be Skeete's Last Stand.

My turn came. I walked No Problems into the ring. The bell went. I took a deep breath and pushed the horse into a trot. After the bell goes you can take up to thirty seconds to start. I wanted No Problems to be as relaxed as possible and I used up all the time before breaking into a canter.

We approached the first fence. It was a three-foot-nine double-oxer – two poles set close together to make one wide jump. No Problems went into it smoothly and I knew he had the right stride.

Learning to see a stride is the secret of good showjumping. The way you approach a jump matters more than the height of the fence. After two and a half years in the sport I was only just learning the technicalities of a stride. It was a feeling that had taken hours to develop.

A course-builder will design a course with calculated distances between jumps. These are based on the theory that the average horse has a twelve-foot stride. The best way of illustrating how a stride works is to put it in human terms: I put up a little cross-pole for you to jump. You run at it and your body knows how much it can cope with and tells you when to leave the ground so that you can jump the pole. But if I hold on to the back of your shirt and stop you from going at the pace at which your body feels comfortable to jump, you say 'Hang on a mo, I'm not having any of that', and you either stop, crash into the pole or dart round the side of the obstacle.

A horse is like that. A horse has rhythm and the rider's skill is in allowing the horse to go on the stride at which it is most comfortable. You must understand your horse. Some horses like to go into jumps quickly and others will take their time. The trick is to capitalise on the horse's assets. Inexperienced riders make the mistake of using 60 per cent of their input and only 40 per cent of the horse. What you need is 80 per cent of horse and 20 per cent of rider.

I remembered everything I had been taught about strides. I squeezed No Problems' flanks and he soared over the first fence.

191

I began to relax. The horse seemed to have recovered from yesterday's jitters. Perhaps he was enjoying the attention of the crowd. Whatever the reason, this round was going to be better than I could ever have dreamed of.

The horse landed and I immediately looked up. This is one of the golden rules of showjumping – always look up to see where you're going as soon as you've completed a jump. It's hard at first because you're tempted to watch your horse's feet.

We wheeled round and I pushed No Problems into the second fence, a pink four-foot upright. I caught the stride from five strides out and it felt brilliant. He cleared the jump easily. Then it was a quick left turn to the next fence, another oxer. We jumped it perfectly and swerved sharp right towards fence number four. This was a double combination – an oxer followed by an upright with two strides between them. We flew over it and I could hear a ripple of applause from the crowd. The way I was jumping felt good, and if it feels good, it's going to look good. Much to my surprise, this horse was turning out OK. I wondered what I'd been worrying about.

I soon found out when we reached the fifth fence and I made my first mistake. It was a simple gate but I missed the stride and the horse took off too early. As we soared over, No Problems' hooves clipped the top bar and the gate crashed down. The crowd gave a little groan. It was good to know they were on my side.

The sixth fence was a tricky spread fence with three rows of poles. The first pole was a foot off the floor, the next two foot and the third four foot. This was the classic showjumping fence where the horse appears to climb almost vertically into the air.

The difficulty with a jump like this is that you're trying to get the horse in as deep as you can at the first pole while the horse is looking at the last pole. No Problems lived up to his name and we cleared it perfectly. And he took the next hurdle, an upright six strides away, just as effortlessly.

Now we were heading for the exit. Some horses go funny at this point. They think they have finished and you have to ride more firmly to let them know their job is not over yet.

Thankfully, No Problems was keen to continue. We passed the exit and headed for the biggest fence of the class, a treble combination featuring an oxer, an upright, another oxer and out. We glided over the first one and landed. I sat up, squeezed for the upright and we went over that. As we reached the last part of the fence it all began to feel a bit weird. The horse was going faster and faster and he was taking little notice of the bitless bridle. The approach into the oxer was OK but for some reason I still don't understand the horse jumped too high, as if he was trying to escape. My intention was to land and gently bring him round to the final fence. But No Problems had other ideas. I think the bridle was causing him pain and he suddenly veered to the right as if trying to pull the reins out of my hand.

I felt myself sliding from the saddle. Falling off a horse seems to happen in slow motion. Your immediate reaction is to try to stop yourself, but when you realise you can't you have to go with it. As I said, I have this uncanny knack of landing on my feet when I fall – and that is exactly what happened then. I slithered off No Problems' back and landed straight in a pile of horse shit. There was a nasty squelching sound and my jodhpurs were streaked with muck.

I wasn't going to allow a setback like this to ruin my day. I pulled No Problems to a halt, gathered up the reins, jumped up and hauled myself on to the saddle cowboy-style. I slipped my feet back into the stirrups and we were back in business.

I steered the horse into the last jump, a simple plank. Many people who fall off during the showjumping round will kick their horse and go for a flyer. But I was later praised for getting No Problems under control and riding steadily into the final fence. He took it beautifully and the round was over. It had taken a little over sixty seconds.

Nick Smith congratulated me outside the ring. He slapped me on the back and said I was 'bloody brilliant'. Strangers came up and said it had been a great piece of riding. They could see how hard I had worked and even if I was unlikely to become the world's top rider I was learning how to do the job.

The judges penalised me with four faults for knocking down the gate and another three and a quarter time faults for taking too long to finish. My riding was finished for the day and I had too many faults to get into the jump-off. But considering that practically everything had been against me, it was one of the best rounds of my life.

For someone who had been competing for only two years I hadn't done badly. I had arrived at Royal Windsor surrounded by hype and I had got away with it. And, most importantly, I had proved to my fellow showjumpers that I could see a stride, the most difficult aspect of the sport.

After my round, one of the BSJA stewards took me aside and did a random check on my boots to make sure they did not have any chemicals on them. Some riders have been known to doctor their boots with chemicals that burn the horse's legs and make it jump higher. I knew this steward because he had checked me eighteen months earlier at Gleneagles. We had a good laugh about it.

I adopted a Jamaican drawl. 'You keep picking on me, doncha? It's 'cos I'm black, ain't it?'

''Course it is,' he replied brightly. These BSJA officials amuse me. They always have a good, dry sense of humour.

A couple of days later I returned to Royal Windsor as the guest of a Cheshire-based promotions man called Andy Egan. Andy had introduced himself after I left the ring. He was a former stuntman who had worked with the TV star Noel Edmonds and the Crinkley Bottom team on various money-raising schemes. He was astonished when I told him how difficult it was proving to be to find sponsorship and said that he might be able to help.

'You've got such a high profile that I'm amazed people aren't showering you with cash,' he said. 'You've been in practically every magazine, you're all over the telly, so what's the problem?'

'You tell me,' I sighed. 'Maybe it's because of my time in jail.'

'No, I don't think that would make much difference.'

'Or because I'm black.'

'I would have thought that was your strong point.'

'Or maybe people think I'm just a flash in the pan and that every-body will soon lose interest.'

'Well, are you a flash in the pan?'

'No chance. I'm here to stay.'

Andy hinted that my problem could be my manager, Frank Maloney. 'Frank's a fantastic businessman but I'm not sure that you need to be associated with the boxing world. A lot of people think that boxing is the underworld.'

Andy proposed a deal. He said he didn't want to be my manager or agent. All he would do was find me sponsorship and take 15 per cent of the proceeds. I wasn't convinced because I had been bullshitted so much in the past, but it sounded interesting.

I accepted Andy's invitation to lunch at Royal Windsor. To many people, lunch in a box at the Royal Windsor Horse Show probably sounds good fun. But to me, a former car-sprayer from Hanwell, it was bloody amazing. I'd never seen a spread of food like it: big round tables set with beautiful cutlery and loaded with lobster, huge sides of salmon and bucketfuls of champagne. The year before I'd been at Royal Windsor as just another punter in the stands. I'd looked across the ring and wondered what went on in those boxes. Now I had made it to a box myself and that showed me I was getting somewhere.

The Queen was having her own lunch only three boxes away. As far as I was concerned, that was as good as mixing with royalty. The last time I'd seen a member of the royal family at such close quarters was sixteen months earlier when Princess Anne had visited Chelmsford Prison. It's funny how your world can change so fast.

It was a great lunch but I realised I was not dressed correctly. I looked pretty smart in a Kenzo shirt, white waistcoat and grey flannels, but it wasn't quite right. I had neither the blue blazer nor the club tie, both essential items if you want to get on in showjumping. These people had an unwritten dress code and I was going to have to learn it.

195

10

'THE SHOWJUMPER FROM HELL'

The public reaction to the news that I was broke was amazing. People rang up offering to lend me horses. What was more, most of them were prepared to pay me £30-a-week livery costs to cover food and keep. I was knocked out, especially since these owners were not rich people. They just wanted to give me a chance and their generosity touched me greatly.

Timmy turned up after his owner had seen me on *The Chrystal Rose Show*. He was a 16.1-hand thoroughbred ex-eventer who came from the New Forest. He was weak and thin when he arrived at Alison's yard but I saw that he had a chance of becoming a good horse.

I built him up slowly. He was bug-eyed and docile and a delightful, if pedestrian, ride. He used to stand all day asleep in his stable and I had to shake him to wake him up. Something must have gone wrong in his genes because he was the antithesis of most thoroughbreds, which tend to be hyped-up and ready to go at the slightest encouragement.

Despite Timmy's size, I had no qualms abut Aloma and Keilly riding him. It didn't take me long to realise that he was not championship material but he was perfect for novice classes at the smaller shows.

And then Sara arrived.

My relationship with Sara was to become one of the great love affairs of my life. She was a massive 17.2-hand Hanoverian bay mare and possibly the worst-behaved horse I have met. She was another loan from a well-wisher who had seen me on TV and evidently thought, that Oliver Skeete's so skint, he won't mind what sort of horses he gets.

Sara's owner was an accountant called Susan Hayes who lived outside Norwich in Norfolk. Susan agreed to pay for the livery until I found a sponsor. This was kind of her since there wasn't much in it for her except the fun of seeing how Sara turned out. And of course there was a slim chance that Sara might end up as a top-class showjumper and therefore become worth a lot of money.

But for the time being the only class that Sara was likely to win was a donkey derby on Blackpool beach. Susan had kept her as a pet, and at 17.2 hands she was some pet! She had been broken in aged six, which is too late – a horse should start learning at three. She had then been turned out into a field and left there. She was now seven years old and had hardly been ridden. Susan must have thought she was being nice to her, but it was no kinder than spoiling a child. The horse was completely wasted.

Sara was a monster at first. She knew she was a big horse and she used her size against me, pushing me around in the stable when I tried to saddle her up. The first time I rode her I could see she was pig-ignorant. I led her into the ring at Alison's yard and climbed on to her back. Alison leaned on the fence, watching us.

I settled into the saddle. Sara gave a rebellious snort. How dare anyone consider riding her? I expected her to buck me off but the opposite happened.

I gave her a gentle kick in the ribs. She emitted a long, rumbling fart and continued to stand there. I kicked harder. Still nothing. She just stood there stupidly, her head bowed towards the ground like a carthorse that has spent too long in the sun. I wondered what on earth I was doing. OK, I was strapped for cash but this was going too far. It was very nice of Susan to give me a free horse to ride but this one was a dog.

I dismounted. Alison handed me a riding crop. She had been watching my efforts to make Sara move and was trying to stop herself from laughing. I waved the crop in front of Sara and gave her a good talking-to. I held her nose and stared into her eyes. 'Look, bitch,' I said. 'You're going to move if it's the last thing I do. Got that?' Sara gave me a mean look and tried to break away from my grasp. 'I don't like women who mess me around,' I added.

I got back into the saddle and gave her an almighty kick with both feet. Success! Sara reluctantly began to lumber forward. She slowly walked down the side of the ring. As we reached the corner I gently took the reins and tugged to the right. The whole concept of reins was evidently new to Sara and she kept walking . . . and walking . . . and walking . . . right into the boundary rails.

I swore under my breath. 'Oh, God. Got a right one here.'

A 17.2-hand horse that is completely out of control can cause a lot of damage. Amid a noisy splintering of wood Sara ploughed through the rails into the field beyond. I hauled on the reins with all the strength I could muster and she stopped. She was not the slightest bit concerned. She lowered her head to the ground and lazily munched on a few blades of grass.

Alison had seen it all. She was giggling uncontrollably. 'Nice horse, Oliver,' she said. 'Can't wait to take her to a show.'

Since Sara had no intention of turning round while I was still on her back, I climbed off and she allowed me to pull her back into the ring. She stood there as placidly as ever. I picked a couple of splinters from her coat. Otherwise, she seemed none the worse for her ordeal.

I rode her every day after that. I couldn't believe how dumb she was. She ran into fences so often that I thought maybe she was short-sighted. Alison assured me that the horse was simply uneducated – 'She's like you, Oliver. Hardly been near a school in her life.'

I would put my left leg on Sara to turn right and there would be no response. Either that or she turned left. When I tried to kick her forward she didn't know what to do and stared blankly at the ground. And there was no chance of a trot.

After a couple of weeks during which I nearly tore out my dread-locks in frustration, she seemed a little better. She began to realise that she was expected to go around the ring rather than through it, and with liberal use of a crop I managed to persuade her to canter.

When I'd knocked it into her that she was no longer a pet, but a working horse, I tried her over the jumps.

The first attempt was disastrous. I set up a cross-bar no more than a foot high in the middle of the ring. I steered Sara into it and kicked her forward. She feebly attempted to jump the pole – and plunged into it. I went flying. Sara tripped and I rolled clear a split second before she crashed on to the ground next to me. I opened my eyes to see the undignified sight of my horse flat on her back with her legs kicking in the air.

A few days later a professional showjumping trainer called Ernest Dillon visited me at the yard. I had met Ernest a year before when I had contacted him to ask if he would train me when my sponsorship money came through. Ernest was one of the top jump trainers in Britain. A former member of the British showjumping team, he was much in demand on the professional circuit and was one of only forty-five fellows of the British Horse Society.

Ernest was a squat, muscular man of about fifty. Years in the saddle had given him bandy legs. He had great charisma, bright blue eyes and sounded like he knew what he was talking about. He was dressed in a leather waistcoat with a red-spotted cowboy bandanna around his neck. With his weatherbeaten face he looked like a cut-down version of John Wayne.

Over a cup of coffee in Alison's kitchen, Ernest brought me down to earth with a stern lecture on the direction my career should be taking. This media coverage was all very well, but I still needed to learn to ride properly.

'Everything's loaded against you,' he told me bluntly. 'You've got enthusiasm, courage and athletic ability but you need help. I've seen you at shows and frankly you need proper training. But that costs money, so without sponsorship you're dead at the starting post.'

'Thanks for telling me,' I said sulkily.

Ernest went on, 'I'm not saying you're useless because I think you're very brave and good at what you do. Characters like you are always good for showjumping because they draw the crowds, and without the crowds there wouldn't be a sport. In the past there were these old jokers like Harvey Smith, George Hobbs and Freddie Welch, but they've gone now and everyone in the BSJA has become so serious.'

He gave me valuable advice about my image. I must be careful not to make a prat of myself. It was one thing to be a character, but I must not be a clown. 'You certainly don't want to be the Eddie the Eagle of showjumping. Eddie was virtually thrown out of ski-jumping because he was bringing the sport into disrepute.'

The mere fact of my existence was character enough. 'Being a six-foot-one Rastafarian showjumper is sufficient and the last thing you should do is make a fool of yourself in the ring. You must take the job to the point of such clear focus that you don't talk to anyone when you're walking the course before a class.

'You have a minute in the ring to either live or die and your concentration span has to be one hundred and twenty per cent for a very short time. It sounds easy but it's not. A Buddhist monk takes thirty years to develop his total concentration for thirty seconds.'

Ernest brightened up. 'So, let's see what you're riding at the moment.'

We walked over to the stables and inspected Timmy and Sara. Ernest took one look at Timmy and screwed up his nose in disgust. 'Ha!' he said. 'Riding-school horse.'

'I beg your pardon?' I said.

'He looks wrong. Can tell he's not going to do anything just by looking at him.'

'Thanks a lot.' I patted Timmy on the nose. He eyed Ernest scornfully. Riding-school horse, indeed!

Ernest pontificated on the subject of what makes a good jumper. 'This is gospel. If your horse doesn't want to get to the other side of the fence clear more than you do, it's not a showjumper. I can spend a minute on a horse and know whether it's good enough. It's something you feel. And it doesn't matter about the height of the fence, it's the way the horse comes off the floor.'

He added with a sigh, 'Getting the right horse is damned difficult. I can't find the right horse and I've been thirty years in the job. Remember, there's nothing worse in showjumping than being seen on a bad horse.'

We moved on to Sara. She peered over her stable door with that lazy look.

'Bloody great thing,' Ernest sniffed. 'Can she jump?'

'Well, sort of.' I looked at Alison out of the corner of my eye. She sniggered.

'If you've any doubts about whether a horse can jump, then it's not a jumper,' Ernest went on.

'Why don't you try her?' I suggested.

Ernest looked remarkably unenthusiastic. 'Go on, give it a try,' I repeated. He didn't look keen but I pushed him into it. I led Sara out of the stable and saddled her up. When she was ready I gave Ernest a leg-up on to her back.

Sara was up to her old tricks. He kicked her gently. No response. He kicked her harder. Still no response.

'This is ridiculous,' Ernest muttered. 'I've put on enough leg to drive a baby elephant through a brick wall and she still won't move.' He lifted his legs and gave Sara a whacking great kick. She blinked and ambled forward.

Ernest tugged on the reins to make her go left. She went right. He tried to stop her. She kept going and bulldozed her bulk into the rails. Then she sharply reversed and started bucking. 'Oh, God,' I murmured to myself. I turned away in embarrassment.

Ernest hung on until she quietened down. Then he hopped off her and dragged her back to me. 'Useless old goat,' he said. 'The only reason you've been sent this load of rubbish is because nobody else will take it. You're wasting your time. Put it in the field and tell the owner to pick it up.'

'Maybe she'll get better,' I suggested. 'I think she just needs some proper training.'

'Don't waste your time. She's a half-witted git. You can't make something out of nothing. It's like going to a lunatic asylum and asking one of the inmates to be your accountant.'

I struggled to remove Sara's bridle. She was whipping her head around. She looked crazy. I snarled at her to be quiet.

Ernest piped up, 'Any horse that's going to put you in that sort of mood just taking the bridle off ain't going to make it.'

I had to see the funny side. I began laughing. 'Well, at least she's better than when she arrived.'

Ernest shook his head. 'You'd need a sponsor to ride that, what with the number of poles you'd break! They'd pay you to stay away from the shows.'

Before he left, Ernest delivered another lecture. He told me I had as much talent as I was born with and that however hard I tried, I would not give my horses any more talent. 'You can learn to use your talent, but horses don't have that sort of brain. They can either do it or they can't.'

Ernest's comments about Sara stung me. I felt protective towards the horse. It wasn't her fault that she was ignorant. She had received no education and neither had I. I had been given a chance to prove myself and I intended to give Sara the same chance. And anyway, beggars couldn't be choosers. Timmy and Sara were my only horses and I couldn't afford anything better.

I was determined to prove Ernest wrong. I wanted to show people that you don't need a millionaire daddy to be a showjumper. And so what if I had to go grubbing in the fields of Norfolk looking for free rides? I have never given up easily and I wasn't going to start now. Sara might have been a 'useless goat' but she deserved the opportunity to learn. I embarked on a rigorous training programme.

In the middle of summer 1994, I moved my horses to a stables next to the M4 at Shinfield in Berkshire. It was more convenient and closer to London. The yard was run by a girl in her early twenties called Tracey Hedges. Tracey had lived and breathed horses since she was a tot and she was delighted to look after Sara and Timmy for me.

Tracey shared my belief that all Sara needed was discipline and tender, loving care. Like me, Tracey was hard up and struggling to keep her yard going. She too hated the attitude so prevalent in the equestrian world that you should ditch a horse if there seems to be no money in it.

Sara's resistance to change was painful for both her and me. But she gradually stopped barging into the rails and began to understand my commands. I had doubts about Ernest's views on my horses. OK, Sara was never going to make a top jumper, but she was reaching the point where she would be capable of holding her own in a novice class.

I worked her in the ring for at least an hour every day. Perhaps it was my love and attention, perhaps it was the presence of my riding crop, but whatever the reason, I couldn't believe the change in her.

She turned out to be a constant surprise. One day I lined up half a dozen jumps and took her into them. She went over every one as if she had been jumping all her life. It proved what I had always said about her: that she was backward for a seven-year-old and merely needed to be educated.

She was like me, a late developer, and the two of us were learning together. It had cut through me when people like Ernest said she was dumb and didn't have a hope. I had a painful memory of myself as a fifteen-year-old school-leaver, when everybody said I didn't have a hope either.

Schooling Sara was the hardest thing I had ever done. I constantly swore at her through our lessons and she stretched my patience to the limit. It was ironic that she had only been given the chance to improve because I hadn't received sponsorship to buy other horses. I wouldn't have looked twice at her if I had had the cash to buy something better. But now I felt that I wouldn't give her up for a million pounds.

Working with a novice like Sara gave me invaluable experience that I would recommend to anyone starting out with horses. My success with her helped my confidence and proved that I was a far better horseman than I thought I was.

After a couple of months I took Sara to her first show, at Smith's Lawn, Windsor. I didn't enter her in any classes but I rode her round the ring to give her a feel of the crowds and the other horses. She scored only four faults and didn't stop once – incredible for a horse that had barely known how to trot just 100 days earlier. She behaved impeccably and seemed to thoroughly enjoy herself. I bumped into several friends who had seen her when she had first arrived from Norfolk. No one could believe the miracle. I was so proud of what I had achieved.

Throughout the summer of 1994 I quietly plugged away at my riding. Most weekends I competed at shows in the south, the west or in the Midlands, entering in discovery, newcomers' and foxhunter classes. Like Sara, Timmy was showing great progress and I either rode him or borrowed a friend's horse. Timmy was never going to be a great jumper and was one of the most laid-back horses I had ever met. But he livened up the moment he got into the ring and we won a few rosettes together.

Tracey and I shared the costs of her horsebox and we trundled down endless motorways to showgrounds of varying sizes. But the long, slow journeys were worth the effort. Sometimes we'd stay overnight for two-day competitions and join the other riders in the evening for barbecues and karaoke sessions. I made many friends and settled into life with the country set. I didn't plan to stay at this level forever – Hickstead and Olympia were too tempting for that – but I enjoyed the buzz of the small shows and they were doing me good.

Sometimes, while I was waiting for my class to start, I would sit alone on a straw bale at the edge of the show ring. I would look at the trees, hear the birds singing, and reflect on how extraordinary it was that a West Indian city boy in his mid-thirties had ended up in the countryside. I couldn't have been further from my roots. This was the world of inherited money, country estates and pheasant for dinner. It was a long way from an Acton semi and court appearances for joyriding.

I often thought to myself, what in heaven's name am I doing here, stuck out in the sticks? But I learned to love the quiet of rural England. I looked forward to finding a place in the country where I could settle down with my family. My days of running around the London clubs were over. It had taken me a long time to discover it, but the city held little attraction for me. It was a good feeling leaving the streets for open fields and clean air.

Sometimes these country people would come and sit next to me on the straw bale. We would talk and I would discover how little they knew about life. They could talk about the land, animals, horseboxes and tractors, but they didn't know much else. They were isolated in their little parochial world, which probably wasn't such a bad space to be in. I mocked them in my mind but I had to concede that their lives were so much better than mine. When I wake up in the morning and go out of my front door I see dog shit and gloom. They see fields and sky, and that can't be bad.

My publicity wagon continued to roll. I was in more magazines and on more television shows. The ITV children's show *Gimme Five* invited me up to their studios in Newcastle, where I was 'gunged' on Saturday-morning live TV. I had always wondered what was in those TV gunge buckets and now I can tell you. It's porridge coloured with vegetable dye – and it took days to get the oatflakes out of my dreadlocks. Timmy and Sara couldn't keep their noses out of my hair.

Andy fixed me up with some celebrity appearances. I went to Cheshire to present the showjumping prizes at the Cheshire County Show. That was a laugh. I was standing by the ring when I noticed a horse being ridden by a man wearing a long, Rastafarian wig.

When I looked closer I saw that it was John Whitaker. He rode into the ring and did his class in the wig. The judge joined in the fun and kept referring to him as Oliver Skeete.

The spectators didn't know if they should laugh or not. They glanced at me nervously to gauge my reaction. I thought it was hilarious and the moment I laughed everybody else did.

A couple of weeks later I was at a charity dinner at Lytham St Anne's in Lancashire. It was attended by sporting celebrities such as Jimmy Greaves. There was one of those old-fashioned blue comedians called Ron Lancaster. He took the piss out of me throughout his after-dinner turn: 'Oi! Don't those dreadlocks irritate your missus's thighs? Anyone turned you upside town and used you as a mop?' Not particularly funny, but that's the level of humour you get at these sporting dinners. I could see he was only trying to tell jokes so I laughed like everyone else. There was no point in getting angry. But if the geezer had come up to me in the street and said that, he'd have got a punch on the nose.

I've been mixing with royalty, too. In September 1994 I met Princess Michael of Kent at the races. She was giving away the prizes at the St Leger Classic at Doncaster. Beautiful woman, Princess Michael. I was invited into the Royal Box and introduced to her. We had a long chat. She knew all about my struggles. She was very sympathetic and we talked about George Bowman, the Olympic carriage-driving champion, and how even he couldn't find a sponsor. We agreed that if he couldn't find the cash, it was hardly surprising that I was having difficulties.

Training Timmy and Sara was a joy but the big money question remained on my mind. Things improved when Andy Egan and his colleagues managed to rustle up some equipment sponsorship. Thermatex presented me with monogrammed horse rugs and I was given Regent leather boots, Goringe jodhpurs and an R. H. Mears jacket.

A Midlands firm called Cliff Barnsby Saddles gave me a made-to-measure saddle and I was topped off with a Champion hard hat. Then things brightened up further with the news that a company called Misbourne was to lend me a horsebox. It was a great help to have my own transport.

This level of sponsorship was not going to buy me horses but it was a start. People had faith in me and that was what mattered most.

I spent a day at the Royal Show at Stoneleigh, near Birmingham, trailing round the stands asking motor companies if they'd sponsor me. I tried Mitsubishi, Land Rover, Vauxhall, Mercedes – the list was endless. The response was always the same. The salesmen said they'd love to help but their companies were already tied up in other sponsorship deals. It was Catch 22. The firms wouldn't give me sponsorship until they'd seen me achieving results on the professional circuit, but I couldn't achieve those results without good horses and I needed a sponsor's money to buy them.

Yet I refused to be defeated. I kept telling myself that sooner or later someone would come through with the cash and then I'd kick myself and wonder what I'd been worrying about.

As I finish writing this book, the good news is that I've climbed the competition ladder and I've gone up a class. I'm now competing in grade C events with a new horse I've been lent called Smithy. He's a beautiful 16.3-hand, grey gelding, and we've been getting on really well together.

At the end of 1994 I had the most brilliant bit of publicity I've had so far – a full-page article in *Horse and Hound*. Now *that* was magic. I felt I'd really made it in the horse world. I mean, that magazine is for serious horsey people who know what's what. Even better, the article quoted the British Show Jumping Association Secretary General, Andrew Finding, who said, 'By generating a public profile, Oliver Skeete is bringing the sport publicity which cannot be bad for the sport at all'.

And, oh yes, I finally met David Broome at the Royal International Horse Show at Olympia just before Christmas 1994. Any bad feeling he might have had towards me in the past seemed to have been forgotten. He came up to me, introduced himself and we had a chat. I also met Harvey Smith the same evening. Now, that man is a cracker. We'd never set eyes on each other before, yet in half a minute if felt as though we were good mates. It was like the two showmen of showjumping meeting for the first time. I think we could both see a lot of ourselves in each other.

Sponsorship remains a problem. I've had more than £40,000 worth of goods from eleven different sponsors but I'm still chasing the big money to buy new horses. I'm still finding it a struggle to make ends meet and I've been surviving on the fees I've been getting from my TV and radio appearances (pretty small they are too). What is certain is that lack of money will not stop me from riding. In the early days, Nigel Mansell mortgaged his home to finance his bid to be a racing driver, and I'm prepared to do the same to be a showjumper.

Reluctantly, I have to admit that I'm probably even further away from cash sponsorship than I was six months ago, and of course it worries me. But I realise I was pretty naive when I first started looking for sponsors. I thought people would be climbing over each other to take me on, but that wasn't the case, and I'm having to look towards other options. One idea is to find a rich owner who will pay me to ride his horses and take them to shows. I can see that happening more quickly than a sponsor giving me a wad of cash to go and buy my own horses.

But I reckon I've done brilliantly when you consider everything that's been loaded against me. After all, there aren't many riders out there who have gone from nothing to grade C in three years. If I was the token black but couldn't ride, that would be a problem. But the fact that I'm beginning to have some success means that I can't be dismissed as a novelty any longer. I'm the first to admit that there are many showjumpers who can teach me about riding ... but there's not one who can teach me anything about public relations.

The main thing is that my riding is getting better all the time. I've learned a lot and my expectations are more realistic now. It might take a little time, but I reckon I've got a good chance of making it as a top showjumper. My ambition is to ride in the 1996 Atlanta Olympics. Getting carried away? I don't think so.

There's little chance the British team will pick me. I'm the first to accept that Britain's got too many great riders like the Whitaker brothers to pick a relative novice like me . . . despite the fact that I could attract more publicity to the team than they could ever dream of.

But I've had a word with the Barbados sports authorities and they've said that I can ride at Atlanta under the Barbadian flag. I'll be there – no question! It will be the first time a West Indian island has sent a showjumper to the Olympics and I can't wait to show that I mean business. I'll have to qualify at the Panama Games first, but with a bit of luck that shouldn't be a problem. If you talk to people on the horse circuit they'll tell you I'm dead serious. I know my limitations and I don't try to boast that I'm something I'm not. Of course, I'm not Olympic standard yet, but with hard work, a good trainer and the right horses, I will be.

I know I'm taking a big risk, but that's what living is about. My attitude hasn't changed since my days of joyriding although now I take risks within the law. And if kids read this book, then don't do what I did, do as I say.

When I look back on my life, I realise how much my lack of formal education has hindered me. I didn't do too well in English at school and I have trouble speaking properly and finding the right words. I'm sure that when I speak to my showjumping friends they can tell I didn't pass my English exams, but that doesn't bother me, because what you see is what you get. I'm a black boy from the city. So when the showjumping crowd hear me say, 'Wow, yo, w'appen', that's me. And when I hear them say, 'OK, yah', that's them. I'll never speak like they do and I'll never be quite like them, but I can tell you one thing for certain: I'm having the best time of my life.

POSTSCRIPT

Many of my old West London haunts have gone. The Dread House was knocked down years ago. There's a block of flats there now. And all those bombsites in Ealing where I used to play with Clydie Macallam have been cleared up and developed. I don't know what happened to Clydie. I bumped into him briefly ten years ago but we never kept up our friendship. I see very few of my other friends from my schooldays. Most of them have been in and out of jail countless times. Some are still inside.

My parents returned to Barbados in 1987. For their last fifteen years in London Dad worked for London Transport along with Mum. Their combined pensions and the sale of their house in London enabled them to build a lovely house with sea views in a new development at Ashton Hall, a mile from The Whim.

The Whim hasn't changed much and the young people are quicker than ever to leave these days. There's only old people left. As she reaches her nineties Great-Aunt Emelyn continues to farm her two-acre plot and Great-Aunt Pearl still puts on her straw cloche hat and praises the Lord most days in the village church. My old policeman uncle, Sylvan, the man who first introduced me to a horse, is in his eighties. He's nearly blind now and he doesn't walk too well. He's not half as big as I remember him, all hunched and old. Yet when I was a child he seemed like a giant.

I'm happy that Mum and Dad are back on 'the Rock'. Dad never really settled in England and they both seem happier than they've ever been. Mum is still a seamstress and she makes the wedding dresses for the local brides just as she did in her twenties. Dad looks after his garden and grows all his own vegetables. He's become soft in his old age. It's as if his life was put on hold in 1961 until the day he retired and came home.

I get on much better with my parents than I ever did before. But they still treat me like a child, bless 'em, and their views about my dreadlocks haven't changed. Whenever I go back to Barbados the first thing Mum says to me is: 'Boy, when are you gettin' dem tings cut?' But they're very proud of my showjumping achievements. Of their sons, I was the last one they expected to make anything of his life.

My relationship with my older brothers, Kennedy and Bentley, has greatly improved. Kennedy is still a keen Jehovah's Witness but we have a silent agreement not to discuss religion. He's married with two children and works in computers in Barbados. He's so straight – collar and tie, neat moustache – but he has a good life. Bentley also returned to Barbados. He's the co-pilot of a submarine that takes tourists down to look at the coral reef. As for the rest of my siblings, my eldest sister, Glenda, lives in California. She is a widow and grandmother and lives there with her boyfriend. Judy was recently divorced from her husband, Noel, after twenty-eight years of marriage. She is a civil servant and lives in west London. Jennifer is married, the mother of four boys and lives in Barbados. My disabled sister, Sandra, lives with my parents on the island. My little sister, Claudia, has also moved to Barbados, where she works in a supermarket. My two younger brothers, Ricky and Elvis, have remained in England. They are both panel beaters in west London. I get on well with all of them these days although I think they still see me as the odd one out, the one who would never conform.

The biggest sadness of my life is that my first girlfriend and my first great love, Jennifer Brown, is dead. She died in 1991 of the blood disorder lupus. I think about her often. We had many happy times together. My grandmother, Rosalie, died in 1986. Our relationship changed in the last years of her life and we hugged and made up. All those painful times when I was growing up with her were forgotten. I now see her as a lovely woman who had to cope with an exceptionally difficult child.

All the problems I went through as a teenager have made me protective of my own children. If I see any of them heading for trouble I warn them about what happened to me. I tell them to be careful who they mix with and not to ape their friends. I want to see my daughters going to university and getting degrees. I don't want them getting pregnant at sixteen like so many girls I've known.

And Sue? We're still not married but we might make it to the altar eventually. I asked her to marry me when we were both very young, but she said no. 'I'll only ask once again,' I said, and she said no for the second time. I'll marry her when I've made it in life but not right now.

Sue's a very special person, very different to all my other girl-friends. She was much more of a challenge. I liked that. Nothing like a girl with common sense.